STRESS BUSTERS

D0169499

By the same author:

Laughter, The Best Medicine

STRESS BUSTERS

101 Ways to Inner Calm

Robert Holden

Thorsons
An Imprint of HarperCollinsPublishers

Thorsons
An Imprint of HarperCollins*Publishers*
77–85 Fulham Palace Road,
Hammersmith, London W6 8JB

First published by Thorsons 1992
This edition 1998
7 9 10 8 6

© Robert Holden 1992

Robert Holden asserts the moral right to
be identified as the author of this work

A catalogue record for this book
is available from the British Library

ISBN 0 7225 2632 6

Printed in Great Britain by
Caledonian International Book Manufacturing, Glasgow

Dedicated to my exceptionally lovely mum,
Sally Holden,
and to my brother and dearest friend,
David Holden

CONTENTS

ACKNOWLEDGEMENTS

There are many people I would like to thank for their much valued personal and professional assistance in the writing of *Stress Busters*. First and foremost, thank you to Anita Patel for encouraging me to set up the first Stress Buster workshops through the West Birmingham Health Authority. Her support throughout will always be remembered. Thank you to Dr Michael Kirkman who has acted as my medical consultant for the book as a whole. Thank you also to the following for their particular help with sections of the book: RELATE for kind assistance in Relationship Stress; Parentline for co-operation in Parental Stress; Radiance Strathdee of Gingerbread for her guidance for Single-parent Stress; Bryan Craig, Wendy Wilson of CRUSE and The Compassionate Friends for help on Bereavement Stress; the Health Education Council for help with the exercise sections; QUIT for support with 'No-smoking'; Gill Whitehurst and the Slade Road Centre for help with Tranquillizers; the Migraine Trust for assistance for Headaches and Migraines; Dr I. Mclean Baird and the British Heart Foundation for help with High Blood-pressure; NAPS and Women's Health Concern for help with Premenstrual Syndrome; Rosalie Everatt and SHIP for support with Pain Relief. And last, but not least, thank you to Erica Smith, my editor, for all of her support and inspiration throughout this project.

FOREWORD

Two-and-a-half ladies attended my first NHS Stress Buster workshop. I say two-and-a-half because one lady, Annie, could only stay for the first nine minutes. Halfway through our first relaxation exercise, while we were all lying comfortably on the floor, Annie sat bolt upright, screamed 'I can hear my bus,' and dashed out the door saying, 'Thanks, that was brilliant. I'll come again.' None of us saw Annie ever again. Now I was down to two.

My Stress Buster workshops are held at a modern house converted into a Health Centre in Handsworth, Birmingham. The health promotion management team, in their wisdom, named the centre *Health Shop*, despite the fact that every service on offer at the Health Shop is free. My two remaining clients had wandered into the Health Shop looking for seaweed, organic yoghurt and alfalfa sprouts. They agreed to settle for Stress Busters instead.

Three years on, some 1,500 people have attended a Stress Buster workshop of one sort or another. The Stress Buster philosophy is a simple one. To put the philosophy into words, it reads: *'To treat myself magnificently well, especially during times of stress, I give myself a better chance to cope and to be well.'* Unfortunately, too often the reverse is true: too many of us, when wounded, neglect ourselves terribly; we are often so preoccupied with the wound that we forget to search for a medicine, a healing or a cure. When things go wrong, treat yourself right!

The essential aim of every Stress Buster workshop is *positive personal empowerment*, or, in other words, inspiring a person to take the appropriate practical steps that will help that person to begin to feel happy, relaxed, self-accepting and confident again. Because remedies, solutions and answers are never the same for any two people, my Stress Buster workshops aim to explore as many effective coping strategies as possible. The approach is always practical, creative and challenging – in a friendly sort of way! *Stress Busters*, the book, adopts the same sort of approach.

The Stress Buster philosophy also embraces a fundamentally spiritual idea that, *'To live well with the world around me, I must learn to live well with the world within me.'* In other words, if I am prepared to look after myself very well, I will be prepared to look after my life, and the people who are a part of my life, that much better. Evelyn Underhill put it very well when he said, 'After all it is those who have a deep and real inner life who are best able to deal with the "irritating details of outer life." ' Ultimately, then, *Stress Busters* is not just about stress management; it is about self-management, and, better still, life management.

Robert Holden
Birmingham, September 1992

INTRODUCTION

Stress Busters introduces you to approximately 101 effective coping strategies for better personal health, happiness and control during times of stress. Allow these ideas to inspire you!

Chapter One, 'The Harmony Principle', is a brief introduction to the potential impact of stress on your life. This chapter identifies common causes of stress, explores specific symptoms of stress, outlines physical and mental reactions to stress, and describes the potential vicious circle of stress. Chapter One sets the scene.

Chapter Two, 'Positive Personal Empowerment', introduces 29 practical, effective techniques and tactics, each one a potentially wonderful resource for enhancing positive personal coping during times of excessive demands. These empowerment practices are designed to support you during almost any type of stress, be it job stress, relationship stress, health stress, the stress of change, or any other stress of life.

Deep relaxation remains one of the most effective personal resources for stress relief, stress release and stress control. Chapter Three, 'Relax, Release and Let Go', introduces you to eight easy-to-learn and easy-to-practise full relaxation techniques. This chapter also includes ten 'portable relaxer' techniques and ten 'portable energizer' techniques.

Chapter Four, 'Coping Well with Change', explores the relationship between stress, change and effective personal coping. This chapter includes a practical guide to anxiety management and also an introduction to a coping concept called *stability zones*. Many of the strategies outlined earlier in Chapter Two can also be very useful for coping well with change.

Chapter Five, 'Life-event Stress', provides coping strategies for some of the most common causes of stress in everyday living, such as relationship stress, parental stress and job stress. Ten practical actions are introduced for each of the specific life-event stresses mentioned. Once again, the coping strategies outlined in Chapter Two can also be of value here.

Chapter Six, 'Stress-related Illnesses', offers practical, healthy support for some of the most common stress-connected symptoms and illnesses, such as poor sleeping, exhaustion, PMS and pain. Chapters Two, Three, Seven and Eight also give additional exercises, techniques and methods that can be helpful for better personal health.

Chapter Seven, 'Diet and Nutrition', offers a sensible guide to healthy eating during times of stress. This chapter outlines the 'stress-aggravating' foods and the 'stress-helpful' foods. It also includes guidelines for a 'stress-friendly diet' as well as a recommended 7-Day Stress-buster Diet.

Chapter Eight, 'Naturally Does It', is a brief, practical survey of some of the most popular complementary medicine therapies for successful stress control. This chapter includes subjects such as music therapy, light therapy, the power of prayer and Love Medicine, all of which aim to restore health, harmony and happiness, naturally.

Stress is now increasingly recognized by the healing professions as a serious medical condition. The recommendations outlined throughout this book are general guidelines only; they are in no way intended to replace the function of your doctor, psychotherapist or counsellor. During times of personal stress, you would be most wise to consult a qualified professional.

1

THE HARMONY PRINCIPLE

I can live well, within myself.

One lazy Sunday afternoon a businessman was hard at work entertaining a potential client at his home. The businessman had a young son of about six years old called David who would occasionally run in and inadvertently disturb the proceedings.

David was bored. It was raining. Mum was out. His best friend had flu. He expected that Daddy and his friend might like to play a game of something either now, soon, or some time later (like in two or three minutes).

Each time David came into the room his father gave him something from the table to go away and play with: first a pen, then a calculator, then a paperweight and then the *Financial Times*. Finally, David was reprimanded.

A little while later David was back again, and this time, his father was prepared. On the table was a large full-colour picture of the world carefully torn into a hundred small pieces. He gave David a roll of sticky tape and asked him to play with the world until he had stuck it all back together again. That, surely, was the end of David!

Much to his father's astonishment, David returned after about ten minutes with the picture of the world complete again. 'How did you manage that so quickly, and so well?', asked his father. David replied, 'Oh, on the back of the picture of the world I had already drawn a big picture of myself, and, when I put myself together the world came together also.'

Life, the human adventure, is a truly poignant, bittersweet affair, made from a mixed marriage of both ups and downs, high points and low points, happy times and sad times, smiles and frowns. Experience can never be 'all good' or 'all bad' – it is, inevitably, a mixture of both. As we turn the pages of our lives we will witness the wonders of the world, and we will also experience its sadness and its pain. Stress is all part of the service!

Just as the natural order of the world created both sun and rain, both daylight and darkness, summertime and wintertime, blossoming and bareness, life and death, so, we too, learn to appreciate that life is an 'all-or-nothing deal' that dictates, quite simply, that pleasure cannot be measured without pain, joy has no meaning without sorrow, and laughter has no humour without tears. Truly, it is the hurts of life that give meaning and context to the happiness of life.

No one can ever be immune to close encounters of the stressful kind. Stress is the unique experience we all share. The pressures, stresses and strains of life are decidedly double-edged: they are often the architects of ruin and disaster, yet they can also be the vital agents that herald achievement, personal discovery and self-growth. Stress can never be avoided; it can, however, be managed and controlled. And, if life is an art, then part of it is to ensure that *you control your stress and your stress does not control you*.

WHAT IS STRESS?

The word 'stress' is an umbrella term for a comprehensive catalogue of words that includes anxiety, tension, arousal, conflict, pressure, burden, fatigue, exhaustion, discord, strain, panic, upset, nervousness, tearfulness, unhappiness and powerlessness. Some people will even go as far as to say, *Stress is Life!*

The linguist uses the word 'stress' to mean 'emphasis'; the psychologist uses 'stress' to describe 'mental anxiety' and 'anguish'; the physicist and the mechanic both use 'stress' to mean 'strain' and 'pressure'; the biologist and surgeon use it to describe a type of fracture; and the physiotherapist will commonly use the word 'stress' to mean 'muscle tension'.

As well as there being different meanings for the word 'stress', there are also different types of stress. For instance, pain, muscle tension and cell deterioration are forms of physical stress; jealousy, insecurity and a sense of inferiority may be forms of emotional stress; and decision-making, poor concentration and mental disorientation can be forms of mental stress.

To complicate the picture a little further, stress can be sub-divided into relationship stresses, environmental stresses, life-event stresses, occupational stresses and health stresses – all of which might contain elements of physical, emotional and mental stress. There is also such a thing as spiritual stress, which afflicts those of us who fail to find meaning, purpose or direction in life.

The multifarious synonyms, symptoms and sources of stress all point to moments in time when our perceived demands threaten to outweigh our perceived resources. Essentially put, stress is a reaction to a basic threat, and the basic threat is *a perceived inability to cope*.

Coping is imperative and vital to the human condition. To perceive yourself as an efficient and effective coper, able to achieve, deserving of happiness and capable of self-determination, is often made to be a necessary prerequisite of personal self-acceptance, positive self-worth and high self-esteem. The happiness of life, the wholeness of life and the harmonies of life so often rest upon this rock of a perceived ability to cope.

Our ability to cope will be called into question whenever our perceived demands threaten to outweigh our perceived resources. We will experience some type of stress whenever our ability to cope is challenged or threatened in some way, for, if our coping collapses, then, so too, so often, may our self-acceptance, our self-worth and our self-esteem collapse. To empower our capacity to cope is, by definition then, an essential aim of successful stress control.

A UNIQUE EXPERIENCE

The stress reaction is a unique personal experience, triggered by our unique personal perceptions of the world. Your experience of stress is, quite genuinely, unique – no other person alive experiences stress in quite the same way as you. What you choose to define as stress, how you choose to react to stress, and how well you control stress, are all governed to a large extent by your unique perceptions of others, and by your unique perceptions of yourself. The same is also true of personal happiness.

The perception factor is that mysterious variable that can often make 'one man's poison another man's pleasure'. An apparently identical external experience can inspire quite different internal responses, because of perception. Hence, some of us will reach for an opportunity because we perceive a chance of success, while others will refrain because they perceive only failure; some of us accept, reward and praise ourselves because we perceive we are deserving, while others will withhold all praise because they perceive they are not; and some of us will take a risk because we perceive the risk is worth taking, while others will adjudge that same risk not worth the effort.

How we perceive life is so often determined by the way we perceive ourselves. Reality is not made *for* us, but *by* us. Depending upon our perceptions, therefore, some of us will choose to rise to the challenge of adversity, while others may choose to avoid it; some of us choose to thrive in chaos, while others may choose to collapse in chaos; and some of us will choose to enjoy confrontation, while others may choose to avoid it and evade it, whenever, whatever and however. Perception makes the play.

Personal perceptions can easily change on a day-to-day basis, or even between any given moments within a single day. Certain people, places and events can be, therefore, 'a poison' at one time and 'a pleasure' at another. It could be that these people, places and events all change at exactly the same time; more likely, however, it is your own perception that has changed. When you change; the world changes.

To put it another way, people change, and their problems change when their perceptions change.

HELPFUL STRESS?

Imagine if someone was suddenly to shout to you, 'fire!', 'watch out!' or, 'thief!' – would you experience any tension? If a car was to come careering down the road towards you, would you show any concern? If, on a dark, starless night, on your way home, you heard heavy footsteps approaching from behind, would you feel fear? If your home smoke alarm sounded, would you not become alert? If your doctor said you were heading for a coronary, would you not be upset?

In each of these hypothetical instances, the failure to experience or to take note of stress could place you at great risk and in serious danger. Stress has a positive function in that it can act as a warning signal, rather like a red light on a car dashboard, so as to encourage you to be alert, prepared and ready to act appropriately. It would certainly be most unwise if, for instance, on smelling smoke bellowing from your kitchen you performed your favourite deep meditation exercise.

Stress, arousal and pressure can also often be the activating agents of achievement that help to motivate and to inspire outstanding positive personal performance. A practical, positive response to a perceived inability to cope can often inspire a person to tap resources, realize potential and achieve success way beyond his or her usual limits. The fear of failure has many times motivated successful examination results, good interviews, inspirational art, excellent company reports, impressive presentations, powerful performances and rewarding personal achievement.

It is an essential aim of life to nurture a creative tension that helps to ignite inspiration, facilitate achievement, support self-growth and reinforce self-respect. To get the most out of life and to push yourself well in life is an entirely natural, healthy, positive response to living. The trick is to create a balance that insures you do not push yourself too far. Without sufficient self-awareness and consistent self-care, creative tension can easily slip and subside into harmful, debilitating stress.

The stress reaction is not, of itself, therefore, implicitly good or bad. Rather, it is often how you choose to respond to your stress and how you choose to manage your stress that ultimately determine whether stress will be a creative, helpful friend or a destructive, ruinous foe. A perceived inability to cope can be the messenger that brings out the confident best in you, or it can be the signal that triggers uncertainty, insecurity and self-doubt. Your perceptions, your beliefs and your reactions are what will make the good, good, or the bad, bad.

HARMFUL STRESS?

Too much repeated or prolonged exposure to stress, to tension and to pressure can leave a person open, prone and more vulnerable to physical dis-ease, emotional imbalance, mental disorders and spiritual unrest. This may be especially true if there is also little or no allowance for balancing activities of rest, relaxation and recreation in life. So often, an absence of harmony accelerates a disturbance of health and a deterioration of coping.

Stress can be particularly harmful when it is a misjudged behaviour. As previously stated, your personal perception is the trigger that activates the stress reaction: if you perceive a threat, the stress alarm will sound. It is possible, however, for your perception to issue judgements that are mis-calculated, incorrect or unreliable. Sometimes the focus of our personal perception lens can be obscured by the clouds of low confidence, by the dusts of tiredness and fatigue, and by the mists of anxiety and worry. Perception is quite capable of deception – particularly during times of stress.

Stress can also be harmful when it is an entirely in-appropriate and impractical behaviour. Have you ever, for instance, had a trantrum while sitting tight in a traffic tail-back that's moving nowhere fast? Have you ever gone wild while waiting and waiting for a bus, a train or a plane? When was the last time you saw red at a set of traffic lights? Have you ever kicked the cat because the dog has run away? In each of these circumstances, a stress reaction cannot affect the desired outcome, and yet we still persist with these in-appropriate, impractical, non-helpful and decidedly un-healthy actions.

Above all, perhaps, stress can be harmful to you if you insist on hanging on to it and not letting it go, even after the perceived stress has long passed. Anxiety, anger, guilt and fear are manifestations of stress that can commonly replay and persist long after the actual physical event has passed, thereby compounding any potential personal harm. Learning to relax, release and let go of stress is an essential part of harmony, happiness and health. Proper release promotes personal peace.

STRESS: THE VICIOUS CIRCLE

The manner in which you choose to interpret, react to and handle a perceived stress can very often be far more damaging to you than the actual stress could ever be on its own. Our internal thoughts, feelings and beliefs have a power and influence that potentially can be much more harmful to us than almost any single external event, person or experience. For this reason, it is always worth asking the question, 'Are my perceptions, feelings and beliefs adding to my stress in any way?'

The S.L.A.P. formula describes a self-defeating, 'vicious circle' stress reaction. The letter 'S' stands for a stress perceived. There is no denying that certain stresses, such as bereavement, divorce, separation and redundancy for instance, are, of themselves, potentially undesirable, disrupting and disorientating. However, the challenge still stands that it is the way in which we perceive, react to and handle these stresses that can be, if we are not careful, even more defeating, debilitating and distressing.

The greatest threat to an ability to cope with a stress perceived is a lack of personal poise, inward composure and central calm. Inner harmony is your greatest protection and resource for controlling and ordering outer chaos. So often, however, the most frequent serious side-effect of stress is a concerted bout of low-level inner harmony. 'L' stands for this low-level inner harmony. When you are at odds with

S.L.A.P.

The Vicious Circle

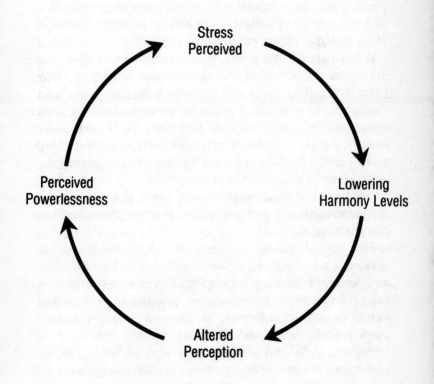

Stress
Perceived

Lowering
Harmony Levels

Altered
Perception

Perceived
Powerlessness

yourself it is very difficult to be even with others and with the world around you.

Stress habituates where self-harmony fails. Very often, stress is not so much a fully fledged illness in its own right, but, rather, a symptom or consequence of a far greater illness, which is a lack of inner, self-harmony. To quote Aristotle, 'Health is harmony; dis-ease is discord.' Harmony, or personal poise, is the basis for creative thinking, fresh perception, decision-making, problem-solving, relaxation and so many other skills that can help to promote successful stress control. Harmony helps to heal.

When your harmony fails, your perception fails also. 'The eye obeys the action of the mind,' wrote Emerson. Once there is a stress perceived, low-level harmony can alter perception so as to effect perceived powerlessness, or, poor self-image. 'A' stands for altered perception; 'P' stands for perceived powerlessness. Perception is focused, controlled and operated by harmony: the quality of your perception depends upon the quality of your harmony. During low-level harmony, personal perception can easily default so as to disorientate, disarm and disillusion. Perceived powerlessness can then set in.

The typical action of perceived powerlessness is to maximize the perceived demands of stress and to minimize any perceived resources for coping. Perceived powerlessness can turn molehills into mountains, puddles into oceans and raindrops into cloudbursts; at the same time, perceived powerlessness will overlook your internal resources of strengths, skills and attributes. If you perceive you are powerless, you may believe you are powerless and, therefore, you will achieve powerlessness. 'Men are disturbed not by the things that happen, but by their opinion of the things that happen,' wrote the Greek philosopher, Epictetus.

The essential purpose of successful stress control is to aim for a restoration of internal order and harmony so as to achieve a metamorphosis of perceived powerlessness into perceived powerfulness. By learning to look after yourself well – in particular, your perceptions, attitudes and beliefs – you will be better positioned to adapt to and look after your world well. Live well within yourself, and you will learn to live well with the world around you.

FIGHT, FLIGHT OR FREEZE

The stress reaction usually begins with a carefully controlled, lightning-quick explosion of physical energy, arousal and power, and within mirco-seconds of a stress perceived, your bloodstream is transformed into a network for thousands of chemical messenger hormones hurrying orders, information and updates to vital centres of control. The 'alarm signal' has sounded, and now the whole of you is alert, expectant and fully equipped for 'fight or flight'. There is always, however, the frequent fear of 'freeze'.

The power of your mind, body and brain is now fully primed to cope with the stress perceived. To take the 'fight' option, you may employ energy for application, confrontation, argument, communication, assertiveness, high endeavour or full concentration, for instance. To take the 'flight' option, you may employ energy for retreat, distancing, detachment, walking away, or taking a break or holiday, for instance. Either way, the fear of 'freeze' forever follows.

Any engine inspired by an intense injection of energy, arousal and power must bear a risk of backfire and breakdown. When the tension gets too tight, the fine tuning can flit, falter and finally 'freeze'. The 'freeze' option may manifest any number of paralysing behaviours and beliefs, including procrastination, indecision, worry, anxiety, fear of self-doubt, abdicated self-responsibility, and, worst of all,

Fight, Flight or Freeze Table

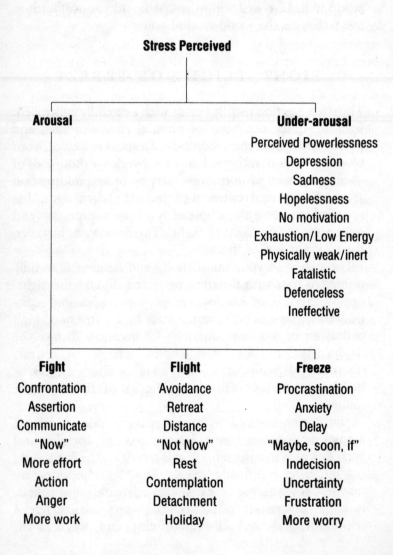

Stress Perceived

Arousal	Under-arousal
	Perceived Powerlessness
	Depression
	Sadness
	Hopelessness
	No motivation
	Exhaustion/Low Energy
	Physically weak/inert
	Fatalistic
	Defenceless
	Ineffective

Fight	Flight	Freeze
Confrontation	Avoidance	Procrastination
Assertion	Retreat	Anxiety
Communicate	Distance	Delay
"Now"	"Not Now"	"Maybe, soon, if"
More effort	Rest	Indecision
Action	Contemplation	Uncertainty
Anger	Detachment	Frustration
More work	Holiday	More worry

perceived powerlessness. The most dangerous manifestation of the 'freeze' option is the erroneous personal belief that you are powerless. 'Freeze' sends the vicious circle of stress spinning.

The full physiological stress reaction is a marvellously complex, fast-moving drama featuring, in particular, the nervous system, the muscle system, lungs, heart and hormones in starring roles. One of the main protagonists is the swashbuckling cavalier, the adrenalin hormone. The presence of adrenalin in the bloodstream can conjure any number of effects, including quickening heart rate, raised blood-pressure, a release of essential body nutrients, muscle tension, nerve activation and alert breathing rhythms.

Adrenalin is only one of a number of arousal activating agents, or 'AAAs', that energize, charge and fuel the stress reaction effort. Noradrenalin and cortisol are, like adrenalin, released from the adrenal glands into the bloodstream. Noradrenalin is thought to be associated with positive, happy and ecstatic arousal – unlike adrenalin, which is more fear-based. A major effect of cortisol is to increase the blood sugar levels which provide essential fuel for a mind, body and brain on red alert. And then there is the sex hormone, testosterone, produced in much larger quantities in men than in women, that also supports drive, determination and decided effort.

Thyroxin is another essential chemical hormone released into the bloodstream, this time via the thyroid gland. Its most important function during stress is to stimulate and to increase the metabolic rate of your body, and to regulate oxygen consumption. Increased metabolism means increased food supplies for greater energy and peak performance.

The other significant guest appearance of the stress reaction is made by endorphins, released by the hypothalamus gland (the stress reaction control centre). Endorphins are your body's own brand of natural painkiller. They will help to delay any immediate effects of pain and distress that might interfere with a peak positive performance. Boxers, for instance, will tell you they feel little or no pain during a fight; the full effects of a punishing ordeal will instead reveal themselves gradually over the following few hours, days or even weeks – well after the perceived stress has passed.

Like every other system in your body, the chemical hormone system (or endocrine system) requires a certain evenness and equilibrium to achieve positive, helpful effects. Any chemical hormone that plays for too much, too often or for too long can begin to effect negative instead of positive reactions. Peak personal performance and outstanding positive accomplishment are the fruits of poise, balance and harmony in action.

Too much adrenalin can leave you irritable, tired and agitated. Too much noradrenalin can leave you high, floating and unearthed. And too much cortisol can suppress the function of your immune system, your body's natural defence mechanism, thus leaving you prone, open and vulnerable to more illness, disease and stress. Without rest, recreation and time for recovery, and without the necessary poise, balance and harmony, the stress reaction can become a chain reaction of stress upon stress upon stress. A sense of perceived powerlessness is one of the most dangerous side-effects of a tired, overworked and exhausted endocrine system. Balance is your best defence.

THE STRESS REACTION: 'A.P.E.'

The extraordinarily quick and complex stress reaction can be divided into a general three-stage process, called A.P.E., which stands for the Arousal stage, the Pressure stage and the Exhaustion stage. Each of these three stages has significant symptoms and exclusive effects which can also be divided into groups: physical effects, emotional effects, mental effects and behavioural effects.

In the initial arousal or positive stage, the whole of your mind, body and brain can be illuminated and inspired by an injection and inrush of energy, arousal and power. During the arousal stage a person will feel alert, primed, poised and ready to act. Generally speaking, he or she will have reserves of energy, resources for coping and remedies for most obstacles. Perception is clear, thinking is quick and creativity is high.

Arousal is a creative, inventive lifeforce that inspires performance, coping and control. Arousal is the spark that fires peak personal performance and outstanding positive accomplishment. Without arousal, personal aim, achievement and accomplishment are mere ideal daydreams. The chief guideline for arousal is: *arousal works best when in harmony with rest*. To put it another way, the quality of your arousal, effort and endeavour is only as good as the quality of your rest, relaxation and recreation. Arousal and rest are, in effect, complementary opposites.

In the intermediate pressure stage of the stress reaction, a person may begin to feel the burden of having to sustain constant arousal. The natural 'high' and initial alertness of the arousal stage are beginning to flag a little. The pressure stage only comes into force, therefore, when there has been insufficient care taken to create a balance of arousal, effort and endeavour with the required rest, relaxation and recreation.

Symptoms of the pressure stage may include fatigue, tiredness, concentration lapses, irritability and energy failures. The pressures of the moment accumulate and accelerate so as to turn natural arousal into potentially negative stress. It is as if a 40-watt bulb were attempting to match the output of a 60-watt bulb. All great performances

Stress "A.P.E"

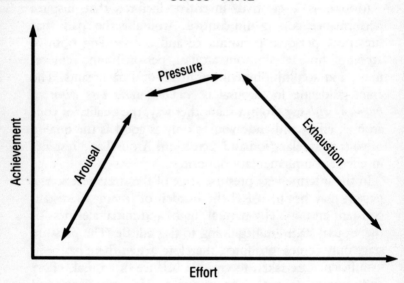

incorporate time and space for interludes. Indeed, interludes are often the catalysts that inspire a performance. Efficient effort output requires regular rest input!

The exhaustion or negative stage of the stress reaction tends only to happen if the demands for arousal, effort and endeavour continue to overwhelm the supply of rest, relaxation and recreation. Repeated or prolonged over-arousal will now deplete physical, mental and emotional resources and reserves so as to effect exhaustion, vulnerability, disorientation, illness and probably collapse. The overworked 40-watt bulb is about to burst. Perceived powerlessness turns to believed powerlessness during the exhausted stage of the stress reaction.

Physical symptoms and effects

forehead tenses
pupils dilate
eyes strain
migraines
head aches
head feels hollow
mouth feels dry
jaws and teeth are clenched
distressed facial complexion
neck strain
shoulder tension
upper back hunches
fast, shallow, irregular breathing
heart pumps faster
palpitations and heart flutter
chest pains
nausea
abdominal pain
stomach 'butterflies'

nervous indigestion
sexual difficulties
cold hands and cold feet
palms become sweaty
body perspires
muscle tension
restricted physical mobility

Emotional symptoms and effects

high anxiety
floating fear
uptight
panicky
edgy
irritable
lonely
unnerved
unsettled
disorientation
limbo
frustration
anger
insecurity
depression
helplessness
powerlessness
loss of hope
tearfulness

Mental symptoms and effects

muddled perceptions
inconsistent priorities
excessive self-criticism

lowering of self-esteem
loss of mental agility
poor concentration
short bursts of energy rather than sustained
  mental endeavour
poor decision making
wavering attention span
an inability to listen well
obsessive hunt for blame
poor time management
mental fatigue
procrastination
poor delegation
inconsistent communication
poor direction setting
more accident/mistake prone
reluctant adaptation to change
more 'ego' centred, less group centred
poor memory and recall
inability to assess one's work and decisions properly

Behavioural effects and symptoms

drooped head
rapid eye movements
forever talking
facial tension lines
clenched teeth
increased smoking
increased alcohol
nail biting
skin picking
hair fiddling
comfort eating
reduced eating

leaning shoulders
collapsed chest
folded arms over the heart
abdomen held in
hand gripping
hand play
legs entwined
foot tapping
general fidgeting
a general inability to sit still for long

A-Z of stress-related diseases

- abdominal pain
- acne
- alcoholism
- allergies
- angina
- apnoea (breathlessness)
- arthritis (rheumatoid)
- asthma
- backache
- cancers
- candidiasis (thrush)
- colds
- constipation
- diarrhoea
- drug addictions
- eczema
- gall stones
- headaches
- heart attacks
- hyperventilation
- impotence
- immune system depression

- incontinence
- indigestion
- insomnia
- irritable bowel syndrome
- menstrual conditions
- migraines
- neuralgia
- neuro-dermatitis
- phobias
- post-viral fatigue syndrome (formerly M.E.)
- premenstrual syndrome
- psoriasis
- shingles (Herpes sp)
- skin eruptions
- strokes
- ulcerative colitis

The word 'health' is derived from several old European words meaning 'whole'. 'Whole' refers to your natural state of living where all the vital organs and internal systems of your being, such as the brain, heart, lungs, muscles and nerves, are operating in perfect order and harmony. One of the more sinister effects of the exhaustion stage of the stress reaction is an absence of essential *homoeostasis*, or harmony, that, in turn, can leave you prone, open and vulnerable to stress-related illnesses.

Throughout the three general stages of the stress reaction you will experience a pattern of stress symptoms and stress effects that is particular only to you. Your ability to read, to detect and to heed these signals, especially during the initial onset stages, is a crucial key to successful stress control and to positive personal coping. Self-knowledge is a prerequisite to personal health, personal happiness and personal self-harmony.

THE HARMONY PRINCIPLE

The most effective, successful coping strategies for stress are the exercises and actions that restore and enhance inner calm and personal poise. Controlling the world around you begins by controlling the world within you. Self-harmony is a basis for personal empowerment, a focus for appropriate perception, a catalyst for natural self-confidence, and an inspiration for personal coping and control. Happiness, wholeness and healing begin with harmony.

On the days when your sense of self-harmony and inner happiness is both rich and real, you will find, quite naturally, that your reserves, resources and remedies for coping flow with abundance. Energy, creativity, patience, empathy, understanding and inspiration come through naturally and well. Self-harmony supports a personal perception that puts crises into context, problems in priority and anxieties at ease. All around you is OK because all within you is OK. The advent of major stresses will inspire you to cope, not to collapse.

On the days, however, when the universe within you is turbulent, stormy and unsettled, the world around you appears also to be slightly turbulent, stormy and unsettled. Unsettled self-harmony blocks creativity, dams the natural flow of reserves, resources and remedies, diverts personal perception, and obstructs confidence, coping and control. Low-level self-harmony promotes perceived powerlessness, which, in turn, leaves you prone, open and vulnerable to stress perceived, and thus, the vicious circle starts to spin.

Personal self-harmony, or homoeostasis, is the magic that makes health, healing and happiness possible. Within you, you rely on a series of homoeostatic controls to support life, to promote growth and to give good health. There is the harmony of alkaline and acid in the stomach, tension and rest in the muscles, sympathetic and parasympathetic action in the nervous system, and an exchange of oxygen for carbon dioxide in the lungs. All forms of life are supported by and evolve through this universal law of homoeostasis.

Personal self-harmony not only heals the wear and tear of trials, tensions and tribulations, but also supports positive personal coping. Poise, calm and centredness all inspire natural self-confidence, positive self-image, good work performance, rest and relaxation, effective personal decision-making, creative mental agility, clear and successful communication, purpose and direction, and energy and enthusiasm. From a harbour of harmony, a person can steer and navigate through the stormy seas of stress.

As the American poet, Henry Longfellow, so rightly said:

> *Not in the clamour of the crowded street,*
> *Not in the shouts and plaudits of the throng,*
> *But in ourselves, are triumph and defeat.*

Successful stress control starts, then, not so much with learning to cope with the world around you, but learning to cope with world within you. To quote the Swiss psychologist, Carl Jung, 'Man can meet the demands of outer necessity in an ideal way if he is also adapted to his own inner world, that is, if he is in harmony with himself.'

Personal self-harmony is our greatest priority. Every action we perform in life is motivated by a desire to create and to achieve greater self-harmony, for self-harmony is our personal passport to the experience of health, happiness and wholeness. As Mark Twain once wrote, 'From the cradle to his grave a man never does a single thing which has any first and foremost object save one – to secure peace of mind, spiritual comfort, for himself.'

The philosophy of stress-busting is that personal peace and control within you offers the greatest chance of achieving personal peace and control around you. None of us can directly control the world around us; but we each of us can directly control the world within us, and, by so doing, we can pick and choose how the world will affect us. In effect, therefore, you *have* the power, you *have* the influence and you *can have* control, for, when you change, your world changes also. Essentially put, confidence, coping and successful stress control happen inside out, not outside in.

2

PERSONAL EMPOWERMENT PRACTICES

I can learn to support myself.

BRAVERY

The Wise man in the storm prays God, not for safety from danger, but for deliverance from fear. It is the storm within which endangers him, not the storm without.

Ralph Waldo Emerson

Stress rarely operates without its faithful accomplice – fear. Rarely, if ever, is the reality of stress as frightening and as potentially damaging as the fear of stress. Whenever fear is allowed to cling to the mind and to lodge itself within the heart, a person will always find him- or herself rendered that much more powerless and inept at dealing successfully with stress. When it comes to stress, fear will often block success. You must weather the storm within you in order to allow for blue skies and sunshine around you.

Think for a moment of all the fears that may surround a stress. Fear of failure, fear of anticipation, fear of change, fear of aloneness, fear of poor self-image, even a fear of success – each of these fears betray another more fundamental fear, that is, the fear of not being able to cope. The fear of not being able to cope will often prevent you from even making a start. Acknowledge this fear, then, but do not submit to it. Perhaps the most effective of all remedies for a fear of not being able to cope is to start coping anyway.

Fear, like stress, has both negative and positive qualities. The person without fear lays him- or herself open to multifarious miseries, miscalculations and misdemeanours. For instance, no fear of injury when aiming to journey to the other side of a busy two-way street could easily result in a bump and a bruise, or even worse. No fears about attaching your TV aerial to the chimney would perhaps be tempting fate too far. And, no fear of failure when entering a new business venture, for example, might well provoke a costly calamity. Fear can promote protection; it can also inspire success.

Fear can be negative for you either when it is inappropriate or when it becomes excessive and overwhelming, thereby causing you to freeze. During 'the freeze', fear can strip you of your most valuable resources, such as creativity, mental dexterity, and the ability to make decisions and to perceive choice. Also, curiously, as the South African writer Alan Paton observed in his work, *The Challenge of Fear*, 'When men are ruled by fear, they strive to prevent the very changes that will abate it.' The freeze of fear can often prevent you from finding your own freedom.

Conscious contemplation of the function of fear reveals that, while fear can at times be a useful warning signal, it is rarely, if ever, a sufficient stress solution. Many people use fear consciously, creatively and constructively to achieve a concerted effort and a peak performance. It is possible, therefore, to rule fear – and, thereby, to ensure that fear does not rule you. However, the fact remains that fear on its own is only an alerting device; it is not a stress solution.

Conscious contemplation of the action of fear reveals that the effects of your fears can often be more dangerous to you than the perceived stress could ever be. Fear focuses on the future, conjuring up imaginary sequences and scenarios, most of which predict, picture and anticipate personal misery and a probable inability to cope. Preoccupation with fear of the future in this way can be so harmful because it can prevent and delay preparing to cope with the present. The moment to make a start to cope – any start – is 'now', not 'when' and not 'if'.

Without courage, there are no successful stress solutions. The first step towards successful stress control must be bravery – bravery to acknowledge and bravery to control your fear. Bravery is often an act of faith. There is one certainty, though, and that is, as soon as you invoke bravery, the appearance and complexion of your perceived stress will begin to change. Just as fear alters perceptions, so too does bravery.

Make a stand, and make it now! Admit your fears, by all means, but never once renounce or lose grip of your courage. The moment you can begin to control is this moment, *now*. Future events will be decided by what you do today. The moment before you, the moment you have now, is probably all you need to attend to. By orientating yourself towards the present, and by being more specific and less general, you leave less space for fear to float through. When coping with fear, it is important to entertain the facts, not fiction!

Whatever plan of action you undertake in life, the seeds of success are sown, always, *always,* by your approach and by your attitude. A courageous approach and attitude to successful stress control are essential. Indeed, a courageous approach and attitude are sometimes remedies in themselves. Whatever route you decide to take, it is worthwhile to remember that a most effective remedy for a fear of not being able to cope is *to start coping*. The words of the Greek philosopher, Plato, ring true: 'Courage is a kind of salvation.'

ACKNOWLEDGE IT

The test of a civilized person is first self-awareness, and then depth after depth of sincerity in self-confrontation.

Clarence Day

Such is the sly, insidious and cunning nature of stress, it can oft-times infiltrate and invade our lives without any conscious awareness on our part. We tend to be so preoccupied with just living, surviving and striving, that often we fail to acknowledge the initial onset of stress in our lives. By the time stress has well and truly set in, we often make the mistake of accepting it as 'normal' and as something that is 'part of me', 'the way I am', or simply, 'my misfortune'.

There are many coping strategies or 'defence mechanisms' we commonly employ to avoid awareness and acknowledgement. We may, for instance, consciously use *suppression* or unconsciously use *repression* to hide feelings of hurt. We may, for instance, employ denial so as to avoid facing up to events and to feelings. We may employ *displacement*, which means, for example, kicking the cat when really we want to kick the boss. Kicking the cat is an altogether safer option!

Projection is the deflection of one's own undesirable traits onto another. For example, someone who struggles to control jealousy may believe that he or she is the object and victim of another person's jealousy, if, that is, projection is being used. *Intellectualization* is an attempt to detach and distance yourself from personal feelings and emotions which may be too painful to acknowledge.

Rationalization attempts to justify a lack of success, wealth, happiness and comfort by employing ideas such as, 'happiness is only transient', or 'wealth is misery'. And *reaction formation* employs beliefs and feelings that are the exact opposite of how you really feel. For instance, someone who is, at heart, very sensitive and introverted, may appear to the world as thick-skinned and extroverted.

In each and every case, these defence mechanisms do not allow you to acknowledge your personal discomforts and stresses. Instead, they temporarily cover over and patch up inner wounds. These defence mechanisms can be very useful temporary measures during extreme stress; they are rarely, if ever, successful long-term stress solutions. To know what causes your stress creates a chance to cope and to control. Self-awareness and personal insight are keys to inner and outer control.

It can often be the case that you may not know why an event stresses you; you know only that it does. It can also often be the case that the feelings accompanying an event that happened long ago remain with you today. A simple, powerful exercise in acknowledgement is to describe your stress in the middle of a blank page, and then, to relax and to allow yourself to draw and to write around the page the thoughts you associate with this event. Such an exercise can help you to become aware, to face up to and to begin to release some of the stresses that have or may have been, until now, hidden from view.

Successful stress control is often all about dealing with 'what is' rather than with 'if only'. Acknowledging to yourself – and maybe also to a friend, a confidant or a professional counsellor – the events and the thoughts that surround a perceived stress is often the first step for release, for relief and for letting go. By acknowledging your stress you can be better positioned to abandon your stress.

FEELINGS?

*Go to your bosom; Knock there, and ask your heart what
it doth know.*

Shakespeare, *Measure for Measure* II. ii. 136

The actual events of a stressful encounter are rarely, of
themselves, a principal source of personal hurt and harm.
Rather, it tends to be the feelings that you associate with a
stressful event and that are invoked within you that are far
more damaging. In other words, the self-injury that can be
caused by turbulent emotions and fragile feelings is often a
more harmful source of stress than the actual events and
circumstances can ever be.

Unacknowledged and uncontrolled feelings can exaggerate
stress and can also lengthen and prolong stress. For instance,
one day of failure, one unpleasant conversation or one
unhappy moment can live on for many weeks, months and
years thereafter. This is especially true when feelings are not
acknowledged and then worked through. If you can
acknowledge how you feel, you will be better able to deal
with the way you feel.

When you aim for successful stress control it is very often
more important to focus on *feelings before facts*. For instance,
a person who fails a driving examination will say that the test
was 'really difficult'. In truth, driving skills are quite basic.
What can be 'really difficult' is learning to steer and to drive
past fears of failure, nervous self-doubt and poor self-esteem.
The same can be true of interviews, presentations,
appointments, meetings, social engagements, relationships,
contests, competitions and other potentially stressful events.

There is nothing quite so comforting and so fortifying as
a feeling; nor is there anything quite so ruinous and
corrosive. For instance, a person may deny his or her heart
to another forever because of the living memory of hurt,

resentment or mistrust that he or she may still associate with a relationship that was over and done with long ago. Here, once again, the main protagonist is not the event itself, but rather the feelings that surrounded and were invoked by the event.

Each of us carries an emotional universe deep within our hearts, the harmony and order of which can easily be disturbed by stress. To keep the climate of your emotional universe both still and calm is essential for successful stress control. This inner peace is our single most vital motivation in life.

Failure to acknowledge how your experience of stress is 'making you feel' can serve to compound your misery. Stress is a conjurer: it throws up feelings of uncertainty, low self-worth, personal disorientation, sadness, powerlessness, inadequacy and fear. These feelings must be acknowledged; these feelings must be gently worked through, for they are potentially very damaging if suppressed, repressed, denied or left alone. Self-awareness and self-honesty are essential steps along the journey of self-healing.

LISTENING

Sink in thyself! There ask what ails thee, at that shrine!
Matthew Arnold

The Greek philosopher and healer, Pythagoras, once wrote, 'There is no illness, only ignorance.' These six words hold a key to successful stress control. The ignorance to which Pythagoras referred is principally a lack of self-knowledge and self-understanding. To know yourself and to understand yourself are essential supports for self-kindness and self-healing.

To listen to your heartbeat, to listen to your lungs, to listen to your muscles, to listen to your nerves – to listen to the language of your body, is to learn how to care – for you. Taking the time to sit down and to listen to your body and to your whole Self, for say five minutes at the end of a day, is a creative, self-healing exercise that can help you to live in better harmony with yourself. Sit down, unwind, and just listen. Hear your Self speak.

So many stresses can be either exacerbated or caused by a neglect to listen to your body and to your Self. Exhaustion and fatigue, anxiety and worry, sadness and unhappiness almost always send out an SOS before they strike. Listening to your body and to your Self is for the most part a forgotten art, and so the SOS signals go unnoticed. Listening can so often be a preventive medicine.

During times of stress it is imperative that we learn to listen to ourselves. For instance, to shut off the voice of grief following a bereavement can be a harmful mistake; to press on and on in the face of exhaustion and fatigue is inviting illness; to pursue a career that cannot cater for your talents may lead to catastrophe; to skip meals continually when your stomach is singing for its supper is also unwise.

There is an ancient Oriental belief that deep, deep within each of us there is a still, small voice which acts as a guiding presence of preservation. This still, small voice sends forth its messages to be translated by both body and brain. This ancient belief also explains why we have been given two ears: one ear for the sounds around us, the other ear for the sound of the still, small voice within us.

We all perform to an independent rhythm and to our own personal tune. To know the rhythm and to know the tune are essential to health and essential to wholeness. Listen, for instance, to your creativity; listen to your dreams; listen to words that echo deep within the chamber of your heart. Too often stress can be self-imposed by serious self-neglect and a failure to read yourself well. Listen well and live well.

EXPRESSION

Hold it in, all you like; it will not go away until you let it out.

A Tibetan Healer

The highest, most precious of friends are often good listeners who are content to allow you to explore, to express and to eject the heavy loads of burden that can weigh you down from within. We all need good listeners, especially during times of crisis and despair. Listening lends necessary space and time for 'brainstorms', free associations and clear-cut expression. Truly, an act of listening can be an act of healing.

To suppress, to repress and to hold in all that we fear and all that we feel is indeed a tantalizing temptation during stressful encounters. From far off, the act of holding in resembles an act of considerable control; at close up, this tyrannical attempt to cope falls miserably short of a cure. To keep a lid on stress most often creates an environment and an atmosphere that is rarely conducive to good healing. Indeed, stress thrives upon the soils of suppression and the rains of repression. It is true to say that, the harder you hold on to your stress, the harder your stress will hold on to you.

To express what it is that you fear and to voice what it is that you feel are essential first steps that can then allow you to confront stress, to control stress and, ultimately, to release stress. Learning to relax, to release and to let go is a veritable art, and will often begin with the discovery and control of self-expression.

Confront your stress, and – now – talk it out, draw it out, sing it out, work it out, dance it out, dream it out, visualize it out, laugh it out, cry it out or scream it out. Expression purges the soul. It can help clarify; it can help objectify. It creates distance; it aids discovery. It changes perspectives; it alters proportions. Look for sounding boards, and be prepared to express yourself. Expression can enable a healing to happen.

FRIENDSHIP

This communicating of a man's self to his friend works two contrary effects; for it redoubleth joys, and cutteth griefs in half.

Francis Bacon, *Of Friendship*

To feel consumed by an overriding desire either to shut down, to close off or to push away the world during moments of intense pressure and personal pain is indeed a common reaction to stress. Just as a rabbit will hurry into its hole, a tortoise will snatch back into its shell and a frightened goldfish will lie still beneath a lily pad, human beings also sometimes experience a need to hide and to obscure themselves from the world.

Withdrawal is an ancient survival instinct which aims to secure self-preservation. It can be, for some, an excellent temporary measure for moments of unbearable strain in that it offers space and time to gather oneself together. We must be careful, however, that positive, short-term withdrawal does not whither away into inappropriate long-term procrastination, dangerous escapism or harmful isolation.

Self-imposed separation is a common symptom of stress. It can also be a *cause* of stress, in that it can turn to isolation and loneliness. In shutting ourselves off from the fury and travesty of a 'mean, bad world', it is most important not to shut out friends, companions and soul-mates as well. When our own inner resources have become so perilously low, it is very often the strength and support of friendship that recharges, refuels and redirects us.

The greatest friendships are often those that are forged through the fires of shared adversity. There is not a true friend in the world who does not rise to the roll of 'a friend in need'. To call upon a friendship during times of stress can be profitable to you in so many unimaginable ways. We all have experience of stress, and we all of us, therefore, have a capacity to help one another: rain does not fall on one roof alone.

One of the most dangerous developments of stress is a distorted perception that triggers a type of tunnel vision. Feelings of isolation and loneliness can contrive to create this long, dark, narrow type of perception – a type of perception that can leave you static and entrenched, powerless and immobile. Friendships offer new perspectives and fresh ideas, help and support, space and time, courage and companionship. These are the lights that can sometimes guide you to the end of your tunnel. By giving your friend a chance you give yourself a chance.

SUPPORTERS

People are lonely because they build walls instead of bridges.
Joseph F. Newton

Stress is like a big, fat poker player who operates with cards of perception-tricks stuffed up both sleeves of his shirt. An intense, overwhelming vacuum of perceived loneliness is a common hand of play, especially during moments of pressure, sadness or uncertainty. The experience of loneliness and of isolation can be a dangerous one in that it can censor support, help, subsidy, upliftment and encouragement from others. For as long as you believe there is no support, there will be little or no chance of support.

Stress and loneliness do so often perform a dance of ever-decreasing circles where perceived stress leads to perceived loneliness and perceived loneliness leads to perceived stress, and so on. One of the most dangerous snippets of self-talk you can hear yourself say during stressful times is, 'I can't be helped' or 'I know they won't be able to help.' If you 'know' you cannot be helped, you will probably be right; if, on the other hand, you think there is a chance of help then you will probably give yourself that chance.

There is no such thing as a solo flight. Performances are a product of both actor and audience, individual and team, player and supporter. A practical, empowering exercise for conquering stress can be, therefore, to take pen to paper and to identify every possible source of support in your life. Give everyone and everything every possible chance to be a supporter. Make your verdict *after* the hearing, not before.

Family, friends and partner are often the most immediate, accessible and understanding supporters. Loved ones can be good sounding boards, understanding listeners, empathic confidants, effective distractors, a source of good entertainment, and wise advisors. Do not make the mistake of overlooking the people who love you merely because they are familiar to you. Be prepared to be surprised – help and support can sometimes come from unexpected sources. Also, be prepared to train your loved ones to offer the support you want – let them know so that you can let them help.

It is certainly true that the people who are closest to you can sometimes be too close to be of positive, practical support. You may find, therefore, that you need to look further afield for your supporters. In particular, you may want to explore avenues of professional therapeutic support, such as doctors, counsellors, psychotherapists, stress groups, health centres, clinics, hypnotherapists and certain complementary therapists, for instance. Professional supporters help you to help yourself, so why not help yourself by contacting one?

Supporters can also arrive in the shape of specialist organizations, centres and group networks. Your local library, Citizens' Advice Bureau, your church, your telephone directories, specialist magazines, local 'What's On' guides or social services centres may be able to offer a route to a possible point of contact. Other supporters may be favourite inspirational words, a regular exercise routine, a social club or well-prepared, nutritious meals. By enlisting the help of supporters you help your perceived resources to outweigh perceived demands.

My Supporters

Who can help me?
My parents, perhaps
My Uncle John
My partner
My friend, Sam
My sister, Jo
An information office
My doctor
My Personnel Officer
A book, maybe?
The library

STRESS-MANAGEMENT GROUPS

*Oft-times an individual is best able to recover and renew,
not alone, but among a few.*
Anonymous

Attending a regular stress-management group can provide immeasurable strength and support during difficult periods in your life. More and more groups and meetings of this kind are now being set up in response to the increasingly stressful times we live in. They are usually run by adult education authorities, health promotion units, counselling centres, or by independent psychotherapists, counsellors, psychologists and specialist stress consultants. Large companies are also beginning to employ counselling services, and very often now send their employees on stress-awareness courses as part of their overall training package.

At a typical stress-management group you will explore what stress is, what causes it, and learn to identify the symptoms and effects of stress that are particular to you. You will then learn a variety of techniques that may include relaxation exercises, anxiety management methods, time-management tactics, requirements for a healthy lifestyle, assertiveness and confidence training, communication skills, goal-setting, problem-solving, meditation, and positive thinking – all of which are designed to help you accomplish successful stress control.

The type of people who attend such groups run the gamut of the human race. They may include business executives, single parents, young mothers, teachers, people out of work, librarians, social workers, students preparing for exams, driving test subjects, people with high blood-pressure, health care professionals, people facing retirement, heart attack victims, divorcees, insomniacs, people on tranquillizers, musicians, sportsmen and -women, policemen and -women, and many other types of people, too.

Everybody should attend a stress-management group at least once in their lives because a stress-management course is really all about self-management and life-management. Within the healing atmosphere of a committed group it is possible to share, to communicate, to create, to explore and to release. Everyone is a teacher to everyone else, and within a group setting participants learn to aim for and to embrace appropriate coping strategies that will help them liberate resources and realize potentials.

It is only a matter of time now before a stress-check service will be incorporated into the National Health Service in Great Britain. Indeed, more and more doctors are already beginning to recommend their patients attend local stress-management groups. Within the next few years we shall see the stress-check take on the same importance as a blood-pressure check, a visit to the doctor and an appointment with the dentist.

IS THE STRESS MINE?

Where there are two, one cannot be wretched, and one not.

Euripides

All human conditions and attitudes are as infectious as the common cold, if not more so. To sit straight-faced in a room of smiles is practically impossible. To burp aloud at a reverential gathering is unthinkable. And to remain calm among a crowd of pandemonium, even if there is no real cause for concern, is to be extremely exceptional. Therefore, whenever you experience displeasure and discomfort, one of the very first things you should do is to ask, 'Does this stress belong to me?'

Human beings have a horrible habit of handing their stress on to passers-by. Strangely enough, this behaviour is probably most true of the people in your life whom you love and who are familiar to you. A hot-tempered boss, a grouchy partner, a tired and exhausted parent, a lonely and unhappy friend, a needy grandparent, or a volatile neighbour, for instance, may use you from time to time, knowingly or unknowingly, as a handy human waste disposal system.

Most people in life are good and generous people when they can afford to be, which is usually when they are happy and coping well. But even the most even-tempered, magnanimous and mild-mannered person can have his or her mean moments. Acknowledge other people's feelings, hear them out, offer empathy, talk to them, point out their behaviour, ignore it, laugh it off, warn others, confront it, share a quiet word, or assert yourself, but do not give these people permission to let their stress sink and sow seed within you.

It is so easy to react unthinkingly and unconsciously to the mood of another person. Thoughts, attitudes, feelings and emotions are conveyed easily, effortlessly and quite naturally from one person to another, often without any conscious intention on the one hand or resistance on the other. It is very important for self-preservation, therefore, that you cultivate an awareness and insight into the private moods and motivations of others. It is also important that you retain at all times a clear sense of independent identity.

There will always be people in your life who will choose your moods, your thoughts and your ideas for you if you do not make sure to choose them for yourself. Whenever you encounter anger, blame, impoliteness or impatience, for example, it is always worth while to remember that you have the option of what, when and how to react. Indeed, you do not need to react at all. Calm, objective consideration, and the question 'Is the stress mine?', are a wonderful shield that enables you to choose, to control and to feel fine.

WRITE IT OUT

A poem, a sentence, causes us to see ourselves. I be, and I see my being, at the same time.
Emerson

The simple act of putting pen to paper can work wonders with problem-solving, decision-making, anxiety knots, tension blocks and other forms of mental and emotional stress. Writing can help to externalize and to objectify internal thoughts, feelings, fears and ideas. Sitting before a blank piece of paper is a little like sitting before a mirror. We write to see ourselves in a new light, from a different angle, and with a fresh focus.

By spilling your thoughts out onto paper you can create clarity, distance and space between you and your thoughts and feelings. Writing is a wave of expression that can help you to wander through the unspoken and the undiscovered. It can help to make the subjective more objective, the unconscious more conscious, and the unexpressed, expressed. Mental clarity, objectivity, knowledge, insight, awareness, understanding, perspective and proportion, and the chance to express yourself – these are just some of the benefits of therapeutic writing.

One method of therapeutic writing is to *brainstorm*. To perform brainstorming, take a blank page and give it a heading – something like, 'My Problem', 'Stress', 'Causes of Stress', 'Why?', 'Solutions', or 'Coping Strategies'. Then make a conscious effort to fill the page full with feelings, thoughts and ideas. Write quickly, without editing, without criticism and without pause. When you've finished, fold the paper up and put it away somewhere safe. An hour later, a day later, or even a week later, return to your writing. Try to analyse it objectively and dispassionately, and look to see what your brainstorming has bubbled up.

Another method of therapeutic writing is to *free associate*. The procedure for free association can be almost identical to that for brainstorming, except that you use as little conscious effort as possible. You may, therefore, like to begin by relaxing for a while, by performing a few rounds of relaxed breathing, for instance. Then, when you are very relaxed, allow thoughts to flow through you onto the headed page before you. Words, phrases, drawings, scribbles and patterns are all acceptable. There should be no conscious consideration when free associating. Later, after a space of time has elapsed, return to your page; you can then analyse consciously what you have produced.

Both brainstorming and free association are based upon a belief that we are potentially the greatest experts for our problems because the solutions to all our problems lie deep within our innermost core. All we need do, therefore, is to express and to realize our conscious and unconscious creative options. Brainstorming and free association can enable us to do this. Another technique is to write a daily 'stress diary' so that you can begin to explore and to understand, consciously, what makes you tick and how it is you react to life.

Don't stop before you start! It is so easy to overlook and to overrule the power and effectiveness of these simple writing techniques. Give yourself the permission to give them a go, and soon you may find that it will be ingrained in you to write away your worries and to write for inner wisdom. Remember: *Nothing comes of doing Nothing*. So, Act!

ACT!

The Universe only rewards action.
Robert Redfern

Charles Handy, in his acclaimed modern masterpiece, *The Age of Unreason*, relates a most disturbing story of an animal experiment which begins by putting a frog into a saucepan of cold water. Heat is applied to the saucepan, slowly warming the water. The poor frog, which is completely free to hop out of the saucepan at any point, just sits there. As the water begins to simmer, the frog blisters. As the water boils, the frog eventually dies.

How does this cruel, abhorrent procedure relate to successful stress control?

The experience of stress demands reaction and response. Most often, this reaction and response can be best described as 'fight or flight'. In other words, we will cope using so-called fighting tactics such as confrontation, assertion and positive attitude, or by using so-called flight tactics such as avoidance, relaxation and retreat. There is, however, one other, less often mentioned category of reaction and response that can be best described as 'freeze'.

Practical action and positive self-help can often give way to manifestations of 'freeze' during stressful moments. These manifestations include crippling anxiety, paralysing fear, unparalleled uncertainty, enormous self-doubt and persistent procrastination. The 'freeze response' may also be termed 'the ostrich effect', for all of its manifestations are akin to the ostrich's trick of burying its head in the sand.

The freeze response is a childlike reaction which, when put into language, roughly translates as, 'I hate this. I wish it would all go away.' If we are honest with ourselves, all of us during times of stress pray, 'I wish . . .'. To wish, to will and to want are futile exercises if you are not also prepared to work. To be powerful, to be effective, and to hop out of the saucepan, it is important to resist the temptation to freeze.

Consideration, contemplation, hesitation and deliberation are all acceptable, providing they arise from an honest intention to act. To act frantically can be as dangerous as to freeze. Think slowly; act quickly. Substitute 15 minutes of aimless anxiety for careful contemplation of, 'What can I be doing, right now, to ease my stress?', and you will find that, after 15 minutes of work, you will be that much closer to achieving all that you would wish, will and want for. Remember, *the only time a person can purchase power is in the present*.

STEP BY STEP

*'Begin at the beginning,' the King said, gravely, 'and go
till you come to the end; then stop.'*
Lewis Carroll, *Alice's Adventures in Wonderland*

During stress we often become enamoured of a special sort
of sight that enables us to see with complete clarity the entire
landscape and history of all our problems, all our failings, all
our obstacles and all our unhappiness. The apparent
enormity of the task before us can conjure such deep-rooted
feelings of perceived powerlessness and believed hopelessness
that recovery can be significantly delayed or postponed.

To be both thoroughly disorientated and wholly
dissatisfied with ourselves and with the plight we are in is a
common experience of stress. The more you become
immersed in stress, the more insurmountable it can appear
to you. Your pain may be real, so too may be your fear, your
sadness and your tears, but this insurmountability is naught
but a trick of perception – a perception blurred by tension,
anxiety and upset.

The highest achievements of life are a culmination of well-
measured little steps. A hopeful champion at Wimbledon
must first put every ounce of effort into winning game one
of the first set of the first match. An aspiring millionaire must
first learn to collect pennies in order to collect pounds, while
a person who hopes to lose weight must begin by losing that
first pound.

In order to 'pick up the pieces', it is absolutely essential
to adopt a policy of step-by-step, one-by-one, day-by-day
and moment-by-moment. There are two simple techniques
for such a system. The first technique is to set a course and
then to list your intended actions, one by one. Those people
who have survived the worst stress of their lives often
dedicate their success to this sort of list-making.

List-making organizes you. It takes the whirling, random thoughts from your mind and places them all, quite motionless, upon the surface of a page. List-making supports objectivity. It clears the mind. It helps you to prioritize actions. One by one you attend to the details before you and, one by one, the fingers of stress must loosen their grip and thereby relinquish control.

The second technique is referred to as *token economies*. Each time you complete an item on your list, be sure to give yourself a token economy. A token economy is a form of personal, enjoyable reward, and can be anything from a mental 'well done' to a bar of chocolate, a glass of wine to a moment of rest, or a lovely meal to a time out with friends. You must ensure, of course, that you choose appropriate rewards.

Operating a step-by-step approach, with the help of lists and token economies, can be a very powerful remedy for the sickness of perceived powerlessness. You will, quite naturally, want to run, to skip and to jump, and, indeed, you will be able to do all of these things – once, that is, you first carefully organize, relearn and rehabilitate, so as to walk step-by-step-by-step.

REFRAMING

If you are distressed by anything external, the pain is not due to the thing itself but to your own estimate of it; and this you have the power to revoke at any moment.

Marcus Aurelius

Cool, calm and clear thinking can often give way to hot, murky exasperation during times of unbridled stress. Thoughts can take on a life of their own, enjoying strange flights of fantasy and wild, wandering whims. During an invasion of insidious stress, it can sometimes seem that no matter what directions or decisions we contemplate, we seem always to hit upon mental cul-de-sacs, one-way streets and dead-end alleys. We believe there is no alternative; therefore there *is* no alternative.

Stress can be so harmful to you because it can interfere with and put a plug on proper perspective. Perspective is vital for the healthy functioning of your mind. You need perspective for vital thinking processes, such as judgement and assessment, measurement and association, and interpretation and response. A sense of perspective and sense of mind are but one and the same. To be able to reframe perspective is an essential skill for successful stress survival.

Without perspective you have no real way of knowing how serious, if at all, a problem is. You also have no real way of knowing what is the best way for you to cope. Your perspectives, perceptions and sense of proportion help you to place your stress accordingly so that successful stress control is either made more difficult or more easy. A minute molehill will be as hard to climb as a mighty mountain if your perspective is clouded.

There is always more than one approach to a problem, no matter how much your stress will attempt to convince you otherwise. Whenever you are seriously stressed, you owe it to yourself to hold on to your perspective, clutching it as a drowning passenger would a passing piece of driftwood in a tossing, turning sea. And if your perspective is unhelpful – let it go, and search for another, more helpful angle. Selecting a successful perspective can be the difference between sinking and swimming.

A fresh viewpoint, a new angle, taking a closer look, distancing yourself, time-travelling, seeing the problem through another person's eyes, and using the lens of hope and the power of positive thought are all useful mental games that can help you to exercise and to control your perspective during times of stress. Laughter, relaxation exercises, physical exercise, meditation, prayer, communication, entertainment and pleasant company are also practical methods of successful stress control because they help to order and to balance personal perception.

How you look at life can so often determine how you live it. Elizabeth Bowen, the writer, once observed, 'If you look at life one way, there is always cause for alarm.' To keep your options open, and to set yourself free, you must be prepared to reframe your perceptions, constantly. At no time is this more true than during moments of personal distress.

GO COSMIC!

I murmured because I had no shoes, until I met a man who had no feet.

Persian Proverb

Stress is never so dangerous than when its perceived shape, size and form so overwhelm you that you begin to lose all measure of proportion and perspective. A personal problem will render you powerless so long as proportion and perspective are out of place. Sanity, self-preservation and every effective coping strategy rest upon your skill and ability to put things in their proper place.

During moments of stress, a broad, holistic, group-orientated outlook often gives way to a more singular, sequential, self-orientated in-look. Your field of perception can become so narrow and so self-centred that all proportion and perspective are lost in a bleak moment of tunnel vision: the pain in your heart becomes the pain of the world; the pressure of a moment becomes the pressure of a lifetime. This is your reality because this is all that you perceive.

Every night, as we sit in the comfort of our own homes,

paraded before us on the television news are murders, rapes, earthquake disasters, transport accidents, civil wars, famines and bomb disasters. We see pictures, close-up, of families bereaving, famine victims barely alive, the children of Beruit crippled by landmines, the students of China crushed by their own army, innocent peoples gassed by their governments, the homeless seeking refuge in houses of cardboard – do any of these pictures and stories compare with your own stress?

Comparison is not meant to trivialize your stress. Rather, comparison is a coping strategy that can help you to shrink your stress into appropriate, manageable proportions. The act of comparison can be an effective personal remedy for a collapsed perspective. To ponder the pain of others and to compare your problems with their plights and predicaments is indeed a sobering exercise for a drunken perspective. It can be the trick that helps you to begin to confront and to deal with your stress.

As well as comparing your own problems with the problems of others in the world, you can also compare your problems of today with the problems you have negotiated successfully in the past. This exercise will serve to remind you of how resourceful and resilient you really are. When perceptions alter and when stresses find their true proportion and perspective, you become powerful again and better placed to cope in a positive, practical manner. Comparisons can be a clever, effective coping strategy.

The writer, Dostoevsky, propounded, 'There is no object on earth which cannot be looked at from a cosmic point of view.' It is certainly true that viewing a problem from a great height can reduce that problem to a very small size. Mountain tops, cathedral spires, hot-air balloons, aircraft flights, sailboats, skyscrapers – the experience of these places and adventures can inspire a more cosmic, holistic appreciation and perception.

To think cosmically, so as to place your stress side-by-side with, for instance, the plight of a young bird in the cold winter months, the struggle and suffering of a third world continent, the ageless evolution of our planet and all our ancestors, the birth of a star, or the collapse of a galaxy – this cosmic, holistic thinking can help, to reduce your problem to size and to increase your capacity to cope. Avoid the narrow tunnel vision: Go cosmic!

POSITIVES

It is better to light a candle than to curse the darkness.
Chinese Proverb

During moments of intense personal pressure and pain, our wounded perception can often programme mind and body almost exclusively with negative, debilitating thoughts of dejection, defeat and despair. Because we perceive we are powerless, we are; because we cannot conceive a hope, there is no hope; and because we believe there is no end, there is no end. One cloud is enough to eclipse the light of the sun.

Whatever we perceive and conceive, we believe – this is especially so during times of stress when we are often open, prone and vulnerable to negative suggestion. To perceive and to ponder positives during times of pressure and pain may seem, therefore, pointless. Deep within yourself you may listen to a hundred reasons why there are no positives. Such is the power of a collapsed perception. The truth will begin to change when perceptions and beliefs begin to change.

To alter selective perception, so as to switch focus from negatives to positives, is an essential skill for happiness and successful stress control. Negatives can convince you to collapse and to give in; positives can empower, praise and help you to win. The agony of adversity will begin to pale when the blind acceptance of negatives starts to fail.

One practical perception technique is called STOP, which stands for Strengths, Teachings, Opportunities and Positives. It can be very advantageous, during times of stress, to practise the STOP technique by answering these four questions:

STOP

1. *What are my Strengths?* Identify your skills, attributes and talents. Make a conscious note of all that you are good at. Stop and ignore that part of you that may want to reply, 'Nothing'!
2. *What is my stress trying to Teach me?* Stop looking for blame, punishment, excuses or scapegoats; identify the lessons of your stress – and then make the appropriate moves.
3. *What Opportunities come with this stress?* Stop focusing on the dead-ends and the cul-de-sacs, and start looking for any potential opportunities. Keep open.
4. *What are the potential Positives?* Stop sticking to negatives; start seeking the positives. What can I be doing right now to make a positive change?

Wherever there are negatives, there are positives, such is the law of natural compensation in life. By choosing to select positives you are choosing to empower yourself, positively. Your adversity becomes a teacher and an opportunity, and through the lessons you live you will discover renewed strength. To quote a famous, familiar saying, 'He knows not his own strength that hath not met adversity.' Preoccupy yourself with positives and you will discover that *adversity advances accomplishment*.

Persistence with this exercise will change what you perceive, what you conceive and what you believe. Don't stop until STOP works for you. Give this exercise as long as it takes, because by the end of it you will be beginning to open yourself up to all of the hope, all of the light and all of the strength that you are. Acknowledge the negatives, but live with the positives, and, in time, you will find that *darkness delivers the daylight*.

THE WORST?

To fear the worst, oft cures the worse.
Shakespeare, *Troilus and Cressida* III. ii. 78

Stress severity is often compounded by a conscious failure to confront and to measure the possible worst. By failing to meet the stare of your stress you can leave yourself open and vulnerable to its teases, its taunts and its threats. The 'unknown enemy' can render you powerless and uncomfortable with all that is unspoken, unexpressed, unacknowledged and uncertain. Concealed in a cloak of invisibility, the 'unknown enemy' is free to spread its chaos and confusion.

Often the most positive and practical path to pursue is to open up to your stress and to confront it, head on: this supports a belief that *the only way out is through*. To fear the worst or to ignore the worst is often far more harmful than attempting to know the worst. Stress can often become so much more severe when your uncontrolled imagination takes hold or when you fail repeatedly to face up to your fears. At least when you know the worst you know where you stand. This in itself can be a tremendous relief.

When tired and exhausted, pessimistic and low, the natural inclination is to avoid the adversary. Retreat and relaxation, distance and detachment, quiet times and inaction can all enhance your capacity to cope, but so too can action-orientated techniques such as cool confrontation. Confrontation demands that the cloak of invisibility is lifted away from your insidious stress. It demands that your stress stands alone, before you, in full view.

So often when you confront a stress it will begin to collapse before you. The act of cool confrontation clarifies. The fruitless paths of worry, anxiety and fear give way to practical coping strategies and a positive personal outlook. Confrontation changes things because you accept control and responsibility for your health, for your happiness and for yourself. Confrontation changes your stress because confrontation changes you. Stress appears as you find it and not as you fear – often there is a world of difference.

Until you confront a stress, your ability to control it will depend upon circumstance, luck and good fortune, if, indeed, such things exist. To take an example, a person receives a bank statement through the post. He fears that he might be overdrawn. To confront his fears he should open the bank statement; instead, he leaves it unopened so as to avoid his fears. From now on, his fears will continue to weigh and to prey upon his mind. He will not know if his actions are appropriate or inappropriate because he does not know if his fears are real or unreal. Until he opens his bank statement he cannot take the appropriate, necessary measures to regain control. He lives in limbo.

A courageous and direct three-step approach to successful stress control is to acknowledge, to express and to confront your stress. It does take a special kind of strength and character to be so direct and determined. Very often, though, people say it takes less bravery to confront a stress than it does to live with the perpetual fears, doubts, uncertainty and worry of an unconfronted stress. Also, there is nothing to stop you engaging the help of a friend, partner, counsellor or psychotherapist for guidance and support. Gratefully accept all the help you can get.

INTERNAL MEMOS

We each of us hold the powers of prophecy:
For, deep within ourselves, the words we do say;
do truly shape the way our world will be.

A Kenyan Poet

Unfortunately, we cannot always dictate, select and control the external events we experience in life, but we have got influence and we have got power when it comes to internal responses. We can dictate, select and control our internal responses. This is very important to acknowledge, because our approach to stress and our attitude to stress can often be very much more damaging to us that the actual stress could ever be on its own.

Stress can sometimes be a sickness, a sickness of perceived powerlessness. Perceived powerlessness often communicates itself through a series of internal memos that may suggest and affirm harmful self-criticism, serious self-doubt, excessive self-pity, personal ineffectiveness, give 'air-time' to failures, censor our successes and sweep in gloom and doom. Long after the actual stressful external event is over, self-defeating internal attitudes, thoughts and feelings are often still busy multiplying the misery.

How you choose to think, what you choose to believe and the manner in which you choose to approach your stress can all either increase or decrease the pain. You can pull your own strings. You can own your own feelings. If you push the permission button you can inspire your own recovery by communicating and conveying positive internal memos of hope, strength and empowerment. *Thinking it so is the first essential step towards making it so.*

Positive internal memos that inspire – 'I can . . .' – that promote – 'I will . . .' – and that affirm – 'I am . . .' – offer, in the face of stress, practical prescriptions for health, healing and wholeness. Statements such as, 'I can be happy,' 'I will succeed,' and 'I am capable' are the sorts of nourishment that can feed, fuel and recharge your efforts at coping, recovery and control. When you aim for positivity, you have nothing to lose, except perhaps, your negativity!

You do not need to deny or suppress the unhappy, hurt feelings you associate with your stress, but by giving more air-time to hope, to optimism and to happiness, you may find you are better able to cope with your personal distress. A frost-bitten hand cries 'pain' as the warm blood begins to flow again; so too, when positives challenge the negatives you may experience some initial pain and resistance. Remember, always, though: *Negative attitudes work against you; positive attitudes work for you.*

BLESSINGS

For help when stressed, remember, 'I, too, am blessed.'
A Yogi from Kashmir

Dangerous stress can sometimes result in a harmful conviction – a conviction that your life is littered with burdens and empty of blessings. It is easy and common to allow perceived burdens to gang up and to overthrow perceived blessings during times of stress – the agony of the moment can so easily block out and obscure the positives, the strengths, the hopes and the blessings you need. As a result, perceived demands do definitely outweigh perceived resources.

The blessings of life are a valuable source of strength and protection against the burdens of life. One very practical, positive exercise to perform during periods of stress is to put pen to paper and to list all of the blessings in your life. Your blessings can be a powerful battery of energy and inspiration, but they must first be acknowledged and appreciated before their energy can be activated. Your blessings can, above all, put your burdens into perspective, thus rendering them less threatening, less harmful and more easy to cope with.

If you believe you have no blessings, then you are a victim of a collapsed perception that so often accompanies stress. Can you see? Can you breathe? Can you hear? Can you read? Can you stand? Can you speak? Can you feel? Can you touch? Make a conscious note of every blessing you experience in your life. Aim to blot out the burdens by identifying as many blessings as possible. Acknowledge you are stressed, by all means, but appreciate, rejoice and accept that you are also blessed.

Blessings can also include strengths, attributes, talents, skills, abilities and characteristics. Identify all that you have and all that you are. Friendships, relatives, partner and other social relationships can also be blessings. Take nothing for granted. Identify every source of joy, comfort and quality you have. By broadcasting your blessings you can, thereby, create an atmosphere that will not tolerate or support an invasion of bullying burdens.

With each blessing you identify, you create one more perceived resource to balance the perceived demands. An appreciation of blessings is a simple, powerful remedy for collapsed perception, for distorted perspectives and for failing proportions. Blessings build you up. By making yourself consciously aware of all that you have in life you are better positioned to you use all of your resources to counteract stress. To inspire coping, and to feel less stressed, it can help to remember that, 'I, too, am blessed.'

WELL-FORMED OUTCOMES

*In every affair consider what precedes and follows, and then
undertake it.*

Epictetus

When the stress alarm sounds, adrenalin rises, the stomach
sinks, muscles tense, heartbeat races and the whole of your
mind and your body primes itself so as to be alert and ready
to act. The subsequent build-up of tension and pressure –
physical, emotional and mental – can become unbearable if
action does not follow. During these moments, forethought,
anticipation and a moment's patience can often give way to
exasperation, anger and impetuous inclination. So often,
undue haste can cause untold harm.

To think it through before you act it through is indeed a
wise way to play. Forethought, consideration and anticipation can help to prepare you, to organize you and to
protect you. To take the time to think ahead will save you
time up ahead. Forethought will also help to accommodate
for the expected and the unexpected. Errors, pitfalls,
problems and possible traps can often be found through the
focus of forethought.

To invent your own strategies in life is indeed one of the
most effective, calculated acts for successful stress control.
Forethought allows you to float into the future for a
foretaste. Like the cavalry officer who sends a scout up into
the pass, you can serve yourself well by practising the skill
of forethought. You will then find that the strength of your
strategies will so often save you. It can certainly be true to
say that when it comes to stress, the person without strategy
is a person without defence.

The regular practice of forethought can help to create well-
formed outcomes. To have a destination, to have a purpose,
to know where you are going – all are vital for a healthy

disposition. Many significant stress surveys have found that both a strong sense of direction and a well-formed outcome are powerful inspirations and supports for positive stress-proofing and practical stress-prevention. It has been found at the same time that chaotic disorientation is both a cause and symptom of stress.

To take the time to form objectives, to set up targets, to go for goal and to aim for well-formed outcomes is to practise essential living. Your well-formed outcomes may centre on the spiritual, revolve around values, measure moral maturity, focus on finances, relate to relationships or promote career development, for instance. Whatever the direction, a well-formed outcome is the catalyst for growth, achievement, developing potentials, personal fulfilment and inner happiness.

It is always worth remembering that *'To think is to act.'* Thinking is, in other words, a practical pursuit and effective endeavour. Skilful forethought can solve perceived problems, deal with decisions, alleviate unnecessary anxieties, conserve energy, alter perceptions, overcome future fears and seek out fresh solutions. Remember, to think a thing through before you act a thing through is a very wise way to play.

SWEAT

> *Regimen is superior to medicine.*
> Voltaire, *A Philosophical Dictionary*

During moments of high anxiety, a tired, unhappy mind will tend to gather and to entertain all manner of thoughts to itself. Your mind can become like a circular racetrack, thought after thought vying for pole position. Thousands of thoughts can quickly accumulate in no time at all, spinning, whirling, roaming, speeding up, accelerating and overtaking one another. Your mind begins to overheat and overcharge as each little thought begins to develop a mind of its own.

To solve your stress, as best as you are able, it is essential to give your conscious mind the very best environment and right amount of time to collect itself, to collate the findings and to come up with a solution. What is needed, then, is some measure of 'traffic control'. Effective traffic control techniques include meditation, creative visualization, hypnotherapy, mental affirmation, communication and music.

Very often, in times of stress, the mind can call upon its faithful companion, the body, to help to ease mental congestion. Therefore, one of the very best things you can do during times of excessive mental tension is to leave the conscious mind alone and to concentrate on physical, bodily tasks such as housework, a brisk walk, gardening, DIY pursuits, stretching, golf, tennis, a quick shower, a trip to the gymnasium, skipping, swimming, and so on. Perspiration promotes inspiration!

Mind blocks and mental knots can often undo themselves when your body is engaged in physical pursuit and healthy activity. Your conscious mind and, more importantly, your unconscious mind, are free to do the necessary filing while you fill your time with physical exercise. Exercising creates distance, distraction and detachment. It can also help to unfold, unknot and untie. The health and harmony of your body supports the health and harmony of your mind, and vice versa. *The light of your mind and the light of your body are as a single flame.*

Logically it might not seem to make sense, but when you leave your thoughts alone you create an opportunity for the future in which you will think faster, more clearly and more appropriately. By investing time and effort in physical labour and exercise you can create a better space within for coping and for control. When you sweat your perspiration pours off, and so too will your stress, leaving your mind free to set up your success. *Don't theorize; exercise!* When it comes to stress and exercise, you can only make it (the stress) go, if you are prepared to give it (exercise) a go.

QUIET TIMES

*If we have not quiet in our minds, outward comfort will
do no more for us than a golden slipper on a gouty foot.*

John Bunyan

Moments of quiet, periods of calm and space for solitude can act as wonderful counterbalances to the action, activity and ambition of a world that appears only to advocate and to accept continually hectic, 'no-time, must-rush' routines.

The failure to punctuate the activity of daily living with moments of rest, relaxation and recreation can seriously undermine personal performance, wholeness and health. Every major lifestyle research programme that has investigated stress-risk has found that an absence of sufficient quiet times (or *QTs*) can be both a significant primary cause of stress and illness and a significant block against rapid rehabilitation and recovery.

Cultivating a capacity to appreciate consciously and to practise continually the practical art of composure, tranquillity and serenity can be an ideal support for successful stress control. Quiet times allow you to take time out so that you can recharge, refuel and rebound back into life again. By allowing yourself to rest, it will help to ensure you can give of your best.

Quiet times can be used to practise relaxation exercises, meditation techniques, creative visualizations or relaxed breathing, for example. Alternatively, this might be a time for a crossword, a warm drink, a cool drink, knitting, a mental pause, music, a meal, a siesta or simply stillness and serenity. Quiet times allow you to collect your thoughts, to absorb the moment and to prepare for moments to come.

Just as there is always a slight, almost imperceptible pause between each breath you take, so too it is a good idea to develop a policy and a schedule that allows for brief moments of rest and reflection along the way. Quiet times appear to be time-wasters only to those who convince themselves they 'haven't the time' to practise them. These people tend to find that stress, ill-health and poor performance are the greatest time-wasters of all. When it comes to practising quiet times, benefits start when *you* start.

NON-ACTION

To do nothing is also a good remedy.

Hippocrates, *Aphorisms 1*

To be a good, kind and wise friend to yourself is of paramount importance during times of stress in your life. You deserve to give yourself every possible care and consideration to help convalesce. It is also important to work out a system or series of coping strategies that will help to restore health and happiness. The most effective coping strategies are almost always action-orientated. Non-action, doing nothing, is a valuable exception to this rule.

The healing process generally, as a rule, requires two essential ingredients: rest and time. This is particularly true for certain specific causes of stress, such as bereavement, separation, divorce, illness and heart attacks, all of which require careful, considered convalescence. Sufficient rest and sufficient time help to create the correct *en-vironment* and *in-vironment* for healing and for building up personal strength and inner resolve.

The healing process can be interrupted by the most honest of intentions: impatience, guilty conscience, too much activity, a willingness to contribute, attempts to carry on as normal and excessive self-expectations, for example. The art of non-action is sometimes the most sensible measure because the instinctive self-healing mechanisms within require the essential ingredients of rest and time for the magic of mending.

Non-action is not an abdication of self-responsibility, nor is it an excuse for persistent procrastination or excessive escapism. On the contrary, non-action is often the most appropriate of all actions, particularly where the healing of body, mind and emotions is concerned. A stable environment of harmony, calm and quiet is vital for personal well-being. The quicker you submit to a course of non-action, the more time you will probably save.

Time is traditionally described as a healer, not because we forget the pain, but because time helps us to digest the pain and to create sufficient strength and inner resolve to begin again. 'Pulling yourself together' in a short space of time is often unfair and unrealistic. Emotions, in particular, require the security of rest, space and time in order to make a complete and full recovery. Short-cuts during convalescence often forecast bad weather up ahead. Let the motto, 'Take time to make time' be your guide, and be not ashamed to follow the words of Shakespeare:

> *O Time, thou must untangle this, not I;*
> *It is too hard a knot for me t'untie!*
>
> *Twelfth Night* II.ii. 38–9

DISTANCE

The field cannot well be seen from within the field.

Emerson, *Circles*

It is possible to enhance dramatically both your resolve and your ability to cope with stress simply by creating a little distance between you and your problems. Stress is often very much more intimidating, deceiving and debilitating close up than it is when viewed from afar. Even a moment's distance can often be enough to help you to rest, to recharge and to reassert yourself.

Distance can deflate the dangers and dilemmas of immediate stressful encounters. Distance can provide distraction, rest, safety, breathing space and time to reflect. A little bit of space between you and your stress can help you to muster new resolve, to set up strategies and to engage help, advice and opinion. Very often a different surrounding will prompt different thoughts, different ideas and vital different perceptions.

An evening out with friends, a meal at a restaurant, a weekend break, a trip to the cinema, a country walk, fun at a fairground, some exercise, recreation, looking up an old friend, a sports event, shopping, or even a holiday, if appropriate, are all excellent distancers. Distancing does not demand isolation and recluse: you can employ your friends to help create distance, distraction and different ideas for you.

Distancing does not require any great amount of time: a cup of tea, leaving the room for a moment, making a telephone call or taking a brisk walk can all help. Distancing does not even require physical travel: deep breathing, relaxation, a drink, some music, a stretch, a yawn, a moment's conversation, a shared joke, a new work task, a competitive mental board game, a crossword, a television programme or a good novel can all help to create distance.

Distancing yourself from you and your problems can prompt a profound change of perception. Space alters perspective. It rearranges priorities. A little bit of distance can allow you to be detached and dispassionate so that you can think more clearly. The complexions and complexities of perceived stress often change when you can transport yourself to a new environment and a safe haven. This is because, as Samuel Johnson said, 'Distance has the same effect on the mind as on the eye.'

RETREAT

Oh that I had wings like a dove! for then would I fly away,
and be at rest.

Psalms, 55: 6

To 'head for the hills' is a time-honoured healing instinct during times of human woe and suffering. The ancient physicians of Greece, the healers of Tibet and China, the medicine priests of the Mayan cultures and the doctors of Victorian Britain, for instance, did not hesitate to prescribe rest and retreat for a tired and weary soul. Retreat can help to relax, refresh, recharge and re-energize the human battery of internal resources that is so often at risk of serious depletion during times of stress.

An oasis, a safe haven, a private patch, a place of beauty, or simply a change of scene, can so often be the catalyst that creates a change, nurtures new thought, aids adjustment, facilitates fun, rekindles resolve, promotes positive perspective, fuels fresh intention and inspires imagination. To rest, to retire and to retreat can rapidly lead to recovery. Retreat is not to escape or to run away; but, rather, to regather so as to march on.

One of the most common causes of personal discomfort and distress is a fundamental lack of quality personal space and quality personal time. We serve others, we attend to others, we work for others, we even live for others, and very often we do so at our own peril, neglecting ourselves. Our supremely social existence can often force us to lose sight of ourselves and of who we are. Personal priorities, aims and achievements, spiritual fulfilment, a sense of satisfaction, wholeness and happiness can all become hazy or hidden in our attempts to cope with the hustle and bustle of modern living.

A practice of regular retreat, or to retreat when coping calls for it, can help to prevent and to cure personal stresses of turmoil and strife. To take a holiday, to visit a retreat centre, to embark upon a weekend break, to take a day off or maybe to visit somewhere new, can serve to take you away from your own personal arena of agony. Things have a funny way of rearranging themselves when you return from retreat. In truth, it is you who have changed, not the events; it is you who have returned rebuilt and renewed, ready to tackle the issues at hand.

Retreat does not need to take up huge amounts of your time. Nor is retreat a time-waster. Regular retreat can be a walk in the park, a stroll by the river, a few moments alone during your morning rituals before work, time in the garden alone, a quiet cup of tea, an absorbing novel, a trip to the letter box, a visit to the local shops, a photograph, picture or painting.

Retreat can also come in the form of a 'magnificent memory'. Magnificent memories are positive moments of private recollection and personal reflection reserved for times when it is truly comforting to feel blessed. Pleasant past memories can magnetize, emblazon and empower the personal present moment so as to inspire and promote a renewed ability to cope.

SERVICE

If you yourself would feel fine, heal and serve and give from time to time.

Native North American Wisdom

It is indeed seemingly strange how a single act of selfless service to another can so often support the server in his or her own times of sorrow. Personal pressures pacify and inner tensions calm when gaze and focus turn away to settle and to serve another in a moment of qualm. Services to others are as shining stars that can sometimes steer and see you through the stormy seas of your own personal sadness and suffering.

Preoccupying yourself with the pains, problems and perceptions of another person can so often serve you well, especially when the motive is sincere and genuine, and meant. You can lose yourself when listening to another. Detachment, distance and disassociation develop as you delve into another person's dilemmas. You can identify with another person's pain and suffering when you involve yourself in his or her world. As a result, your personal problems can, consciously and unconsciously, so often find their true place.

By listening, comforting and sharing with a friend, relative or stranger, you aim to assist and to empower that person so that he or she might take effective action. Your advice, your assistance and your actions, for others, can so often spark a personal revival and re-empowerment. How often have the words you have spoken to others, really, in truth, sounded more like the words you have been longing to say to yourself?

Help and humanity extend far beyond the four walls of any home. To donate your time, your work and your support to the international campaigns that aim to stop the suffering of the hungry, the suffering of the homeless, the suffering of animals and the suffering of the environment, for instance, is also a service that can help you. Although personal gain could not be further from your mind, you cannot help but be empowered by all your actions that are kind.

For some people, especially professional carers and the

unofficial 'agony aunts', stress can be created by a personal neglect that is caused by continual, unceasing care and attention for others. Achieving the appropriate balance and protection of adequate personal space and enough personal time is, therefore, a fundamental aim and necessity of successful stress control. Too much or too little leaves a person feeling brittle. Aim, always, therefore, for the bounty of balance.

NATURE

Gie me ae spark o' Nature's fire,
That's a' the learning I desire.
Robert Burns

To see into the sparkle of a star set upon a blue backcloth of night-time sky; to listen and to hear the hush of a breeze through leaves of mighty oak; to walk along the wavelines of a windswept, golden shore; to stand before the fires and flames of orange, yellow and red that are the glory of the blessed sun; to taste, to touch and to take in the tranquil blue of a clear summer sky; and to walk barefoot upon a natural rug of hilltop grass: Mother Nature; Mother Nurse.

Humanity's greatest misfortune has been to alienate itself from the adoring arms of Mother Nature. The beauties and bounties of Mother Nature and Mother Earth are all but lost, shut out and blacked by the images and illusions that crowd our 'civilized', political, economic existence. Only the poets are left to praise pleasures of peace and personal healing as administered through Mother Nature; Mother Nurse.

In the ancient healing books of Asia there is a prescription for sadness which reads, 'Let your sad heart beat in harmony and in time with Mother Nature's Mind'. Mother Nature offers retreat. She offers solitude. She gives us space. She lends us time. She parades great beauty. She organizes distraction. She provides perspective. It was Byron who wrote, 'There is pleasure in the pathless woods; There is a rapture on the lonely shore; There is society, where none intrudes; By the deep Sea, and Music in its roar; I love not Man the less, but Nature more.'

To walk along a canal footpath, to meander by a river, to wander through a wood, to picnic in a park, to follow public paths through fields and fields and fields, to hug a huge oak, to sail upon the seas, to explore the nearest hills, to lie upon the garden grass, to repot a household plant, to listen to the chorus of crow, blackbird and thrush, to enjoy a fragrance of jasmine, honeysuckle or rose – whatever you wish, tune in and hand over your problems for a while to Mother Nature; Mother Nurse.

Mother Nature's weather, wind and water, Her seasons, sun and snow – they offer tremendous beauty, great power and natural repose. Nature is not for our eyes, but for our hearts. To return to a place of nature can so often soothe, comfort and console so as to effect better successful stress control. Before you go, you cannot know what it is to be with Mother Nature; Mother Nurse. The rewards and returns are always rich. 'Come forth into the light of things,' wrote William Wordsworth, 'Let Nature be your teacher.'

CREATE

Creativity cures the chaos in the heart.
Tibetan proverb

Continual creative expression and a well-developed sense of appreciation and respect for creativity are hallmarks of personal health, happiness and wholeness. To make the time and space to allow for creativity, even when that time and space may not appear to be there, is also a fundamental factor that feeds self-worth and self-development, and that also can facilitate successful stress control.

We are, all of us, creative sparks. Creativity is as natural as breathing. Creating is synonymous with living. And yet, most of modern humanity persists in preventing a natural, personal full flow of creative expression. We have somehow been tricked into thinking that creativity is reserved only for the genius and for the artist. Creativity is your birthright. Creativity can also be your salvation, your therapy and your liberation.

Creative, positive thoughts and actions can help you to survive the snares of stress. Tensions, pressures and adversity often necessitate mental dexterity. To raise new questions, to focus afresh, to promote new possibilities, to alter the angle, to challenge perceptions and to invoke inspiration all require creative control. Problem-solving, decision-making, mental knots and emotional wounds are like cages to the person who will ignore the enterprise of his or her own positive creative potential.

Creativity is a therapy. To express your problems through written words, painted pictures, music, movement and dance is often a first essential step towards healing and wholeness. In recent times, the growths of art therapy, music therapy, drama therapy, yoga therapy and dance therapy, for instance, have rediscovered creativity's central, curative role in the process of healing and wholeness. To create is to live; to create is to heal.

We are, all of us, creative sparks. Your choice of clothes, the style of your hair, the foods you cook, the decoration of your home, the plants in each room, the arrangement of your garden or window box, the car you drive, your favourite colours, the music you attune to, the books you read, your interests and your hobbies – these are all expressions of your natural, creative expression. To cultivate this expression in a conscious fashion is to fill your life with a greater fullness.

To engage in a creative pursuit has so many untold pleasures and benefits. To write, to sing, to dance, to draw, to paint, to etch, to stitch, to weave, to sculpt, to carve, to shape and to design adds to the fullness of self-expression. So many stresses are caused by what is unspoken, unseen, unheard and untouched. Creative self-expression can enable a person to explore and to experience him- or herself, fully. The right creative environment is both enriching and inspiring.

Entertainment is one of the most profound and enriching healers of all. It is no wonder that, for instance, the ancient Greeks built their large open-air theatres next to their impressive healing temples. Theatre, opera, a symphony, an absorbing novel, a radio play, the cinema and other similar forms of entertainment can help you to detach, to relax, to enjoy, to uplift, to forget for a while, to distance, and later on, maybe, to perceive things differently. Personal treats during a personal trauma can so often trigger and enhance a person's capacity to cope.

PHILOSOPHY

Oh God, make us children of quietness, and heirs of peace.
St Clement of Alexandria

The light of personal philosophy soothes the might of personal pain. Our capacity to cope with calamity can so easily be enhanced by a spiritual conviction, a spiritual faith and a spiritual philosophy. To practise a spiritual philosophy can provide a person with the understanding, the tolerance, the perspective and the firm inner purpose that puts personal pain in its place. The right philosophy can set a person free.

To cope well with the world, it can certainly help to invest your trust, your efforts and your hopes in something that is by far and away much bigger than the world. Philosophy can lift a person up. Creative, spiritual contemplation can promote a fear-free focus, heightened perception, holistic sight, renewed resolve and inner light. A concept of Creator, expressed perhaps as God, Brahma, Allah, Father/Mother, Sun or Jehovah, is an inspiration that can console, comfort and give rest.

Spiritual philosophy advocates the need for peace, for composure, a quiet mind, solitude, relaxation and tranquillity; spiritual endeavour can enhance successful stress control because it helps to create such qualities. Prayer, contemplation, meditation, service, learning, wise words, parables and readings can all help to create a battery of spiritual strength that can support mind, body and emotion. We all have an inner, rechargeable spiritual battery. Like any other rechargeable battery, though, it must first be filled in order to flow.

To give expression to your spiritual self is to give expression to your whole self. Spiritual philosophy is about practice, not platitudes. To invest in the spiritual can certainly serve to enhance understanding and control of the physical, the mental and the emotional. Spiritual *outlook* and *inlook* can support a perception that helps to put things in their place and can create a realization that stirs resources, reserves and remedies for coping. To live a life without philosophy is to run the risk of being dashed over and over against the rocks by a cruel, rugged sea. Personal philosophy and spiritual realization provide compass, map and stars – the tools of navigation.

'DON'T QUIT'

'Don't Quit' is a model example of the importance of a sustained positive approach to personal stress. It has served as an inspiration and comfort to many people over the years. If you read it carefully it does not advocate effort, effort and more effort. Rather, it encourages a balance between rest and effort; above all, it encourages a person to create and to maintain a vision that, if held firmly enough, must eventually become reality.

Stress disorientates us; it obscures our perception; it creates uncertainty and fear; it can also sap our motivation and will. 'Don't Quit' encourages us not to surrender to and be controlled by stress. It says we must always remain defiant, holding on to a vision of hope and belief that will in itself be instrumental in helping to create a happy and rewarding future. Without that vision of hope and belief we may never inherit the future we deserve – a future that may at this time be a lot closer to us than our stress is allowing us to see.

> *When things go wrong, as they sometimes will,*
> *When the road you're trudging seems all up hill,*
> *When the funds are low and the debts are high,*
> *And you want to smile, but you have to sigh,*
> *When care is pressing you down a bit,*
> *Rest, if you must – but don't you quit.*
>
> *Life is queer with its twists and turns,*
> *As any one of us sometimes learns,*
> *And many a failure turns about*
> *When he might have won had he stuck it out;*
> *Don't give up though the pace seems slow –*
> *you might succeed with another blow.*
>
> *Often the goal is nearer than it seems*
> *To a faint and faltering person,*
> *Often the struggler has given up*
> *When he might have captured the victor's cup.*
> *And he learned too late when the night slipped down,*
> *How close he was to the golden crown.*

Success is failure turned inside out –
The silver tint of the clouds of doubt,
And you never can tell how close you are,
It may be near when it seems afar;
So stick to the fight when you're hardest hit –
It's when things seem worst that you mustn't quit.

3

RELAX, RELEASE AND LET GO

I can be calm, relaxed and confident.

RELAXED BREATHING

A normal, healthy breathing pattern tends to falter and collapse at the first sign of harm or threat. The initial impact of stress is, therefore, often accelerated and made worse by a bothered and battered breathing pattern. Stressed breathing can easily accentuate perceived powerlessness, add to mental disorientation and increase emotional uncertainty, all of which can, in turn, perpetuate more stressed breathing. To control your breath is very often, therefore, a first step towards successful stress control.

The medical term *hyperventilation* describes a quick, shallow, irregular pattern of over-breathing. Very occasionally, it is also used to describe patterns of under-breathing. Over-breathing seems to happen most often when we perceive or experience high anxiety, panic and phobia, exhaustion and fatigue, anger and arousal, and fear and fright. Under-breathing seems to happen most often when we experience moments of shock, sadness, depression or dejection, during which the lungs may suffer from a state of mild paralysis. Indeed, the breathing can become so slow and so shallow as to be almost unnoticeable.

Mental composure and emotional calm can also suffer as

a result of stressed breathing. Undue or heightened emotional sensitivity, feeling weepy, dark pools of perception, poor and patchy perspective, racing chariots of thought, cloudy concentration, a reluctance to rest and to relax, willowy self-worth, and a failure to see the wood for the trees, may all ensue as a result of uneven, stressed breathing. To be relaxed and easy, it is important to allow your breathing to be relaxed and easy.

Relaxed breathing is, by contrast, an entirely natural method of breathing which is performed with a deep, long and regular rhythm. Like the gentle waves of sea lapping a golden shore, or like the measured swing of a pendulum, relaxed breathing has all the certainty, balance and poise necessary for supporting the essential order and harmony of both mind and body. Many people who take the time to change the way they breathe say they experience a greater rest, relaxation and ease.

10 Physical Effects of Poor Breathing

- Deprives your body of nourishment
- Drains your nervous system
- Evaporates your energy
- Makes muscles tense
- Raises or lowers blood-pressure
- Inhibits circulatory flow
- Creates an 'anaemic' look
- Promotes poor posture
- Disturbs and unsettles digestion
- Can lead to colds, bronchitis and asthma

Relaxed breathing can be, therefore, a powerful prevention and natural antidote for stress. To balance your breath can help to promote relaxation, support energy production, reduce muscle tension, soothe nervous strain, support body circulation, heal the heart, aid digestion, and generally help to maintain your body balance. The same is also true for the homoeostasis, or balance, of your mind and your emotions.

Relaxed breathing is an essential cornerstone of most popular, deep relaxation techniques, including progressive relaxation, meditation, autogenics and hypnotherapy. It is an exercise that facilitates relaxation induction, making it easier to begin and to get into relaxation. It also acts as a relaxation deepener. In other words, the better you perform relaxed breathing, the better you can relax; and the better you relax, the better you can perform relaxed breathing.

Relaxed Breathing Exercise

1. Find a comfortable spot where you can lie down or sit down, and where you know you will not be disturbed. Ensure lighting is low, any tight clothes are loose, and that you are entirely comfortable, both physically and mentally.
2. Place your arms by your sides, palms facing the ceiling. Ensure your head, neck and spine are neatly aligned. Try also to distribute the weight of your body evenly on both the right-hand and left-hand sides.
3. Close your eyes, if you wish. Tune in to the stillness of your body. Focus your awareness on the moment of 'here and now'. Turn your attention to your breathing.
4. To create a deep, long, slow rhythm, allow your breathing to become deeper, longer and slower. Allow yourself to breathe down deep in the abdomen area, pushing the stomach out as you breathe in and letting the stomach sink back down again as you breathe out.
5. Repeat as you inhale, 'Deep and long and slow'. As you exhale, repeat, 'Slow and long and deep'. Whenever your

mind wanders, gently bring it back to your breathing again. You are now performing relaxed breathing.

6. As the lungs continue to breathe deeper, longer and slower, become aware of how the whole of your body begins to breathe deeper, longer and slower. As you inhale, imbibe pure energy; as you exhale, eject your stress.

7. End your relaxation as deliberately as you began it. First, stir the body gently; second, open your eyes; third, sit up and stand up carefully. Five minutes of relaxed breathing is plenty for the first few days. Increase the time thereafter as you see fit.

To perform relaxed breathing first thing in the morning can help to set you up for the rest of your day, and to perform relaxed breathing last thing at night can help to promote a refreshing, healing, deep sleep. Once you have the measure of the relaxed breathing, you will find you are able to perform it anywhere and at any time without attracting any undue attention or feelings of embarrassment. You may also eventually find yourself performing relaxed breathing quite naturally, without any conscious awareness or concern, even during stressful encounters. This is perfectly OK because relaxed breathing is the natural, healing way to breathe.

THE MUSCLE TENSION CHECK

The word 'stress' is partly derived from a Latin word *stringere*, which means to bind and to draw tight. You may very often find you use words such as 'strained', 'stretched' and 'tense' to describe the way you are feeling when stressed. It is interesting to note that these words correspond in particular to the way the muscles of your body react to stressful encounters.

The muscles of your body work in groups, each group

S. C. A. R.
A four step negative stress cycle

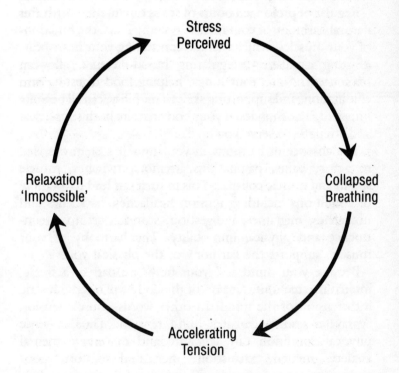

Stress
Perceived

Collapsed
Breathing

Accelerating
Tension

Relaxation
'Impossible'

operating in natural opposition to another group so as to create harmony. For instance, when you straighten your arm, your tricep muscles contract and your bicep muscles relax; when you bend your arm, your biceps contract and your triceps relax. In this way, the muscles of your body can hopefully achieve a natural balance between exertion and rest, and thus they avoid harmful levels of over-arousal or under-arousal. Once again, another type of homoeostasis, or natural harmony, is at work.

Regular or prolonged bouts of stress can interfere with this natural harmony of your muscle system. Thus, the functions of your muscles, which include controlling your heart beat, assisting circulation, regulating blood-pressure, allowing oxygen entry into your lungs, helping food digestion and elimination, and supporting skeletal mobility, can all become impaired. The muscles of your body require both suppleness and strength to serve you well.

The absence of harmony in your muscle system can lead to aches, pains, palpitations, tremors, twitches, muscle spasm and muscle collapse. This in turn can lead to a variety of conditions including tension headaches, backaches and neckaches, migraines, indigestion, stomach cramp, incontinence and physical immobility. The harmony of your muscles supports the harmony of the physical you.

Because your mind and your body are part of a single, interconnected unit, tension of the body will often translate into tension of the mind. In other words, muscle tension aggravates and exacerbates mind tension. Thus, a tense physical condition can aggravate and exacerbate mental anxiety, mental exhaustion, mental discomfort, poor concentration and general ineffectiveness and disorientation.

To care for the muscles of your body on a day-to-day basis is both a useful stress prevention exercise and effective stress remedy. Performing a regular *Muscle Tension Check* throughout the day can help to ensure that muscle tension is reduced, released and avoided. As you relax, release and let go of your muscle tension, you may also find that you relax, release and let go of your mental tension.

You can prepare for the Muscle Tension Check as you would for a full relaxation routine, or, otherwise, perform it as an on-the-spot, of-the-minute exercise.

Muscle Tension Check

1. As you breathe in, focus your attention on the frontalis muscle across your forehead. As you breathe out, mentally and physically relax, release and let go. During the exhalation, you may wish to repeat silently, 'relax, release and let go'.
2. As you breathe in, focus your attention on the sterno-mastoid muscle of your neck. As you breathe out, mentally and physically relax, release and let go. Enhance the exhalation by repeating silently, 'relax, release and let go'.
3. As you breathe in, focus your attention on the trapezius and deltoid muscles of your shoulders. As you breathe out, mentally and physically relax, release and let go. Silently repeat, 'relax, release and let go.'
4. As you breathe in, focus your attention on the pectoralis major muscle of your chest. As you breathe out, mentally and physically relax, release and let go. Say, 'relax, release and let go.'
5. As you breathe in, focus your attention on the latissimus dorsi muscle of your back. As you breathe out, mentally and physically relax, release and let go. Add, 'relax, release and let go.'
6. As you breathe in, focus your attention on the rectus abdominis muscle of your stomach. As you breathe out, mentally and physically relax, release and let go. Affirm, 'relax, release and let go'.

7. As you breathe in, focus your attention on all the various muscles of your feet. As you breathe out, mentally and physically, relax, release and let go. Repeat, 'relax, release and let go'.

Each day, as many times as you like, it is good to take a moment to make sure that what you are doing is supporting the harmony of your muscle system. The four most important points are to ensure that, 1) you assume a healthy, upright sitting position when seated, 2) you walk with a straight, well-aligned posture, 3) your body is stretched, flexed and made supple from time to time, and 4) your breathing is full, deep and relaxed at all times. And remember, also, that relaxed muscle tension inspires relaxed mental tension.

PROGRESSIVE RELAXATION

Progressive relaxation is an ancient relaxation system which has been given a modern name. This short, effective and easy-to-perform therapeutic technique aims to restore harmony to the muscles of your body. It is a particularly good exercise for recognizing and releasing pockets of muscle tension that may accumulate throughout the day around, for instance, your shoulders, your neck, your forehead, your chest, your legs and your feet.

By purposefully relaxing the muscles of your body, relaxation also spreads to your nervous system, to your lungs, to your heart and to the whole of your being. Such is the effectiveness of this simple practice that it is now commonly prescribed by physiologists, clinical psychologists, psycho-therapists and other health care professionals to help treat stress-related illnesses. Many women are first introduced to a variation on this exercise at antenatal clinics.

Progressive relaxation is as much a learning exercise as a practical technique. By performing progressive relaxation you learn to identify the subtle, though definite, difference between a relaxed muscle and a tense muscle. This is significant because relaxation and stress research has shown that for many of us we are so busy coping with the challenges of our day that we fail to register the onset of muscle tension. In other words, stress and muscle tension build-up can catch us by surprise, thus making its impact all the more difficult to cope with.

Progressive relaxation can also help to detect even the most subtle tension in all parts of the body and mind. As many as eight out of every ten people live with high levels of consciously undetected chronic (long-term) muscle tension which has built up and not been dealt with over many years (rather like the action of plaque on teeth).

10 Physical Effects of Muscle Tension

- Tension headaches
- Migraines
- Eye strain
- Neck ache
- Palpitations
- Poor breathing
- Back pain
- Stomach cramps
- Nervous tremor
- Exhaustion

Full Progressive Relaxation Routine

1. Choose a warm place which you feel is conducive to relaxation, and in which you know you will not be

disturbed. Close the door, dim the lights, loosen your clothing, lie down and then close your eyes. If you are lying on the floor you may wish to use a folded blanket to give added comfort.

2. Now that you have prepared the body you should also prepare the mind. You can do this by allowing the mind to concentrate on the performance of several rounds of relaxed breathing. Also, you might wish to picture yourself in your mind's eye as lying down and relaxing on the floor.

3. Once you feel settled, place your attention on your feet. First, as you breathe in, tense the muscles of your feet. Second, as you hold your breath for a moment or two, hold the tension in your feet. Third, as you breathe out, release the tension in your feet and relax.

4. Now move on to your ankles. First, as you breathe in, tense the muscles around your ankles. Second, as you hold your breath for a moment or two, hold the tension around your ankles. Third, as you breathe out, release the tension around your ankles and relax.

5. Next, you may wish to relax your calf muscles. First, as you breathe in, tense your calf muscles. Second, as you hold your breath for a moment or two, hold the tension within your calves. Third, as you breathe out, release the tension within your calves and relax.

6. To continue the practice, you can perform this same relaxation sequence working the length of your body up to the crown of your head. Go next to your knees, your thighs, your pelvis, your buttocks, your hips, your stomach, your chest, your spine; and then your hands, your elbows, your arms, your shoulders, your neck, your face and your forehead.

7. To finish, first tense the whole of your body as you breathe in; second, hold the tension of your body as you retain your breath; and third, relax your entire body as you

breathe out, slowly and deeply. By now you should feel comfortable and gently poised. Resist the temptation to doze or fall asleep unless you are performing this exercise last thing at night. The more active and less dozy your relaxations are, the greater the benefits you will enjoy.

8. Ending a relaxation practice is as important as the preparation. You must always come out of a relaxation gradually and gently. You may wish to wiggle the fingers and toes to begin with. Afterwards, you may also like to stretch your body.

One note of caution: you should not tense your muscles too hard, particularly around your stomach, heart, neck and forehead regions, and especially if you are susceptible to headaches, or have ulcers or a heart condition, for instance. If you are in any doubt at all you should consult your doctor.

NERVE RELAXATION EXERCISES

The part of your nervous system that is most often associated with the stress response is the autonomic nervous system. This system is divided into a sympathetic branch and a parasympathetic branch, both of which co-operate with one other so as to create and to maintain an essential homoeostasis, or natural order, for all of your nerves.

In times of stress, the hypothalamus gland in your brain, otherwise known as the stress response control centre, sends out hormones which activate the sympathetic branch of your nervous system so as to prepare for 'fight or flight'. The action of your sympathetic branch then helps to mobilize your entire body, quickening your heart rate, raising blood-pressure, increasing the production of blood sugar and body food, and activating your muscle system.

Once the perceived stress has passed it is the job of your

parasympathetic branch to recreate the inner order and harmony of your nervous system by slowing the heart rate, lowering blood-pressure, normalizing breathing patterns, relaxing your muscles, etc. Your nervous system can then rest and regenerate in preparation for its next call of command.

If, however, the sympathetic branch has to respond to stress too often or on a prolonged basis, then the nerves of your body can become frayed and tangled. We sometimes use words and phrases such as 'frayed nerves', 'tense and nervy' or 'a bundle of nerves' to describe how we are feeling during these moments. The essential harmony has been broken. Regular or prolonged stress will continue to suppress the parasympathetic branch and to promote excessive activity in the sympathetic branch, thereby exhausting and depleting the vital systems and organs of your body.

Relaxation techniques such as relaxed breathing, meditation, progressive relaxation and autogenics are very often effective because they influence the parasympathetic branch of your nervous system to calm down and to balance out the activity of the sympathetic branch. Medical research seems to suggest that the nervous system can also be trained to respond well to either 'word commands' or 'picture plays'.

Word commands are simple, easy-to-repeat mental prescription formulas such as 'Relaxed, relaxed, relaxed,' 'I am now relaxing my mind and body,' 'Calm, relaxed and confident,' 'Release' and 'My mind and body are serene and still.' By repeating word commands as you relax, you can inspire and create a better atmosphere within you for coping. With regular practice, your word commands can become a personal motto, an anthem and a source of inspiration.

To create your own word command, ensure that the words you choose are honest, positive and easy to remember. To get the maximum therapeutic pleasure from this simple, powerful technique, you may wish in the beginning to prepare for word commands as you would for a standard relaxation exercise. With practice, word commands can be performed anywhere and at any time. Word commands can be performed for as long as 15 minutes at any one time to as little as 15 seconds.

Word Commands

1. Allow yourself to become quiet, comfortable and still. Practise a few rounds of relaxed breathing, allowing yourself to breathe deeper, longer and slower with each and every breath you take.
2. As you inhale, silently repeat your chosen word command. As you exhale, repeat your chosen word command again. For example, breathing in: 'I am calm, relaxed and confident;' breathing out: 'I am calm relaxed and confident.'
3. As you continue with the exercise, engage your creative power of imagination to help transform the word command from lifeless words to a living reality. A sincere belief is the active agent of transformation.
4. If you choose to perform word commands as a full relaxation routine, be sure to end the exercise as gently and as carefully as you prepared for it.

Your creative brain is designed to process and convey information using verbal language and visual language. During each and every moment of your day, your brain is continually feeding a free flow of mental images through your mind. These mental visualizations can have a profound effect on the equilibrium of your entire system – physical, mental, emotional and spiritual. In other words, the pictures of your mind can either be healing or harmful.

'Picture plays' are creative therapeutic exercises that aim to harness the healing power of mental images to help promote harmony, happiness and wholeness. Mental images inspire real effects. Behavioural psychologists employ visualization techniques as a proven strategy for controlling anxiety and phobias, for example. There are other schools of psychology that work exclusively with mental pictures as a healing tool. Mental images can be medicines.

A mental fantasy of a rain forest with a cool blue-white waterfall flowing between rugged rock and lush green vegetation can be a natural, energizing, inspiring healing experience. Another positive picture play might be a personal mental image that affirms a happy you, a calm you, a popular you, feeling relaxed, positive and joyful. Imagining and behaving 'as if' can often inspire new attitudes, new achievements and new realities. Pictures are powerful.

As with word commands, you can perform picture plays as a complete relaxation routine, or you can use them for portable, instant practice, anywhere and at any time. The more you practise picture plays the more you will discover and benefit from the potential of their definite, therapeutic properties. Simply allow your picture plays to relax you, to energize you and to inspire you.

Picture Plays

1. Allow yourself to settle and to become silent and still. Close your eyes, if you wish, and let your body become limp, loose and light.
2. Once you feel comfortably poised, balance your breathing by performing several rounds of long, deep, slow breathing. The more relaxed you are, the easier it is to hold the pictures in your mind.
3. Select a personal picture play and allow yourself to breathe and to flow with the sequence of events. Abandon the critical and embrace the creative. Reach for the pictures and image them as real.

4. Picture plays can be performed for as long as you like and as often as you like. Be sure, though, to end your picture plays as carefully and as gently as you prepared for them.

MEDITATION

The physiological reaction of the body and the psychological reaction of the mind to a well-performed meditation has been found by medical research to be almost the exact opposite to the initial 'fight or flight' reactions conjured up by the stress response. Meditation has a great potential, therefore, as a preventive and curative technique for effecting successful stress control.

The psychological reaction of the mind to a well-performed meditation has also been measured on many occasions. The results seem to show that the mind is able both to relax and to concentrate much better. In other words, the mind is better poised. This poise can profoundly affect your mental and emotional health and performance. Meditation as a psychotherapeutic tool is, for this reason, becoming more and more popular in the counselling and psychotherapy professions.

10 Physical Benefits of Meditation

- Regulates heart beat
- Lowers blood-pressure
- Reduces muscle tension
- Relaxes the breathing
- Soothes the nerves
- Improves body posture
- Calms brainwaves
- Relieves physical pain
- Conserves energy
- Boosts the immune system

The brainwave activity during meditation is also most revealing. Many meditators soon find they are able to develop brainwave patterns that show clear and strong levels of alpha waves, the brainwaves associated with relaxation, energy, detachment, creativity and ideas. Some meditators can even produce brainwaves which are normally associated with deep sleep. Thus, meditation can give you the healing benefits of sleep while you are awake. For this reason, meditation is sometimes called 'waking sleep'.

Many of the most easy-to-master basic meditations, such as *A-to-Z*, are based on simple concentration. By allowing the whole of your attention to focus on a single concentration point, you can allow your mind and body to become silent, centred and still; this is often in stark contrast to the hurry-flurry of a normal daily routine in which your mind and body are put through an assault course of pressures, positions, demands and obstacles. As you begin to achieve this physical and mental poise, so the mind and body are made free to promote rest, relaxation, healing and energy.

Meditation also offers an opportunity for quality personal space and quality personal time. Meditation philosophy states quite clearly that, by regularly taking time out of life, you will find more to put back into life. Meditation often becomes an oasis for mind, body and soul – an opportunity to rest and recharge, to relax and let go, to release and be free. Many people experience meditation as a time of renewal, an inspiration point for a distressed mind, tired body and weary soul. Meditation is a medicine – for mind, body and soul. Meditation can inspire successful stress control.

How to Perform Meditation

Your meditation will only be as good as your preparation for it. The most common obstacle to meditation is tension. It is important, therefore, to allow yourself to settle and to be still. As with your relaxation practice, you should find a quiet, comfortable room where there is little or no noise, and where you know you will not be disturbed.

There are a number of recommended postures for meditation. To begin with, though, you can either sit cross-legged on the floor, sit upright in a comfortable chair, or, if you prefer, lie down on your back. The important thing is to feel the body is comfortable and settled and that your head, neck and spine are aligned. Before you begin a meditation it is very useful to perform a few rounds of relaxed breathing and also to perform a quick Muscle Tension Check. If you have meditated well you will find that by the end you are breathing naturally anyway and that your skeletal muscles are loose and relaxed. Therefore, performing these two practices can be perfect for preparing for meditation.

The timing of your meditation is important. It is recommended that you find space to meditate especially at the beginning of the day. It is remarkable how meditating at this time can set you up for your whole day. It can soon be as important to you as getting dressed. Meditating at midday, if circumstances permit, is a great boost that can help to keep you on the right track. And meditating last thing at night can help to inspire a most relaxing and refreshing deep sleep.

The length of your meditation should be no longer than five minutes to begin with. The abiding rule at all times must be quality, not quantity. We are so often more preoccupied with quantity than quality; indeed this is one reason why we may need to meditate. Resolve to do no more than five minutes at first, and you may find that the influence and effect of a few minutes of good meditation can last for a long, long time.

A-to-Z Meditation

1. Allow yourself to become calm, relaxed and comfortable. Become aware of your breathing pattern, and begin to develop a slower, longer and deeper breath with every inhalation and with every exhalation.
2. Breathe in, breathe out, and mentally repeat, 'A'. Breathe in, breathe out, and mentally repeat, 'B'. Breathe in, breathe out, and mentally repeat, 'C'. Continue through the alphabet up to 'Z'.
3. Your mind will wander, at first. Do not be at all perturbed. Simply go back to 'A' again, and take one letter at a time. Do not try to force concentration; you must allow concentration to happen, naturally.
4. When you have arrived at 'Z' you can either stop or you can perform the sequence in reverse from 'Z' to 'A' and then stop. Ensure that you end your meditation as gently and as carefully as you began it.

SELF-HYPNOSIS AND HYPNOTHERAPY

The term 'hypnosis' describes a condition of profound relaxation that you can either allow yourself to enter, as with self-hypnosis, or that you can allow a professional therapist to guide you into, as with hypnotherapy. The term 'hypnotherapy' describes the use of therapy delivered and received during a condition of profound relaxation and acceptance.

The combination of subtle and profound relaxation with potent and positive suggestion has been found to be a most effective, practical stress control therapy, as described by hundreds and hundreds of medical and scientific trials. Hypnosis can often dissolve the grip of stress that lurks behind presenting conditions such as migraine, high blood-pressure, exhaustion, menstrual problems and allergies.

Many of the common physical symptoms and behaviours of stress, such as nail biting, stuttering, nervous tremor, speech impairments, spots, acne and minor incontinence can also be helped by self-hypnosis and hypnotherapy. Hypnosis can be remarkably effective at healing the habits that can so easily hinder your positive health and well-being.

Hypnosis is very often practised in conjunction with psychotherapy. Hence, another explanation of the term hypnotherapy. Many hypnotherapists are therefore qualified counsellors, psychotherapists, psychiatrists, nurses or doctors. Many emotional and mental forms of stress, such as depression, phobias, loneliness, jealousy, low self-esteem and anger may also be greatly helped by a course of hypnotherapy treatments.

You needn't be ill to benefit from self-hypnosis and hypnotherapy. Self-hypnosis and hypnotherapy can be used to develop self-confidence, to help problem-solving and decision-making, to encourage creative thinking, to adopt good goal-setting, to improve memory, and for becoming a successful speaker, for instance.

Hypnosis theory states that we live in a world of possibilities. Our potential is as great as we can conceive of. There are two obstacles to this potential. One of these obstacles is stress, in any of its multifarious forms. The other obstacle is poor programming. We can gain better access to this potential, however, through a three-step process.

Relaxation – Suggestion – Affirmation

First, you must learn to relax, both physically and mentally. This is essential, because the impact and influence of suggestion are governed by the depth of your relaxation. When you are deeply relaxed, the suggestive or programming power behind all words has an especially powerful effect and influence. Once the seeds of suggestion are planted, they need to be affirmed, again and again, so as to take root and so as eventually to manifest and to flower in your life.

10 Specialist Hypnotherapy Applications

- Successful stress control
- Eliminating phobias
- Promoting relaxation
- Restoring natural self-confidence
- Controlling weight
- Stopping smoking
- Aiding examination success
- Increasing sports performance
- Combatting insomnia
- Promoting creative thinking
- Bettering work performance

'Seven Breaths' Self-Hypnosis Formula

Prepare for this exercise as you would for a normal relaxation practice. Ensure your surroundings are as conducive as possible for deep relaxation, and allow your body to become settled and still.

When you feel ready, allow your mind to focus on your breathing as you perform a few rounds of relaxed breathing. Repeat the following 'relax, release, let go' prescriptions to yourself as you relax. You may if you wish transfer these words onto cassette.

1. 'I take a long, slow, deep breath in, and the tension in my feet becomes limp, loose and light.'
2. 'I take a long, slow, deep breath in, and the tension in my legs becomes limp, loose and light.'

3. 'I take a long, slow, deep breath in, and the tension along my spine becomes limp, loose and light.'
4. 'I take a long, slow, deep breath in, and the tension in my arms becomes limp, loose and light.'
5. 'I take a long, slow, deep breath in, and the tension in my shoulders becomes limp, loose and light.'
6. 'I take a long, slow, deep breath in, and the tension in my neck becomes limp, loose and light.'
7. 'I take a long, slow, deep breath in, and the tension in my head becomes limp, loose and light.'
8. 'One, two – I gently stir my body – three – I begin to stretch my body – four – I begin to open my eyes – five – I open my eyes. I am now fully refreshed, fully relaxed and fully alert – ready to meet the challenges of my day.'

The growth of hypnosis and hypnotherapy has been hindered slightly by a few misconceptions and erroneous beliefs. The most common misunderstanding is that a person loses consciousness during hypnosis. The aim of hypnosis is to achieve a relaxed state of conscious awareness. The only time you might lose consciousness is if you were so tired and so run down that when you relaxed you fell asleep.

The most common erroneous fear of hypnotherapy is that a subject is put under the will and control of somebody else. The truth is, the subject and hypnotherapist form a contract in which the subject allows him- or herself to experience hypnosis. The subject is always in control. You can, of course, use self-hypnosis cassettes if you prefer. However, in truth, all hypnosis is self-hypnosis.

Hypnosis and hypnotherapy aim at liberating your natural, innate freedom and potential. It is not mystical; it will not change you into something you are not. It *will* help you to relax, though. And during your relaxation you will experience the harmony, order and balance which you are –

it is this experience that will gradually help you to give yourself the permission to be who you really want to be and to do more of what you really want to do.

AUTOGENICS

The name *autogenics* is a collective term for a number of simple, therapeutic mental exercises which in differing ways aim to, 'switch off the stress "fight or flight" system of the body, and switch on the rest, relaxation and re-creation system.' There is often particular emphasis in autogenics training on restoring and enhancing the harmony of your mind and body's natural 're-creation system'.

Autogenics was originally devised in the 1920s and 1930s by Johannes H. Schultz, a German psychiatrist and hypnotherapist. His work has since been developed by other leading health care proponents across the world. The technique is a combination of breath control, hypnotherapy and mental affirmation, and may also combine creative visualization and progressive relaxation. Autogenics, thus, embodies a truly eclectic approach to deep relaxation.

The word autogenics is derived from the Greek words *auto*, which means 'self', and *genous*, which means 'originated'. Autogenics places an important emphasis on belief in your own inner, innate capacity and potential for self-control and self-determination. Since the 1930s, well over 3,000 scientific and medical studies and reports on autogenics have been published. There is now more than enough evidence to show that autogenics is a useful and valid form of deep relaxation.

Many of the controlled medical trials on autogenics have established that autogenics can be of great benefit to many of the commonly acknowledged stress-related diseases, such as phobias, anxiety, high blood-pressure, migraines, insomnia, muscle tension, hyperventilation and pain. Autogenics has also found to be very helpful in developing creativity and improving concentration and co-ordination, and for improving the body's capacity to cope with jet-lag and other forms of physical and mental exhaustion and fatigue.

To achieve the maximum therapeutic benefit from the following autogenics exercise, prepare as you would for a standard deep relaxation routine. Use a space in which you know you will not be disturbed unexpectedly. Dim the lights, loosen any tight clothing, and then lie down on your back, placing your arms at your sides with palms facing upwards. Take a moment to allow your body to nestle into the floor, sofa or bed beneath you and you will then be ready to begin.

An Autogenics Relaxation Exercise

1. Focus all of your attention on your breathing, and as you inhale, silently repeat, 'Deeper, longer slower.' As you exhale, repeat again, 'Deeper, longer, slower.' Perform this sequence seven times.
2. Focus all your attention on your left shoulder, and silently repeat, 'My left shoulder is heavy and relaxed; my left shoulder is heavy and relaxed.' For the next five seconds or so allow all the muscles of your left shoulder to feel heavy and relaxed.
3. Focus all your attention on your right shoulder, and silently repeat, 'My right shoulder is heavy and relaxed; my right shoulder is heavy and relaxed.' For the next five seconds or so allow all the muscles of your right shoulder to feel heavy and relaxed.
4. Perform the same sequence as you focus all your attention on your left arm, right arm; left hand, right hand. Then

perform the same sequence for your left hip, right hip; left leg, right leg; left foot, right foot.

5. Allow your mind to rest upon your heart now, as you repeat, 'My heart is warm and easy; my heart is warm and easy.' For the next five seconds or so, allow your heart to feel warm and easy.

6. If you wish, you can repeat the same sequence, this time using the autogenic prescription of 'relaxed and warm'. Begin with the left shoulder, then the right shoulder; the left arm, the right arm; the left hand, the right hand; the left hip, the right hip; the left leg, the right leg; the left foot, the right foot.

7. Allow your mind to rest upon your heart now, as you repeat, 'My heart is warm and easy; my heart is warm and easy.' For the next five seconds or so, allow your heart to feel warm and easy.

8. Finally, allow your whole body to feel warm, relaxed and easy. First, repeat to yourself a few times, 'My whole body feels warm, relaxed and easy; my whole body feels warm, relaxed and easy.' After a few seconds, you should change this to, 'My whole body is warm, relaxed and easy; my whole body is warm, relaxed and easy.'

9. Bathe yourself in the relaxation you have created. When you are ready to finish, allow yourself to complete the exercise gradually, slowly and carefully, so that you return to a normal waking state without any sudden shocks or movements. You are then ready to continue with your day. Or you can, of course, perform this exercise last thing at night to help to promote a deep and refreshing sleep.

Autogenics is promoted as much as a psychotherapeutic technique as a physical relaxation system. For this reason a great majority of trained autogenics practitioners are qualified psychotherapists or counsellors. Through auto-genics, or 'self-orientated' practice, an autogenics practitioner guides a person towards reducing and preventing harmful stress responses, towards building up greater experience and more assured practice of relaxation, and thereby, aims to help a person to restore the essential inner harmony, order and balance necessary for physical, mental and emotional health and well-being.

BIOFEEDBACK RELAXATION THERAPY

When you are relaxing, how do you know you are relaxed? This sounds a very simple question to answer, but, as biofeedback research has often discovered, as many as seven out of ten people who think they are relaxing are, in actual fact, not. Worse still, out of these seven people there are usually three or four who, rather than relaxing, are actually tensing up. There is, therefore, a world of difference between thinking you are relaxed and actually knowing you are relaxed. This difference can be a vital one for successful stress control.

Biofeedback therapy has been used for over 40 years by doctors, psychotherapists, clinical psychologists, nurses, complementary healers and a host of other health care professionals. It is a proven technique that can help you to identify your stress, that can help you to monitor it accurately and objectively, and that can help you to assess how useful your attempts to cope with it are.

Biofeedback means 'feedback, or information, about the inner biological states of the body'. In other words, biofeedback gives 'external feedback to your conscious mind of the activity of the inner, biological states – states that are normally known only to your unconscious mind'.

The main principle of biofeedback is that, by becoming more aware of your internal and normally unconscious biological states, you can begin to control them at will. Biofeedback equipment helps you to do this by giving you a reliable, external measurement of the stress or relaxation of different internal systems of your body, such as the nervous system, the muscle system, blood-pressure, body temperature and brain activity.

Using biofeedback equipment to help a person to help him- or herself has been found to be of very great benefit for many stress-related conditions, including hypertension, pain relief, anxiety attacks, phobias, allergies, heart disease, ulcers, migraines, menstrual difficulties, shaking, sweating, fatigue, under-arousal and backache, for instance.

You needn't be ill, though, to benefit from biofeedback. Biofeedback can help you to help yourself to think more creatively, for instance, or to develop self-confidence, cultivate self-assertiveness, learn to relax more fully, handle relationships with greater ease, speak in public with more assurance, or meditate with greater benefit and control. Biofeedback supplies the essential self-awareness that can be the key to better coping, improved self-confidence and greater control.

Ten 'Portable Relaxers'

The following simple exercises can be very effective at promoting a relaxed, controlled influence over mind and body in a short space of time. You may find that some of these exercises are especially helpful for coping with the moment at hand, for handling pressures of the present, for shock, for surprises, for panic, for unanticipated misadventures, or for performing at your best in meetings, interviews and presentations, where clear, cool, considered communication is called for.

1. *The relaxed breath*. Three rounds of a deep, slow and even type of breathing, each breath a little deeper and slower than the last, can help to instil deep relaxation very quickly. Gently push your abdomen down and your stomach out as you breathe in. As you breathe out, sense your whole body relaxing, releasing and letting go.

2. *Close your eyes*. The simple act of closing the eyes has been found for many people to encourage the type of brainwaves that promote detachment, relaxation and poise. Performed with the relaxed breath, the benefits are even greater. You may also wish to rest your fingers or palms gently over your eyes, exerting a slight pressure on them. This too can be very therapeutic.

3. *Dulcet tones*. Every word you listen to carries a hidden power of suggestion. Very often your mind and your body will work on the suggestions behind words without your being consciously aware of the fact. With a practice of mental affirmation you can create your own suggestions, such as 'I am now relaxing my mind and body,' 'I am calm, relaxed and easy,' or 'I am relaxing, releasing and letting go.' The more you repeat an affirmation to yourself, the more the suggestion can take effect.

4. *Shoulder shrug*. As you breathe in, clench your hands and tighten your shoulder and neck muscles. Hold the tension for a moment as you hold your breath. As you breathe out let go of the tension you have created. Do this twice, once quite quickly and once more slowly. Most of the tension of the body settles in the shoulders and neck. By relaxing these areas you can promote relaxation throughout your whole body.

5. *Feet flexing*. Sit down with your legs outstretched. As you breathe in, tense the muscles of your feet as tightly as you can. Hold the tension as you hold your breath. As you breathe out, let the tension go and feel the

relaxation spread up your legs and throughout your whole body.

6. *A warm cup of tea*. Holding a warm cup of tea is often enough on its own to help calm your body and mind. Drinking a cup of tea is even better! And why not try herbal tea? Warmth is a great relaxant. Also, because we may associate a warm drink with a break, rest, or even with bedtime, it can often encourage us, apparently quite naturally, to slow down, to relax and to recuperate.

7. *Sigh*. A long, deep sigh can do a lot to relieve body tension, particularly around the heart area. It also has a similar, corresponding affect on any mental and emotional strain and tension. Many people with some forms of heart trouble sigh quite naturally, blowing air firmly out of the mouth. This they find allows the heart to settle and to relax.

8. *Yawn*. Yawning is acknowledged by many yoga teachers as a valid yoga exercise in its own right. It helps to stretch, exercise and relax the muscles of your face, which often take a heavy measure of the stresses and burdens of the day. Yawning also exercises the lungs, promotes deep, healthy breathing, and therefore can help to relax your whole body. Making yourself yawn a couple of times can be a pleasantly relaxing and therapeutic exercise.

9. *Tuning in to stillness*. When things get too much, we often become agitated, restless and generally unsettled. By stilling your body and also by consciously focusing and stilling your mind on your body, you can detach and relax out of many of the pressures that confront you. You also save valuable energy which would otherwise be wasted on anxiety, irritability, restlessness and apprehension.

10. *Leave the room*. Take a moment to create a bit of distance and a change of scene so that you can be by yourself. When possible, this can help you to collect your

thoughts and determine how best to tackle stress. Also, a bit of space and a little bit of time away can easily help to clear and to change your perspective. When you change your environment you can also change your thinking.

Ten 'Portable Rechargers'

The following 'portable rechargers' are temporary measures designed to help recharge and uplift a tiring mind and body during moments of stress and strain. Their beneficial effects are only temporary, and they tend to work best when used sparingly. To rely on these energizers on a continual basis or as a sole stress solution will not give you the benefits you are looking for. There may, however, be times in your life when one of these techniques will give you the lift you need to get through.

1. *The arousal breath*. Three rounds of quick, deep breathing, pushing your chest out as you breathe in and pulling your chest in as you breathe out can help to activate and to rejuvenate your mind and your body.
2. *Splash!* Taking a minute to splash your face with water, and then to rub your face vigorously with a towel, is a very good method for taking a break and then starting again. It helps especially to clear and to stimulate a tired and jaded mind.
3. *Thought Power.* A single thought can energize and activate the whole of your being. When your energy levels are running low, prescribe mental affirmations to yourself such as, 'I am now energizing my mind and my body,' 'I enjoy energy in abundance,' 'I am energized,' 'I am vitalized.' Think energy!
4. *Stretch*. Take a moment to stand upright with hands resting gently by your sides. Then breathe in and stretch

The Stress Reaction

Physical Effects of Stress and Relaxation

	Stress Reaction	Relaxation Effect
Muscle Tension	Tight	Relaxed
Nervous System	Tense	Relaxed
Breathing Rate	Fast, shallow	Slow, deep
Heart Rate	Irregular	Regular
Blood Pressure	Up	Down
Digestion	Blocked	Balanced
Circulation	Restricted	Full flowing
Adrenalin	High	Low
Immune System	Dampened	Enhanced

the whole of your body up, taking your hands up over your head. Hold the stretch as you hold your breath, and then, as you breathe out, let go of all the tension, allowing your hands to flop and fall by your sides again. Simple stretches like this can help to awaken, enliven and reactivate your whole body.

5. *A brisk walk*. Walking stimulates and exercises your whole body. Furthermore, it can create physical distance between you and your stress, as well as a mental distance, in that it can help you to detach, forget and let go for a while.

6. *A long cool glass of water*. Taking a moment to drink a glass of water can really help to cleanse and to refresh. In general, we do not drink enough water, which is an added stress for the body, anyway. Empowering this moment, when drinking, with positive thought and attention can enhance the rejuvenating benefits of this simple, effective exercise.

7. *Smile!* Smiling is a natural energizer. It can work particularly well for you when you least feel like it. Take a moment to laugh and to smile to yourself, in front of a mirror if possible, and also with other people. So long as we can smile, a rich supply of energy, tolerance and relaxation can always be available to us.

8. *Singing*. Singing boosts the thyroid gland, which is very influential in controlling your energy levels. Pick any song and start singing. You may find it a reliable battery of strength and energy. If singing is a bit uncomfortable for you, you can always begin with humming or even whistling! Music can also inspire energy or rest.

9. *A quick breath of fresh air*. OK, so the air isn't quite as fresh as it used to be, but it can still be a very powerful source of energy. Taking in air in a cool calm breeze can be a wonderful tonic.

10. *Relax*. The aim of relaxation is not to send you off into

a comatose, sleepy, sluggish state of mind. On the contrary, quick relaxations can be very good for re-energizing and recharging your entire physical and mental system. If your attention and your concentration are active, then your relaxation exercises will become active, practical and powerful ones that will support your ability to think, to work and to exert yourself well.

4

COPING WELL
WITH CHANGE

I can cope well with change.

For what wears out the life of mortal men?
Tis that from change to change their being rolls;
Tis that repeated shocks, again, again,
Exhaust the energy of strongest souls,
And numb the elastic powers.

Matthew Arnold

In a living, dynamic world such as ours, where the only thing that can be said to be truly permanent is change, the art of successful stress control must inevitably include an ability to prepare for, to accept and to cope with change.

A failure to come to terms with change is an occasional cause of personal pain that is common to all of us. A permanent, everlasting harmony and happiness is at heart, perhaps, our most earnest wish; we live, however, in a world that is anything but permanent and everlasting. On the contrary, our world is dynamic, uncertain, transient and changeful. Change is of the essence.

LIFE CHANGES

Some life events we interpret as very pleasing: they therefore promote happiness, they affirm our ability to cope, they support and sustain positive self-image, and they enhance self-harmony. Other life events we interpret as harmful to us: we therefore describe them as 'disturbing' and 'unsettling' because they disturb and unsettle our world and the way we fit into and relate to that world. Change, as a rule, we conclude can be either kind or cruel.

In 1967, two American doctors, T.H. Holmes and R.H. Rahe, published the 'Holmes and Rahe Social Readjustment Rating Scale' in the *Journal of Psychosomatic Research*. This scale lists 43 common life events that their research found to be potentially threatening and harmful to every individual's quality of health, happiness and wholeness. The impact of each of these 41 life events is measured and assessed using a scoring scale of 1 to 100.

This research suggested that if in the course of one full year a person accumulates a score greater than 300, there is an 80 per cent chance that sickness, stress and ill-health might surface at any time during the space of the following two years. If the score accumulated is between 150 and 300 points, then susceptibility to stress and to sickness over the next two years is reduced to 50 per cent. And, if the score accumulated is below 150 points, then there will be only a slight, incidental chance of illness. The full version of The Social Readjustment Rating Scale is on page 120.

Holmes' and Rahe's research is an interesting indicator of the potential impact of perpetual change and readjustment. It highlights obvious causes of stress, such as the death of a spouse, divorce, or personal injury or illness, as well as less obvious causes of stress, such as the Christmas holiday, going away on holiday, or gaining an outstanding personal achievement. Most important of all, the work of Holmes and Rahe has mapped out a measurable, definable relationship between stress, illness and change.

Holmes and Rahe concluded that the challenges of life are often challenges of change. They also observed that a lack of or disturbance of order, harmony and stability in a person's life is a potential health hazard. Human beings require a certain harmony for health, happiness and wholeness to happen. Change can chip away at this harmony so as to effect dis-order, dis-temper and dis-ease. This is particularly true when change is either uncalled for, unaccepted or uncontrolled.

PERCEIVING CHANGE

Attitudes to change are often much more problematic and harmful than the actuality of change. Muddled, emotional perceptions can plague a person so as to create fear, deny reality, instil uncertainty, block creativity, breed anxiety, prevent perspective, delay decision-making, engender fatigued and generally make for misery. In essence, the crisis of change can be further complicated and greatly exacerbated by a problem of perception.

Holmes and Rahe created a points system for impact of change; they could not, however, create a points system for impact of perception. This is because each of us is endowed with our own unique perception of experience. If you refer to the Holmes and Rahe Social Readjustment Rating Scale, you will see that 'Child leaves home' scores 29 points. Now, to the mother who perceives that her world will crack when her child starts to pack, 29 points will be more like 290 points.

How you perceive is how you play. To change with the changes, it can be very helpful, therefore, to attempt to change your perceptions. To achieve a balanced perspective, it is very good to acknowledge formally all of the negatives and all of the positives of change. Do not let nasty negatives eclipse potential positives. Positives will appear if you are prepared to look for them. If you view change solely as a

The Holmes and Rahe Social Readjustment Rating Scale

	Scale
Death of spouse or partner	100
Divorce	73
Marital Separation	65
Jail sentence or being institutionalized	63
Death of close member of family	63
Illness or injury	53
Marriage	50
Loss of job	47
Reconciliation with marriage partner	45
Retirement	45
Health problem of close member of family	44
Pregnancy	40
Sex problems	39
Addition to family	39
Major change at work	39
Change of financial status	39
Death of friend	37
Change in line of work	36
Change in number of marital arguments	35
Large mortgage taken out	31
Mortgage or loan foreclosed	30
Responsibility change	29
Child leaves home	29
In-law problems	29
Personal achievement realized	28
Wife starts or stops work	26
Starting at new school	26
Leaving school	26
Change in living conditions	25
Change in personal habits	24
Trouble with employer	23
Change in working hours	20
Change in residence	20
Change in recreation	19
Change in church activities	19
Change in social activities	18
Small mortgage taken out	17
Change in sleeping habits	16
Change in number of family get-togethers	15
Major change in eating pattern	15
Holiday	13
Christmas	12
Minor violation of law	11

curse, you will be cursed; if you take change as a challenge you may well find you rise to that challenge.

Writing out the positives over and above the negatives can be a painful, difficult exercise. Many people will refrain because their perception and their pain tell them there is no point. Such is the power of personal perception! During any given moment, your perception has a potential to promote and to perpetuate either personal powerlessness or personal empowerment. Adjusting your perceptions promotes your adjustment to change. Don't stop before you start.

ANTICIPATING CHANGE

To change before change happens can be a clever coping strategy for dealing well with anticipated future change. So often, though, the fear and uncertainty imposed by impending change will prevent proper preparation and planning. It is essential, though, to assume the role of *pre-actor* rather than *re-actor*. In other words, you should attempt, where possible, to initiate change on your terms and in your time. By changing before change happens you can help to take the pain out of change.

Retirement, change of residence, marriage, an addition to the family, going on holiday and children leaving home are all examples of change from The Holmes and Rahe Social Readjustment Rating Scale that can usually be clearly identified before they happen. Worry, anxiety and concern are natural reactions to any future change; these feelings should not prevent you, though, from preparing and planning a map of activity to cope and to control the course of these changes.

A Four-Step Plan for Impending Change

1. When will the change happen? All plans point to a deadline date. If you are unsure, make a good conservative estimate.
2. How will the change affect me? What are the negatives? What are the positives? What will be harmful? What will be helpful? What new opportunities may I see as a result of the change?
3. How can I affect the change? Create a 'New for Old' Target Plan so as to establish possible new coping strategies and new actions for old ones.
4. What can I be doing now, today, to change before change? There is no better time to begin a plan of action than during the moment of *now*.

To fill in the gaps before the gaps appear is by far the most pleasant and painless path of action for coping with impending change. Confronting change before change takes effect helps you to 'talk on your terms': change happens *by* you instead of *to* you. By changing before change happens, the passage of change does not have to undermine or overwhelm you. Indeed, the course of change can be a creative, challenging and exciting experience in which *you empower you*.

CREATING CHANGE

Creating change requires courage and conviction, mainly because change carries uncertainty and unknowing. Fear, anxiety and self-doubt can block bravery and corrupt confidence so as to avoid any adjustments being made. This type of reaction to change is another manifestation of the 'freeze' response to stress. The following five-step plan is a helpful catalyst for making a switch from the powerless 'anxiety response' to a more powerful 'action response'.

Five Steps to Positive Change

1. What is the stress? Try to identify the change and, also, try to identify how you feel towards the change.
2. Can I create a change? The answer is always 'yes' – somehow, some way, your thoughts and actions can make some difference.
3. In what ways can I create a change? The more times you perform this exercise, the more ideas will arise.
4. What action will be the most effective? Assess, analyse and prioritize.
5. What can I be doing *now*? The time to create change is the time you are alive in – *Now!*

Sometimes the most powerful action we can take when immersed in a sea of stress is to demonstrate to ourselves that we have both the capacity and the ability to create change, at will. Doing something different, out of the ordinary, if only as a gesture, can be an extraordinarily powerful act of defiance, serving us with courage, conviction, confidence and, above all, with hope.

Going to the cinema, taking a long contemplative walk, contacting an estranged friend, visiting somewhere new, wearing a new outfit, a new hairstyle, doing something silly, cooking something exotic, buying a treat for yourself, a new book, a new television programme, entering a competition, joining a club – whatever you decide to do, create a change for the sake of change so as to remind yourself that you can be powerful, you can be effective, and that you can initiate change – on your terms.

Tomorrow need not be the same as today. Remember,

nothing is permanent except for change. Each day delivers, therefore, new possibilities to the person who is prepared to perceive them. Choosing to create and to control changes can help you to feel liberated, alive and in control. You become pre-active as opposed to a re-active. Rising to the challenge of change can help to increase your capacity to cope.

ACCEPTING CHANGE

A failure to come to terms with change can easily precipitate problems of a personal nature. Non-acceptance may manifest by any manner of means, such as denial, anger, stubbornness, reluctance, procrastination and an inability to forgive. Not confronting a change might mean we live in both a real world of 'life as it is' and an imaginary world of 'life as it was'. This double-day living can give rise to definite difficulties that may only make a personal predicament more painful.

Whereas change may only take a moment to manifest, adjustment to change is often a slow, gradual step-by-step sequence that happens over many moments. When a person is faced with a change he or she did not choose, then this period of adjustment can advance into days, weeks, months and years. Positive, healthy coping with change usually commences when a person is prepared to accept. Acceptance triggers the switch from the imaginary world of 'life as it was' to the real world of 'life as it is'.

In a world characterized by change, knowing the difference between that which can and cannot be changed is an essential skill for happy living. The famous 'Serenity Prayer' of St Francis of Assisi is often reserved for recitation on personal decision days for this very reason.

The Serenity Prayer
'God, grant me the strength to change that which I need
to change,
the patience to accept that which I cannot change,
and, above all,
the wisdom to know the difference.'

Guilt, regret, resentment and sadness can keep us locked up in the past as surely as anxiety, worry, fear and concern can keep us hooked up on the future. If you want to move away from your pain, you must begin to distinguish between the grief of 'if only' and the good sense of 'what is'. A simple written exercise is to draw two columns and head one column 'if only' and the other column 'what is'. Write down all your thoughts and feelings of 'if only' and all the facts and figures of 'what is'. When you have done this, take another page and ask yourself, 'what now?' – ask the question until you hear an answer.

ANXIETY MANAGEMENT

Anxiety does not empty tomorrow of its sorrows, but only
empties today of its strength.
Charles H. Spurgeon

Anxiety, worry and fear are not solutions for stress – they have never, ever solved a single problem for anyone in the whole history of the human race. At best, anxiety will inspire action; at worst, anxiety is an illness of imagined implication. High anxiety can inflict all manner of harm and haphazardness that can render you powerless and generally less effective. Unabated anxiety only adds to adversity.

Like stress, anxiety has a positive function in that it can act as an 'alerting device' for self-preservation. If, for instance, you did not feel anxious when your doctor tells you you are heading for a heart attack, when you are just about to cross a busy road, or when the petrol gauge on your car reads empty, then you would be an absolute fool for you would suffer nasty consequences that need not have happened. Listen to your anxiety, therefore, but do not expect it to solve your problems. No amount of anxiety has ever filled up an empty petrol tank!

Action or Anxiety

Action	Anxiety
Empowerment	Powerlessness
"Open doors"	"Closed doors"
Strength	Exhaustion
Rational Thinking	Irrational Thinking
Less Fear	More Fear
Relaxation	Restlessness

Anxieties alert you; actions save you. Whenever you are stressed, you have a choice between anxiety and action. You can persist with anxiety for a long, long time, but it will still not get you to where you want to go. Unabated anxiety tends not to adjourn of its own accord. On the contrary, without action, it can easily become an illness of imagined implication in that it conjures up a future of fears, the impact of which can leave you completely powerless in the present. 'How much pain have cost us the evils which have never happened?' wrote Thomas Jefferson.

The harmful effects of repeated and prolonged anxiety attacks are much the same as those of stress. Mental effects can include disorientation, thought clouds, emotional darkness, poor perception, fear, fatigue and procrastination. Emotional effects can include low self-worth, escalating self-doubts, fluctuating feelings, emotional sensitivity and consuming unhappiness. Physical effects can include headaches, migraines, high blood-pressure, palpitations, muscle tension and nervous strain.

Seven-Step Anxiety Plan

1. *Identify the anxiety.* If you wish, place the word 'anxiety' in the middle of a blank page and then draw and write around the word so as to uncover a cause.
2. *Why do I worry?* Keep asking yourself 'why?' You may have written down, for example, change of job, but the real reason you are anxious is a fear of failure. Keep looking behind the presenting anxiety, for there you might find the real worry.
3. *What are the benefits of worry?* What wisdom is there in your worry? How will it help you? List all the benefits you can think of for worrying, and then list all the negatives.
4. *Affirm to yourself, 'The Universe only rewards action'.* List all the possible actions you could administer to counteract your anxiety.
5. *Remember, anxiety never once solved a problem for anyone in the whole history of the human race.* If your actions are appropriate, your anxiety will abate.
6. *Which of my actions is the most appropriate?* Develop a plan of priorities for tackling your problem.

7. *What action can I be achieving,* now? Fear of the future can
deny the power of the present. Attending to your anxiety
can only begin at one moment, and that moment is *now*.

The key to switching off anxiety may involve any type of
strategy. Some people enjoy relaxation, for instance: they
find that relaxed breathing, meditation, creative visualization
or self-hypnosis works well. Some people enjoy exercise: they
find that yoga, T'ai Chi, aerobics, running, walking, tennis
or golf, for instance, helps to work off anxiety. Some people,
on the other hand, enjoy company, communication, sharing
and expressing as a way to purge their worry. The keys that
help you to worry less will help you to control better your
stress.

STABILITY ZONES

Good order is the foundation of all things.

Edmund Burke

To aim to create safe havens of stability is a natural human
reaction to living in a dynamic world of perpetual change and
ceaseless transformation. To be able to hold on to something
that is certain, solid and dependable is indeed a worthy
therapy valued most highly. We each of us create, therefore,
quite instinctively, our own oases of order and stability, and
we do this most often through the people, patterns, rituals
and routines of our day-to-day lives. These oases are best
known as *stability zones*, or *comfort corners*.

A single stability zone can be a natural, valuable battery of
personal strength that supplies all the certainty, security and
equilibrium needed to counteract the effects of a changeful,
wayward world. Stability zones give us constancy, a sense of
rootedness, rest, balance and something predictable and

dependable. In other words, when it comes to stability zones, we know what to expect, we know where we stand and it is we who are in control. This is often very different to the usual pattern of events we may experience day to day.

Your stability zones may take the shape of a person, a place or a personal regular ritual. Stability zones can be a parent, a brother or sister, a grandparent, a godparent, an uncle or aunt, a partner, a child, a priest, a teacher, a counsellor, a friend or even a work colleague. Someone who provides dependable strength and support and who is always there for you is an example of a positive stability zone. During times of personal crisis and distress, it is good to call upon these stability zones for comfort, communication and care.

Stability zones in the shape of a place can include your home, your favourite armchair, a park, a golf course, a bath, the local pub, a preferred restaurant, church, a religious site, a countryside place, a regular holiday location, the garden, your place of work, a social club, the cinema or the theatre, perhaps. A place that will always be there, that you can depend upon and that doesn't change too often, is a good example of a stability zone place. Making your home the most comfortable stability zone you know is often the most rewarding of all stability zones.

Stability zones in the shape of regular rituals may include breakfast routines, a daily bath or shower, reading the paper, the first cup of coffee or tea of the day, walking the dog, exercising, reading a novel, meditation, hobbies and interests, relaxation exercises, the news, soap operas, Sunday lunch, mealtimes, a regular evening out, changing your clothes when you get in from work, a regular date with a friend, cooking, ironing or gardening each day, for instance.

Consciously creating stability zones in your life and consciously appreciating them for all the pleasure they give are two of the more practical and natural ways of counteracting the stressful effects of an ever-changing, unpredictable world. Balance, order and harmony help to set stress free – and enjoying something, without obsession, that is regular, predictable, enjoyable and safe is a perfectly natural therapy and effective personal resource for surviving successfully through stress.

'THIS TOO SHALL PASS'

Time cools, time clarifies, no mood can be maintained quite unaltered through the course of the hours.

Thomas Mann

It is so easy to feel and to believe that, with the onset of stress, the strain of mind and the sadness of heart will last on and on, forever and forever. We can, if we are not careful, become so mesmerized and so immersed in the misery of the moment that a wave of never-ending hopelessness can threaten to drown us. And yet, if there is one safe prophesy it is that your stress will change: there will be a bright new dawn, and you will be able to say, 'This too has passed.'

Change is a part of the natural order of the world. The world is supported by change; it evolves through change; and we, as a part of this world, can expect the possibility of change every moment we are alive. Whenever you are stressed, then, you would be wise never to let go of the lifeline of 'This too shall pass.' Always remember that nothing is permanent except for change.

Thoughts, emotions, feelings, perceptions, consequences and events are never permanent. Within them all are the seeds of change – change that can be affected at any moment with the right resolve and considered control. Henry Ward Beecher, the American philosopher, expressed this truth well. He wrote, 'No emotion, any more than a wave, can long retain its own individual form.'

Knowing that 'This too shall pass' can be a wonderful projection during times of personal discomfort. As a stress control strategy, this knowledge cannot really be taught; it can only be learned. It is something that is picked up through experience. Take a moment, now, this minute, to recall some of the stresses from the past that at the time you felt would never abate and would never be resolved. 'These too did pass', did they not? While you do this, try to remember also what helped then, for it may help now.

To be happy and to control stress successfully, you must work with and not against change. Time has but one function: the measurement of change. With the passage of time, all things, including your stress, must beckon to the call of 'This too shall pass.' A change of fortune is inevitable; the finality of stress is mere illusion. Such knowledge offers cool consolation and renewed resolve during times of stress. It can also open you up to a new hope, a fresh determination and a new, positive change.

Your faith in a brighter future will be rewarded by action, not anxiety. As you begin to act step by step and as you begin to control moment by moment, you will so empower yourself to believe that 'This too shall pass.' It is so easy to stand stuck in the muddy misery of the moment – whether you can believe it or not, though, there will come a time when the rains will stop, the sun will shine again, the ground will harden, and you will be able to walk free. The sooner you start, step by step, the sooner the time will come.

5

LIFE EVENT STRESS

I can feel good about myself.

RELATIONSHIP STRESS

Why oh why is it that the people we love the most are often the people who appear to hurt us the most? Close ones, loved ones, the people we are really fond of, appear to be endowed with a special sense of power that can make us laugh and weep. Their influence and their actions seem to be able to make us dance and crawl, to take us up and down, to make us tall and small. Our loved ones have such a lot to answer for, and so have we!

Creating loving relationships is vital to the human condition. We each of us respond, in our different ways, to an ancient need to harmonize, to complete and to feel whole. This innate quest offers marvellous treasures well worth searching for; the adventurous terrain is not without its traumas, though. Getting close to people, and learning to love, can give us the strength, the fulfilment we seek; it can also leave us faltering, tender and, oh so weak.

When any two people meet, greet and relate with one another, they bring with them two worlds of differing perceptions and experiences, differing expectations and memories, and differing needs and wishes. Integration, co-existence and creative mutual growth are delicate, skilful operations, often ongoing over many years, that are not without their tensions, stresses and fears. True: failure rates are high, but that has never been reason enough not to try.

Relating, and creating, are talents that mature through the lessons of days, weeks, months and years. Be it with parents, partners, children or friends, the art of relating is as a colourful rose that demands appropriate continual care, consideration and commitment. To juggle with big words such as 'trust', 'forgiveness', 'honesty', 'loyalty', 'communication', 'understanding' and 'love' is, at times, a heavy load that can rock even the most honest, sincere intentions.

The term *relationship stress* refers most often to a failure to 'fill' or to feel 'full'. In other words, fulfilment, completion and wholeness are not happening. The two worlds do not balance; they collide. The worlds may share a similar vision, yet they may still set a course for collision. Answers as to why can be as many and as varied as the countless stars that light up a night-time sky.

Effective strategies for relationship stress include many of the tips and techniques outlined in Chapter 2 that aim to counteract perceived powerlessness. The following, general guidelines are also offered for personal consideration and creative contemplation.

'Know Thyself'

The measure of harmony between any two people is built upon foundations of personal harmony within each individual. In other words, to be comfortable with another person, it helps to be as comfortable as you can be with yourself. If you are at odds with yourself, it is difficult to be even with others. Invest time, therefore, to understand yourself, to support yourself and to be yourself. Identify your values. Manage your weaknesses. Savour your strengths.

Establish and pursue your aspirations and aims. By managing yourself well, you will be better positioned to manage your relationships well.

Communicate

Poor, unhappy communication is a most widespread symptom and common cause of relationship stress. The quality of personal, intimate communication between two people is an effective barometer for measuring the quality of the entire, overall relationship. Basically put: where communication fails, the relationship fails; where communication works, the relationship works. In order to relate, you must allow a chance of communication. Relationships can evolve if there is a resolve to work and work and work again, at communication.

Express Yourself

Do the people who are closest to you 'know' who you are – the real you? You have a responsibility to tell them; they have a responsibility to listen well. Often we will fail to express ourselves because of an anticipated fear of failure, misunderstanding or rejection; not expressing ourselves can, however, create an incomparable mess. If the relationship you want is honest and true, then you owe it to yourself to communicate and to express the real you. Ask yourself this question: Will the initial personal pain be worth the eventual long-term gain?

Listen Well

Relationship stress can often begin to dissolve and subside when two people prick up their ears, open and wide. Too often we can be too busy making a point, locating a blame, assuming too much, rehearsing our next words and preoccupied with our own feelings to take the time to listen and listen well. The most dangerous assumption anyone can ever make, when it comes to relationship stress, is that he or she already listens enough. The first rule of listening is that there is always something new to hear.

Respect

To be able to relate and to convey respect to the people who 'make your day' are maybe the most valuable gifts there are to give. The human ego is a delicate, sensitive seed that requires all the love, understanding and respect it can feed on. Affirming a person's importance, acknowledging his or her contributions, applauding his or her attributes, communicating 'I love you' and conveying appreciation – now, today, this moment – can, undoubtedly, help to guarantee less relationship stress.

Great Expectations!

Every relationship has to live up to what is usually an unspoken agenda of expectations, standards, commitments and limits. Each person, independently, draws up a conscious and unconscious contract of obligation which he or she then expects 'the other' to abide by without any formal signature of agreement. You must be prepared to communicate your expectations, your hopes and your aspirations, for your own good and for the good of the relationship. Good relations can be swamped by great expectations. In general, people find that the less they need from others, the more they can give to others.

Co-directors!

To be happy, it helps to share responsibility. If two people attempt to accept complete responsibility for a relationship, they are ideally positioned to share that responsibility. Rewarding relationships carry no passengers! By taking responsibility for the way you feel and for the way things are, whether you like them or not, you hold tight to the reins that can steer towards progress, peace and good change. If you are always prepared to ask, 'What am I doing to deserve this mess?', you will be well placed to do all that you can to reduce relationship stress.

Quality Time

Relationships require not just living time, surviving time or quantity time, but quality time. Quality is a bond: the more you share quality with another person the closer the two of you become. Each person sets the other free when he or she purposely steers the relationship towards the golden shores of quality. Too often we forget, we overlook, we delay quality; yet without quality a relationship can easily, quickly get lost at sea. Quality time can keep a relationship well balanced, fine tuned and on course, right down the line.

Personal Space

The threat of relationship stress will often gather apace wherever there is a lack of personal time and personal space. Close, intimate relationships work well when each individual respects and trusts that personal time and personal space are an absolute must. The quality of time spent together so often depends on the quality of time spent apart. A relationship must be allowed to ventilate, to breathe and to rest, so that each individual can enjoy the other at his or her best. You owe it to yourself, and to those whom you care for, to give yourself quality personal time and quality personal space.

Action Replays

Taking the time with each other to review, to revise and to talk over the past can help to plan, prepare for and look forward to the future. Taking out time for 'action replay' can help to contain and to control early on any problems that may crop up along the way. It is also important to review, to revise and to talk over future plans and directions. 'Are we still on course?' 'Is this what we both want?' 'What we both need is . . .?' Cool, calm reflection is a cornerstone of future positive intention.

TOP 10 CAUSES OF RELATIONSHIP STRESS

- A failure of self-love and self-understanding
- Unhealthy, 'make me happy' partner dependency
- Ineffective communication, not listening
- Past patterns upsetting present relationships
- A lack of sufficient quality 'together time'
- 'Great Expectations' syndrome and being judgemental
- Differing sexual and intimate requirements
- Having no plans, no direction and no common purpose
- Failure to show respect, appreciation and love
- Frequent unequal share of responsibility

PARENTAL STRESS

The experience of parenthood is demanding, daunting and delightful. Occasionally you know it to be a blessed joy; more often than not, though, it can feel like a job of hard work – a preoccupation that stretches every parent to the limit! Parenthood is an overnight promotion to management that brings with it long hours of work, complete concentrated commitment, lots and lots of 'paperwork', endless supervisory meetings, vast responsibilities, overtime as standard, and a huge hole in your personal finances. Life as you know it will never be the same again!

Parenting is a romp into the unrehearsed, the unexpected, the unknown and, at times, the unbelievable! There can be no rehearsals for the role of parent, there is little or no opportunity for pre-match practice, and there is no course of training or set of guidelines that can prepare you completely for what you are about to receive. Parenting will bring out the best in you and, occasionally perhaps, it will bring out the test in you. Parenting is a test; it is also a blessing, a joy and reward.

Parenting is a day-by-day discovery of the hidden depths of your personal resources, skills and invention, but still, there will be times when, in spite of your best, or indeed anyone else's best, the perceived demands will outweigh the perceived resources. As a parent, you cannot ever expect to avoid stress totally, but you will find there will always be opportunities to manage it better and to control it better.

The challenges, the demands and the tests of parenting are often exaggerated or complicated by other responsibilities and commitments to partners, family, friends, workplace and finances, for instance. Many parents describe parenting as a juggling act of identities, priorities and responsibilities. Resources of time, energy, creativity, love and attention have to be shared and distributed in a way that is fair both to others and to yourself. On some days the juggling flows beautifully, and on other days it may be clumsy, controversial and uncoordinated. The following guidelines are for happy juggling!

First Aid

One of the most common causes of parental stress is a chronic neglect of personal health, happiness and well-being. The eyes of a small child communicate such helplessness, dependence and vulnerability that parents instinctively respond with love and with sacrifice. Self-sacrifice is a perfectly natural parenting instinct. At times, however, it can be taken to dangerous extremes. Looking after your child does not mean, for instance, you should not look after yourself. On the contrary, the better you look after you, the better you will be able to look after your child. Investing time, effort, energy and space in yourself is a healthy, positive investment for both you and your child. When you are well, things tend to go well for you and your child.

'I am'

The arrival of baby signals an invasion and onslaught of nappies, teddy bears, colic drops, jumpsuits and other associated baby paraphernalia. You become witness to an incredible, overwhelming change, and it dawns on you gradually that nothing will ever be quite the same. Your home is transformed, overnight, into a baby zone. It is no longer yours. And you are no longer you. People forget your name; your best friends, for instance, start calling you 'mummy and daddy'! When out for a walk, people will converse with your baby, while you, who unlike baby understands everything that is said, will often go unnoticed, unacknowledged and ignored! Even at night-time, when baby sleeps, all of the talk still centres around him or her. There will come a time when the original you will want to cry, 'Well, what about me, then?'

To avoid this common manifestation of parental stress, it is important, therefore, to ensure that the role of parent does not completely eclipse or deny your other committed roles as partner, lover, friend, family member and 'me'. Five creative steps towards this healthy goal are:

1. Tell friends, partners and family to call you by your name and not 'mum' or 'dad'.
2. Do not let baby items invade every single room in your home; make space for you.
3. Keep your interests and your hobbies alive, now, today. If, for instance, you played a musical instrument before baby arrived, continue to play.
4. When baby goes to sleep, or even when baby is still awake, ensure that you and your partner or friends talk about non-baby topics.
5. Keep contact with friends, relatives and work colleagues, and be prepared to talk about 'you'. As one parent once said, 'Being a parent is what I do; it's a part of me, but it's not all of me'.

Plan, Prepare and Prioritize

Another common source of parental stress is the common perception that when it comes to caring for a child there is no time for anything else. This potentially harmful perception of 'no time' is rarely, if ever, completely true. One way to dispel the 'no time myth' is to keep a daily time diary and to mark in red the moments when your child comes first and to mark in green the moments when you are free to attend to other priorities. This diary will prove to you that there will be varying times in a day when you need *not* be a parent. Planning, preparing and prioritizing for these precious times is important for your well-being. Some days your plans will go awry, but that does not mean you should not still try. Baby management demands careful, skilful, persistent time management.

Quality Time

So often, when you finally find a moment that is yours, the temptation is to flop, to collapse and to doze. If, however, you are able to plan for these moments and fill them with quality – hobbies, interests, communication, intimacy and other enjoyable engagements, for instance – then this time will be even more valuable to you. Planned and unplanned personal quality time can be a precious battery of strength, hope, reward and renewal for the often debilitating task of parenting. Being able to look forward to constructive, productive and enjoyable moments for yourself, and for you and your partner or friends, can help to make parenting that much more endurable, enjoyable and easy to cope with. Quality time off will help to promote quality time on.

Shared Responsibilities

The failure to share responsibilities well and to define roles clearly are very common causes of stress between parents and partners. Most couples follow an unofficial, unspoken and unconscious contract that evolves naturally through their time together. By taking the time to sit down together to review and to revise each person's role and responsibilities, as both partner and parent, you may find that you can be of greater support and strength to one another than ever before. By identifying what you are both good at and by examining areas that either of you may feel need working at, you allow your relationship to grow through a shared contract of mutual strength and support. This can be especially important when baby arrives, as well as for every major stage of your child's development, such as teething, walking, starting nursery and going to school.

Communicate

The demands of parenting can often mean that a happy, intimate relationship can collapse and deteriorate into a sterile non-communicating co-existence. Any attempt to keep the lines of communication open is a generally healthy and positive contribution to a relationship. The quality of communication together is also very important. Relating to one another as friends, as partners and as lovers can help a couple to relate better to one another as parents. Expressing your love, sharing your feelings, and continuing to court one another can help to make each of you feel happy, loved and wanted. By remembering the qualities that initially brought you together, you can help to improve the quality of your life now and forever. Open, honest, loving and intimate communication can help to make happy partners happy parents.

'Fantastic Failures'

Failure, of itself, is rarely, if ever, a serious cause of personal distress; rather, it is the self-criticism, the self-doubt and the negative self-accusations that follow failure that tend to be really damaging and dangerous. Parenting is all about venturing into uncharted territory and unfamiliar surroundings. Quite naturally, there will be times when you stumble, falter and fall. Being the best possible parent to your child is a natural, universal aspiration all parents share; it is so easy, though, to torture yourself, especially during moments of failure, with an image of the perfect, angelic, mythical parent-ideal. Self-recriminations do little for either you or your child. The words of one particular parent who faced up to her parent-ideal are especially inspiring. She wrote, 'As a parent, I probably fail five, six, seven times a day, and that's a good day; but I have learned to welcome what

I call "fantastic failures" because I now know each failure is, for me, an invitation to grow.'

Moment by Moment

A skilled mountain climber will rarely take a full view of a new mountain he or she is about to ascend, preferring instead to avert eyes, keep head down and begin the ascent, step by step by step. Parenting is a mountainous commitment, and the only sure way to climb is to hold on to the moment and grow, step by step by step. During moments of tension, anxiety and fatigue, it is so easy to translate one mistake into 'Everything is a mistake,' one failure into 'I am a failure,' one hour of the baby's crying into 'Baby always cries,' and one day of failing to cope into 'I'll never be able to cope.' These beliefs, though not true, can overthrow you. It is important, so as not to be overwhelmed by these desperate, bleak affirmations, that you empower yourself by attending to the moment you can control – the moment of now. Take one day at a time, and the weeks, the months and the years will take care of themselves.

On the Plus Side

'He cries a lot,' 'She never sleeps,' 'He's a little devil,' 'She's no angel,' 'Children? – never again!' So often we, as adults, describe and define children in terms of negatives. We shy away from acknowledging, from appreciating and from communicating the many wonderful gifts that children bring. Yes, it is true, children can be very problematic; but they are also very, very precious. During times of parental stress, the negatives can so easily close in, overwhelm and leave you feeling powerless. You can improve your capacity to cope with the negatives by making a conscious effort to remember and to record all of the positives, the pluses and the pleasures that parenting brings. One way to do this is to keep a diary of precious times; another way is to make a point of communicating the good news of parenting to people. Appreciating all of the blessings of parenting can keep you from being overwhelmed by all of the burdens.

Supporters

When the perceived demands outweigh the perceived resources, it is easy to convince yourself that you are all alone, on your own and completely unsupported. This is a common experience of most types of stress, including parental stress. One way to counteract these harmful, negative affirmations is to write out a list of all the possible supporters in your life, tried and untried. Family, friends and partner are the obvious ports of call. Training your loved ones to be better supporters can also be an active, appropriate, positive step forward for you and your family. There are also the professional supporters, such as the support group for parents under stress, called Parentline. Local libraries, Citizens' Advice Bureaux, Relate and various counselling centres may also offer help. Once you have identified possible supporters, do not decide they cannot help at least until you've tried. Check the Useful Addresses section at the back of this book for more possible supporters.

SINGLE-PARENT STRESS

The accelerating demise of the 'normal' nuclear family set-up – that once consisted of two parents, one male and one female, and two and a quarter children – has meant that many parents today are forced to contend with quite different experiences of parental stress than those faced by their own mothers and fathers. This is particularly so for single-parent families, where one adult has to shoulder the responsibility and burdens of two.

Different experiences of parental stress arise from different family dynamics. For instance, the one-parent family where the mother is the primary carer will encounter different tensions to the one-parent family where the primary carer is the father; the one-parent family with a working mother will have to grapple with different pressures to the one-parent family with a working father; and the divorced single parent will experience different strains to the bereaved single parent. It is also true, though, that all single parents will also share experiences of stress that are particular to single-parenting.

There will always be times when a single parent experiences a perceived inability to cope. Perceived demands will, at times, outweigh the perceived resources. Single parents have to contend not only with the pressures of family but also with the pressures of society where they may meet with isolation, stigma, discrimination, judgement, inadequate childcare, a lack of employment opportunity and financial hardship. Society provides well for couples; it so often falls short for singles, particularly single parents and their families.

Empowerment

Because a single parent has to shoulder the responsibilities normally shared by two parents, it is absolutely essential that he or she learns the art of self-care. Learning to be the best possible friend you can be to yourself is a necessary act of self-preservation. By learning to care for yourself you create a greater capacity for caring for your dependents. Gingerbread, a leading organization for all lone parents and their children, promotes a philosophy that states, 'Lone parents who are confident, supported and feel good about themselves, make better parents than those who are lonely, unhappy and feel a victim of circumstance.' Bypass the guilt, eliminate excuses and prioritize personal self-care – *when you empower you, you improve everything you do.*

Advantages

The adversities of single-parenting often become easier to contend with as a person develops increased awareness and appreciation of the advantages of single-parenting. Many single parents are able to testify to the many privileges and positives of their role. 'Setting my own standards', 'making my own decisions', 'giving more time to me and to my children', 'cultivating and nurturing self-confidence', 'growing broad shoulders', 'more love and less arguing', 'the family working as a team' and 'learning to be a good, effective parent' are just a few of the common personal testimonies of single parents. Hold on to the advantages so that you can let go of the adversities.

Opportunities

One of the most dangerous behaviours caused by stress is focusing on the restrictions of circumstance, so much so that this can eclipse and deny freedom of opportunity. Single-parenting is often defined in terms of restrictions, limitations and handicaps, yet many single parents are able to say that their experience has been one of growth, development and opportunity. One of the very best ways to perceive any hardship or adversity is to tackle it head on as a challenge, a test and an opportunity. Single-parenting can offer many new opportunities, such as new friends, new groups, self-growth, a change of direction, new priorities and new goals. What opportunities are opening up for you?

Strengths

Pressure is a personal food that can feed the seeds of strength that lie deep and innate within you. What strengths have you developed as a single parent? A conscious awareness and appreciation of your strengths can help to manage and to offset weaknesses. Single parents become a witness to their own innate strengths. They speak of discovering self-reliance, exploring new talents, developing assertiveness, gaining self-insight, holding the reins of control, handling responsibility and being able to give more to new relationships. Standing next to the strengths can help to prevent wilting next to the weaknesses.

Rewards

Putting more into it enables getting more out of it. While not denying the ever-increasing workloads of parenting, single parents are able to recognize the rewards they receive for their endeavours and care. Before you can receive rewards you must be able to recognize rewards. What rewards do you recognize as a single parent? Single parents often point out that it is also very important to give self-praise, self-congratulation and self-reward, not least because there is often no one else around to provide it. Like all parents, single parents succeed every day a thousand different ways. It is very important that you recognize these successes so that success is not overshadowed by failure. Reward yourself so as to preserve yourself.

Helpers

Creating a network of willing cushions, carriers and supporters to help bear the load is a sensible technique of self-support and of self-preservation. Some helpers might need to be trained by you; others will already be raring to go. Typical helpers might include relatives and family, friends, your children's teachers, other parents, neighbours, counselling services, social services workers, health visitors, your ex-partner and local single-parent groups. Lone-parenting need not be a lonely experience. If you begin by tracking down potential helpers, and then communicate your needs to them, you will be better positioned to find support from people who are prepared to carry the load.

Oases

Oases, 'time for me' and 'responsibility-free zones' are important for relaxation, release and letting go. Many single parents convince themselves there is no 'time for me'. For people who believe there is no time, there is no time; for those who are prepared to make the time, they find the time. If you create a time diary, you will find there are times in the day that you can take for you. Single parents often become adept at managing these times. It is important that you take time out to relax, to unwind and to recuperate. Enrol the help of your carriers to help you to recharge from time to time. The time is always there if you really look for it.

Networking

Maintaining and expanding a network of friends, family and other social contacts is often a valuable therapy and essential lifeline for single parents. The opportunity to get out, to change your environment, to receive guests, to meet, to talk and to socialize is often a tonic and elixir. Often you will feel too tired to make the effort, and often you will feel that your friends make assumptions that you are too busy, but you must not let this stop you from making contact. The energy you expend will be returned to you again and again. A network of faithfuls can beam a light onto the darkness of the day. Rewards are a return for effort.

Organizers

The single-parent family manager has to be an adept time-manager as well. Time is of the essence. It is absolutely vital therefore that you carry out a project in your household to identify any lurking time drains. It is also important to explore and to experiment with any possible time-savers. Single parents often become very proficient at creating routines, time frames and deadlines. When it comes to time, maximum efficiency is the key. Taking the time to identify and to pursue organizers will not really take up any time at all; on the contrary, it will save you time. Organization is a time-saver. If you are wise, you will understand that there is always more you can do to organize.

Goals

As a single parent it is very easy to free-wheel throughout the days, the weeks and the months, consumed by and preoccupied with the demands of the moment. Taking time to set goals might appear, at first, only to increase your burden of pressure and responsibility. With a little more thought, it becomes apparent that goal-setting can help to plan and to prioritize your life – better, perhaps, than you do now. By making personal goals and family goals you create direction, you identify priorities, you harness energy, you organize well, and along the way, you will find that you grow and develop in so many ways. Taking the time to establish your goals will help you to achieve your goals – goals that you and your family would wish to aspire to. All proficient managers make time for goals.

CHRISTMAS AND HOLIDAY STRESS

Counselling centres generally report that they receive more crisis calls at Christmas time than on any other occasion in the year. The school holidays are other times in the year when counsellors and therapists witness a sudden surge in distress calls. Christmas cheer and holiday wholesomeness, far from being fun and fulfilling, can end up being a time of disorder, depression and dread. For so many people, the two common 'high points' in the year are often, in reality, the two personal 'low points' in the year.

There is an old saying that goes, 'Christmas comes, but once a year is enough!' It is a sad, ironic fact that Christmas, supposedly a spiritual safehaven of 'peace and goodwill', should be a catalyst for so much personal crisis and calamity. Prescriptions for anti-depressants and tranquillizers often soar during the Christmas season. Marriage guidance centres can be inundated with requests for help from desperate and dejected men and women. Counselling centres, charities and churches alike can all have their work cut out coping with the crises of Christmas.

Horrors of the holiday season often run a close parallel to the tensions of Christmas time. Many people feel that the one thing they long for on returning home from a holiday, is a holiday! Quite clearly, then, both the Christmas season and the holiday season are not without their dangers of discord, dissonance and disruption. It is important to understand, however, that Christmas time and holiday time are neither implicitly 'good' or 'bad'; rather, it is our approach, our attitude and our actions that will tend to bring out the 'good' or the 'bad'. We can, if we are careful enough, clasp the reins of control. We can, in other words, 'make it good' or 'make it bad'.

Great Expectations

In his play *All's Well that Ends Well*, Shakespeare advises us, 'Oft expectation fails and most oft there where most it promises; and oft it hits where hope is coldest and despair most fits.' The great expectations of a 'perfect' or 'near-perfect' Christmas or holiday can turn even the smallest, most trivial incident into a test, a trial and a trauma. A dud cracker, too much salt in the stuffing, missing the opening credits on the James Bond film, a Christmas card which reads 'with love' instead of 'much love', and piles of pine needles in your slippers are just a few examples of the many minor misdemeanours which can dampen a merry Christmas.

As for holiday time, glossy brochures, TV recommend-ations and travel agency staff often encourage great expectations that are rarely experienced. The trip from Romance to Reality Airport can turn turquoise seas to a basic brown, tantalizing à la carte menus to transport caravan meals, and open-air paradises into cramped chalets with holes in the roof. High expectations can leave us prone, open and vulnerable to low tolerance thresholds, below par boredom and heavy disappointments. The lesson of great expectations is that 'perfection' is not delivered to you, but *by* you. Be clear on this from the start, and come what may, you can still end up happy at heart.

Careful Choices

Making correct choices can be the difference between make or break when it comes to Christmas and holiday stress. Presents that are personally chosen, thought about and appropriate are the most treasured of all. The material cost is rarely as important as the meaningful thought. And when it comes to the kids, if big Simon likes football and little Tim likes trains, don't buy Tim a goalkeeper shirt. Choices about where to have Christmas and whom to entertain must also be considered carefully. You may even have to choose to be assertive so as to protect your choices. What you choose to compromise on is another important consideration.

One of the most stress-provoking experiences of holiday-making is choosing where, 'on Earth', to go. Will it be sun, or somewhere cool? Will it be beach, or mountains, perhaps? Will it be commercial, or unspoilt, maybe? Other crucial choices can be choosing whom to go with, how long to go for, and what to do on holiday. Different types of people prefer different types of holidays. Do all that you can, therefore, to make an informed and considered choice. Once the choice is made, choose to make the very best of it all.

Forward Planning

Special moments require special planning. If your Christmas planning begins on Christmas Eve, it will most likely fall apart by mid-morning Christmas Day. Christmas festivity can so easily disintegrate into Christmas frenzy if your party plans are really only partly-plans. Make your lists in October, save your monies in November, and go for broke, though not quite, in December. Christmas is a time to organize and then relax; to relax and then organize rarely works as well.

For several days, weeks or months you will know when and where you are travelling to, so don't leave it until the last minute to get there. Passport checks, flight number checks and traveller's cheque checks are a good idea if you really do want to go away! Planning a holiday can be as much fun as going on holiday, particularly if you make it a policy to plan well. Pack all you can into the planning so that when you get there you can unpack as much fun and pleasure as possible.

Contingency Plans

Cater for emergencies by creating your own Christmas and holiday contingency kits. Happiness at Christmas can be a tough game to play, so it is a good idea to have one or two reserves and substitutes on the team bench. Extra crackers for the kids, a secret store of more brandy butter, universal 'surprise gifts' for universal 'surprise visitors', replacement fuses for the fairy lights, and batteries for the really big present that won't work without them, will all help to raise Christmas cheer.

Sick bags are essential for happy holidays! So too are plaster kits, a spare tyre without puncture, essential telephone numbers, and games for the children and reading for you when it rains. The more children you have, the more contingencies you make! Plain sailing, smooth rides and free flight are exceptions on holiday, not the rule. Whatever the exception and whatever the rule, plan for both. If all goes well, the more homework you do, the less holiday-work there will be to do.

Shared Responsibilities

The ultimate Christmas nightmare: what happens when it's nobody's turn to do the washing-up? Do not attempt to be a Christmas martyr, unless, that is, you are happy to become one. Too many Christmas Day ding-dongs and Boxing Day bash-ups are a result of the failure to share responsibilities fairly. Identify responsibilities, and share them. The chores of cooking, carving and cleaning, for instance, require a committed contribution from all parties concerned. The same is true of holiday responsibilities. Too many school holidays are named after Saints – do not attempt to add yourself to the list. Know what response you desire, and divide the responsibilities accordingly.

Give and Take

Many of the lessons of Christmas time and holidays are to do with give and take, and compromise. On the occasion of Christmas, it seems appropriate to see what the Bible says. In Acts 20: 35 it is written, 'It is more blessed to give than to receive.' Learning to give is a pleasure, a reward in itself, and a talent. How well do you give? Do you give well enough and often enough? Do you give too much? When it comes to taking, do you take the time to appreciate all that you get, or do you take it for granted? Giving, taking and compromising for Christmas is a shared effort and a shared responsibility.

What do you give to your holidays? What do you expect to take from your holidays? Holidays, like Christmas time, cannot be made only of 'all me' moments. The joys and the pleasures of holiday-making are precisely what you make of it all; they are inspired, in particular, by learning the lessons of personal giving, personal taking and personal compromise. Caring well and sharing well, together, are wonderful healers for handling the stresses and strains of potential holiday heat.

Money Management

To be financially generous and carefree at Christmas time is a potential pressure which, if we allow ourselves to succumb to it, can result in a plenitude of personal pains, upsets and unpleasantries. The pressure to spend for affection is perpetrated in particular by a relentless media campaign that penetrates our homes from October onwards via TV, radio and press. Five strategies for Christmas cash management include, 1) make a monthly investment throughout the year into a Christmas/Birthdays bank account; 2) wherever possible, spend cash rather than use credit; 3) agree upon a money spending pass-not; 4) use all of your discrimination to avoid buying 'play-with-once-only', unimaginative, over-priced toys for children; 5) remember that, when it comes to buying presents, feelings are more appropriate and better appreciated than finances.

A monthly investment into a separate bank account throughout the year is also a good idea for spreading the cost of a holiday. Five more strategies for sensible holiday budgeting include, 1) assessing the true cost of 'hidden extras' such as local travel, picnic equipment, swimming extras, heating meters, equipment rentals, and payments for use of a hotel safe, for instance; 2) deciding a personal daily budget for ice creams, snacks, fruit machines, meals out and drinks, for instance; 3) creating a collective budget for odds and ends so as to ensure a fair distribution of generosity; 4) taking small containers of domestic cleaners and refreshments so as to avoid a big shopping bill on arrival; 5) when travelling abroad, know your currency exchange rates exactly, not approximately.

Travel Stress

Travel can so easily be a source of stress during the Christmas and holiday seasons. Whom to travel to, where to travel to, when to travel, travel timetables, how to travel and travel maps and travel routes all need to be carefully planned, steered and controlled. Five important questions to answer include, 1) who drinks; who drives? 2) has the car had a recent service? 3) weather complications? 4) any contingencies for travel delays? 5) travel money? The old English proverb speaks the truth: 'The heaviest baggage for a traveller is an empty purse.' Travel insurance, your driver's licence and emergency breakdown cover may save your holiday in any number of ways. Basically put, the more effort you make to prepare the less effort it will take to get you there. Also, just in case, be prepared to laugh a lot!

Personal Space

To avoid the high anxiety of Christmas and holiday stress it is occasionally necessary to retreat from time to time away from the hilarity of paper hats, cans of spray-string, party poppers and festive frolicking fun and games. At Christmas time and holiday time we tend to put on our public face of host or entertainer and proceed then to attend to absolutely everything save our very own self. Our personal daily routines are obstructed, our time and our space are invaded, and personal moments alone are denied us.

Time to relax, reflect, recharge and re-create, for the sake of ourselves, are often denied for the sake of others. We can all enjoy the prospect of a happy, respectable time if we are prepared to respect our own and others' individual preferences, different paces, heart-felt wishes and personal space. Christmas and holidays are not always appropriate times for fun and for giving, especially if, for instance, a person has recently experienced loss, separation or bereavement. Make space for your true feelings, and then you and your true friends can make space for you.

Beware Anti-climax

Many of the stresses of Christmas and holiday time happen not before or during the event, but after. Planning the end as thoughtfully and as thoroughly as you planned the beginning can help to cater well for the inevitable feelings of deflation, tiredness and anti-climax. If you are the type of person who suffers from Boxing Day blues at Christmas or touchdown depression at the airport, then it is a good idea to plan events so as to ensure that your happiness does not hurry to a horrible halt. Plan for the 'moments after' *before* the event actually begins. Give yourself every opportunity to find your feet again in a way that is happy, enjoyable and kind to you.

Common Causes of Christmas Calamity
and Holiday Horror

- Financial pressure problems
- Great expectations syndrome
- Conflicting family loyalties
- Communication complacencies
- Poor planning and preparation
- Unfair responsibility rotas
- Little or no personal space
- Temporary 'saintliness' roles
- Attempted personal martyrdom
- High spirits/low tolerances

INTERVIEW, EXAM AND
TEST STRESS

Interviews, exams and tests are easy; the fears, the doubts and the uncertainties that surround these events often are not. For example, the basic skills required to pass a driving test are very simple: almost any IQ score will do, and you don't even need both of your arms, legs or eyes. However, the fear of failure, the nervous anticipation and the worrying self-doubts can, if not carefully managed, metamorphose the most harmless, menial of tasks into a truly horrendous, insurmountable challenge.

Most people who fail their driving test do so not because of the traffic on the road but because of the traffic in their mind. The same is true of any other type of 'test' in life, be it school examinations, college degrees, job interviews, professional qualifications, artistic auditions, first aid-training, court appearances, social club entrance interviews, work presentations, quizzes, competitions, media interviews or sports events, for instance.

The fear of failure can inspire two main responses: doubt or determination. We can be so infected by the insidious disease of doubt that any effort to succeed is negated and nullified by negative non-belief. On the other hand, the fear of failure can ignite intention, inspire dedication and make for an heroic, strong single-mindedness. The fears of failure must be strictly controlled before one can enjoy the heights of success.

Of all the doubts in the world, self-doubt is often the most difficult to overcome. So often, when it comes to interviews, exams and tests, the real challenge is about you – in particular, it is about your desire to succeed, your belief in yourself, your personal self-esteem. If you handle yourself well, you are more likely to handle your challenge well. To put it another way, 'When I manage "Me" well, I am better positioned to manage the moment well.'

Preparation

Quality of preparation inspires and supports both quality of progress and quality of performance. Preparation that begins five minutes before a test will usually fail five minutes into the test. Test-management requires time-management. Make time to plan the time leading up to your interview, exam or test. Do your best to do your best. Give yourself every opportunity to make the most of your opportunity. Establish a learning routine; work on your weak spots; consolidate your strengths; and devise yourself a strategy. Prepare well and you will be better positioned to perform well.

Practice

There is an amusing ancient Hindu proverb which reads, 'He who tastes a grain of mustard seed knows more of its flavour than he who sees an elephant-load of it.' Practise your performance so as to improve your performance – before and not after your big day. Practising can help to identify problem areas, to patch up weaknesses, to develop your strengths and to build up personal confidence. Practising well can help you to promote yourself well. Good practice tends to promote good progress. The most potent form of personal learning is practice – practise your skills, practise success and practise control of your stress. Practice makes perfect.

Effort

It was the Greek dramatist Euripides who coined the phrase, 'Much effort, much prosperity'. How much effort are you willing to invest to achieve your desired dividends? How committed are you to your cause? What can you be doing, right now, to improve your chances of success? You must have the willingness to expend effort and the wisdom to expend the right kind of effort. What you give will help to determine what you get. If your energy, your enthusiasm and your efforts are committed, sincere and consistent, then these attributes will be your success, irrespective of any result.

Trust

If you prepare yourself well, practise frequently and invest the right effort, then you are entitled to trust in yourself. If you build yourself up well, you cannot let yourself down badly. Trust in self is a reward you reap for self-responsibility, self-care and self-discipline. Learning to trust your training and your talents can help you to tackle a task skilfully and well. Trusting is also a mental trick that can help you to dispel worry, fear, anxiety and uncertainty, all of which are manifestations of personal mistrust. First, do the best for yourself; second, trust that the best is about to happen.

Censorship

When it comes to passing interviews, exams and tests, worry doesn't work. No one has ever achieved a pass, an acceptance or a success by worry alone, no matter how proficient he or she was at worrying! Do not ever let worry get in the way of your work. Censor the doubts, the fears, the worry and the negatives; substitute determination, work, hope and positives. Take every chance to give yourself the chance to do well. You will almost always feel feelings of fear, worry and uncertainty, but that does not mean you need to subscribe to them, believe in them, or afford them permission to take control. Censor the negatives; capitalize on the positives.

Affirmation

Affirm, at all times and in all ways, your ability to achieve abundant success. Think 'I can' do well; believe 'I can' do well; behave so that 'I can' do well; and talk as if 'I can' do well. Approach, attitude and action are often self-fulfilling prophesies. Beware that you are not, right now, talking or thinking yourself into defeat. Affirm your ability to achieve – think and affirm, believe and affirm, behave and affirm, and talk and affirm. Affirming positives is by far and away more pleasant and more productive than affirming negatives.

Appearance

Presentation is an important part of any personal perform-ance. The way you appear is a statement about the way you are. Presentation is a very powerful and persuasive language, and how you appear will determine in part how you are received, read, and judged. An appropriate appearance can also help to inspire a good personal presentation. Take a look at your presentation – be it a letter, your personal dress, a planned talk, or a phone call, for instance – and use time, thought and effort to ensure you create the right appearance for the right effect.

Relax

To be inwardly relaxed during times of personal pressure is so often the key to a good performance. A well-practised relaxation technique can help a person to plan clearly, to think clearly, to disperse negative personal tensions and to communicate well. Many professionals practise a relaxation technique, such as meditation, autogenics, hypnotherapy or good breath control, so as to handle positively the pressure of personal performance (See Chapter 3). To be poised under pressure can help a person to perform under pressure. If you relax well you may find you are better positioned to react well.

Communication

Practise and develop your communication skills – for every event and for all occasions. Your ability to communicate well can inspire your ability to conduct yourself well. Clarity and conciseness are keynotes of all types of communication. Other important pointers are relaxation, fine body posture, good voice intonation, steady eye contact, good appearance, neat presentation and an absence of nervous gestures. Look, study and listen to yourself communicating. Answer the following question, now: What can I do to enhance the way I communicate? To command yourself well, it helps to communicate well.

Rewards

It is so important to look after yourself the best you possibly can when faced with a personal trial or test. To reward yourself continually when preparing for an imminent challenge can have a tremendous, positive impact on personal morale, motivation and esteem. It can also be good to plan a reward for after the event, such as a long hot bath, a meal out with friends or buying yourself a gift, for instance. Having something to look forward to 'afterwards' can also lift the spirits. Let your motto be, 'do well for myself; be well for myself'.

Causes of Interview, Exam and Test Tension

- Excessive self-doubt
- Fear of failure
- Fear of success
- Risk of rejection
- Negative beliefs
- An inability to relax
- Not enough practice
- Worry rather than work
- Unhelpful preparation
- Not enough hard work

JOB STRESS

The wonderful world of work weaves a very fine line between productive pressure and destructive stress.

Pressure is an essential ingredient of good work: the pressure to perform well can inspire creativity, achievement and success; the pressure of a tight deadline can spark increased effort, energy and drive; excessive demands upon our time can help us to prioritize effectively, to delegate well and to offload time-wasters; and pressures of finance can inspire good goal-setting, creative change and new, more effective policies.

The positive stimulation of the workplace offers a rich potential of personal and collective pay-offs, such as learning new skills, discovering personal potentials, improving self-esteem, learning about teamwork, making friends, enjoying excellent achievements, handling failure, acquiring strength through crisis and learning to communicate well. Productive pressure and positive stimulation are the batteries that power our personal professional performances. We all have our moments when we dream of and wish for a stress-free job in a workplace without pressure; but work without sufficient stimulation or without the appropriate tension or drive can be very boring and very stressful. Boredom at work is a definite health hazard; having no pressure or responsibility can corrode personal confidence; lazy complacency leads to accidents; and no new challenges can often lead to a stale, unsatisfactory performance.

Rather like a pain barrier, each of us has our own stress barrier which when broken turns productive pressure into a sour, seedless stress. We usually break the stress barrier at times when we perceive and believe our capacity to cope is seriously threatened. Pressures feel too intense; perceived demands outweigh perceived resources; and energy for coping begins to exhaust itself. Learning to protect, to fortify and to extend our own stress barrier is essential for happy, healthy working.

Identifying causes of work stress can prove to be an illusive, confusing exercise: first and foremost, because stress affects every individual in a unique way, there can be no dogmatic, all-true generalizations; secondly, because within any work-place there can be individual stresses, company/corporate stresses, environmental stresses and economic/political stresses, all of which play on one another; thirdly, because many ingredients that make for happiness, and success can also contribute to failure and demise.

Perhaps the biggest single cause of work stress has been a

failure of awareness – how many of us really know how stress affects us at work? How many of us make a conscious effort to manage stress, pressure and tension in the workplace? And how many of us take time and effort to learn to protect, to fortify and to extend our own personal stress barriers? Both company and individual, employer and employee must own the responsibility to create a better awareness and understanding of work stress. Awareness facilitates control.

There are signs that business managers are at last beginning to address stress: there are more Occupational Health Departments in industry than ever before, though many are forced to battle with budgets that are blatantly mean; more and more organizations are beginning to invest in human resources training, such as successful stress control workshops; office environment technicians are occasionally employed to create better, more healthy working environments; a confidential counselling service for employees is also offered by certain big multi-national groups; job share, flexitime, quality circles, job redesign and employee participation and involvement programmes also aim to tackle harmful work stress; and then there are the much publicized troubleshooters, such as Sir John Harvey Jones, who aim to tackle corporate stress and to improve business excellence.

There has always been a strong belief that employers have a moral duty to care and provide for the health and happiness of their employees. For this reason we have Health and Safety Acts and Occupational Health Objectives. In the USA, employers are increasingly being held liable for employees' health problems that are associated specifically with stress. Unfortunately, though, the majority of employers today have still yet to rise to this awareness of stress awareness and stress control.

Stress management also has a lot to do with self-management and self-care. We, as individuals, must also accept some responsibility for our health and happiness. One or two small changes in our work approach and our work routines can make a dramatic difference in the quality of our work performance and our work-happiness. With sufficient awareness and appropriate action, there is always plenty we can do to prevent, release or alleviate our work stress. Of all the help there is, self-help is best.

Self-Management

While others may from time to time mismanage you, mismanaging yourself is something you should never do. This is the first rule of successful stress control in the workplace. Just because your employer, manager or colleague may mismanage you, do not be tempted to take it as a cue to start mismanaging yourself. So many people resort to 'You don't care, I don't care' reactions to stress. When the stress gets tough, you must get tough too – on yourself. Managing yourself well will help you to manage your stress well. Be aware how stress affects you. Become 'answers and actions'-conscious, rather than 'anxiety and adversity'-conscious. You can worry about your stress, or you can work at your stress. Which will you do? Be your own ideal manager – care for yourself. This approach will inspire others to care for you, too.

Organization

Don't agonize; organize. Effective self-organization and organization of others tends to fail badly during times of stress, thereby exacerbating the effects of stress; it is absolutely essential, therefore, that you maintain order and harmony, within and around you, during peak pressure periods. The ability to organize yourself, your office, your desk, your diary, your morning routines, your travel to work and your general working operations does take up time, but not as much time as is wasted if you fail to organize these things. If you feel you can't organize everything, organize what you can. Small steps often yield big bonuses. Order, balance and harmony are cornerstones of consistent long-term achievement.

Time Management

'Our costliest expenditure is time,' wrote the Greek philosopher, Theophrastus. Good time management will often inspire effective, happy professional performance; bad time management so often contributes to poor stress control, and vice versa. Learning to manage yourself well begins with learning to manage your time well. Treasure your time – units of time are, after all, units of life. Make the most of your time: organize and reorganize, yourself; identify and eliminate time-wasters; identify and incorporate time-savers; know your priorities, and stick to them; avoid regularly being too generous with your time, for it is rarely appreciated; delegate fairly, where possible; encourage others, where possible, to treasure their time, too. When it comes to effective time management, you can only notice a difference if you are first prepared to make a difference.

Lifestyle

To dedicate all of your time, effort and energy to work cannot guarantee you will work well – it cannot even guarantee that you will get all the work done. On the contrary, being immersed in your work can cause you to submerge and to drown in a sea of quantities, mistakes, accidents, miscommunications, failures and fatigue – quality, meanwhile, is allowed to sail away. The surest guarantee for working well is to work at living well. Modern performance psychology suggests that 'workstyle' is a faithful reflection of lifestyle.

You will be better able to cope with the burdens of work if you actively pursue and engage yourself in all of the blessings there are to be enjoyed outside of work. The motto is simple: Live well, work well.

Relaxation

The quality of your effort, endeavour and arousal can only ever be as good as the quality of your rest, relaxation and recreation. Effort upon effort, with no time for rest, rarely promotes effectiveness; on the contrary, endless effort tends to exacerbate and to accelerate exhaustion, burn-out, ill health and a faltering performance. Learning to relax well outside of work can help you to relax well inside of work. More and more professionals are taking up relaxation, autogenics, meditation and hypnotherapy (See Chapter 3) as positive steps towards polished professional performance. A cool, calm approach to work can certainly position you well for coping with the chaos and the conflicts of work. Relax well, react well.

Detachment

At the end of the day, when you leave your work, do you really leave your work? Or, does your work follow you home? In many jobs, particularly where unpleasant pressure is part of the normal day-to-day proceedings, learning to detach well is an absolutely essential act of self-preservation. Worrying about work will not lighten the load; on the contrary, persistent night-time worry often leaves a person less effective for coping with the next day – this makes for more worry! When at work, work hard; when at play, play hard. Work to the full; live to the full. Think for a moment how best you can detach at the end of the day. Put an action into effect, and enjoy the effects.

Health

Unhealthy, maladaptive self-management strategies often abound whenever harmful perceived stresses hop up the horizon. In particular, four cornerstones of health so often crumble and collapse at the onset of chaos. They are: diet, rest, sleep and exercise. During times of stress many people resort to junk foods, quick meals, increased alcohol, comfort foods, no relaxation, no quality time, reduced sleep, no recreation, no social time and no play. To live well and to work well it is essential that we eat well, rest well, sleep well and exercise well. Concentrate on these four cornerstones and you will be better positioned to cope with the crises and the conflicts of occupational life.

Communication

Poor communication in the workplace is both a symptom of work stress and a cause of work stress. Communication channels often get clogged when crises, chaos and conflicts arise, thereby adding to the impact of such problems. So many individuals within organizations who suffer from work stress are not prepared to speak of their work stress. Suffering in silence is hardly a satisfactory solution for stress. One reason people feel inhibited about speaking up is that words like stress, tension and pressure are still 'taboo' – if so, then change the words a little, and speak of 'morale', 'motivation', 'directions', 'job satisfaction' and 'time management'. We each have a responsibility for good communication practice within our place of work. Whomever you communicate to, communicate constructively.

Directions

Poorly defined objectives, unclear goals and a dodgy sense of direction are classic symptoms and causes of low morale, under-achievement and poor stress control – on both the individual and corporate levels. Without a precise set of aims, time management is tricky, workloads tend to multiply, wasted resources abound, prioritizing is impractical and measuring success is impossible. How clear are you about your goals? Are your goals reasonable enough? Do you have a written job description? Does it tally with what you do each day? A carefully considered, well-chosen direction is essential for happy, positive work performance. We are, each of us, ultimately responsible for our own directions – sometimes setting the right direction may even mean a change of job.

Purpose

Do you know why you go to work? The standard answer to this question is, 'To pay the rent'! But after that, do you know why you go to work? Do you make your work serve any other purposes for you? How about: learning skills, meeting people, handling responsibility, developing potential, learning about life, enjoying success and learning to cope with failures? Performance psychology research shows that people who do not know why they go to work are often more susceptible to the stresses and strains of work. Do you aspire to standards you have set yourself? Do you give yourself rewards? Can you identify everything that is positive and uplifting about your work role? These sorts of questions – and the answers, more importantly – serve to illuminate our latent, abundant capacity for coping with failure and success, happiness and stress.

Top 10 Symptoms of Harmful Work Stress

- Higher sickness and absenteeism rates
- Higher employee turnover
- Lower motivation and morale

- Poor team spirit
- Fluctuating productivity levels
- Higher incidence of accidents
- Lower quality indicators
- Higher minor disputes or strikes
- Higher early retirement requests
- Fewer training opportunities

Top 10 Causes of Harmful Work Stress

- No formal stress-care awareness policy
- Inconsistent, poorly trained management
- Inconsistent management communication
- Poor management/colleague relationships
- Unhelpful approaches/attitudes to stress
- Unwritten objectives and unclear goals
- Feeling undervalued and unappreciated
- Insufficient employee consultation
- Unrealistic workloads/time schedules
- Poor time management/organization skills

UNEMPLOYMENT STRESS

Redundancy and unemployment are in many ways the working world's equivalent to personal bereavement and loss. The most obvious loss of all is usually a loss of income; however, loss of working income is usually no less damaging than loss of working status, loss of personal identity and loss of self-esteem. The often familiar fears, frustrations and feelings of uncertainty that surround redundancy and unemployment can have just as tangible effects as the financial worries.

Loss of work and loss of income tend to trigger a need for all sorts of personal alterations and life adjustments.

Redundancy and unemployment can deprive a person of a daily routine, of a daily purpose and of a possible daily source of satisfaction and enjoyment; redundancy and unemployment can also prevent access to a daily circle of friends, colleagues and peers. All of these losses often only serve to compound a loss of personal confidence, self-worth and inner esteem.

Many people find they go through certain distinct stages of reaction to redundancy and unemployment. Numbing shock, astonishment, and a sense of disbelief are common initial reactions that may then give way either to disorientation, powerlessness, despondency and procrastination or to anger, denial, outrage and frustration. In truth, many people will feel a mix of most of these feelings, with perhaps one or two feelings tending to predominate. These reactions are often complicated by possible knock-on negative effects for relationships and personal health, all of which adds to the potential damaging impact of redundancy and unemployment.

How we react to redundancy and unemployment is also governed by certain perceptions, beliefs and realities. If, for instance, you perceive that you don't stand a chance of being employed ever, ever again, then this perception will undoubtedly have a severe impact on your life. If, for instance, you believe there are no jobs available and you cannot be bothered to make absolutely, definitely, certainly sure, then this belief will unbalance you. And if, for instance, the reality is that the economy is in recession and jobs really are scarce, then you may have to try harder and longer before you enjoy your just rewards.

React Correctly

How do you feel? How have you chosen to react to the news of your redundancy or unemployment? Are you despondent, upset, angry or low? Do you realize that none of these reactions are actively helping you to make a fresh start? In fact these reactions are probably hindering and obstructing your best efforts. Some reactions will definitely not help you to get what you want; others might. Finding a new job, for instance, is a job of work in itself: it may possibly be the most important job you ever have to undertake. It is essential, therefore, that while you may want to air your frustrations and hurt, you also ensure that you react correctly. Reactions reap rewards. If you react well you give yourself every opportunity to reap the rewards you are working for.

Don't Worry

Worry has never, ever once in the whole history of the human race ever got anyone work – except the doctor, of course, and the nurse, the counsellor, the psychologist, the heart specialist and the funeral director! During times of redundancy and unemployment, if your earnest wish is to resume work, you must become 'work-conscious', not 'worry-conscious'. In other words, you must become action-orientated rather than anxiety-orientated. What can I be doing, right now, to improve my chances of work? Each and every day, this is the key question you need to address. Anxiety and worry will go away the more you act and work towards your goals. While anxiety will more likely gain you sympathy; actions will more likely to gain you employment.

Strategy

Being unemployed is a little bit like being self-employed. For a full eight to ten hours a day you follow nobody's plans, orders or goals, save your own. The way you plan your day determines in part the progress and productiveness of that day. Your strategies, your schemes and your self-organization are as foundations; if your foundations are firm, what you build on them will stand. Plan your work time precisely; plan your rest time carefully; and plan your recreation and leisure time well. Remember, if re-employment is your aim, finding a job is a job of work in itself, so work well and live well and you shall give yourself every chance to do well. Plan properly; progress productively.

Assets

During times of adversity it is easy to lose sight of the assets that can help to alleviate anguish and anxiety. Know your attributes, hold on to your assets and be aware of all of your talents, skills and experience. Make a written list of all of your plus-points – what benefits would a potential employer purchase when you agree to go to work for that employer? If you do not recognize your assets, then no one else is likely to recognize them, either. Promote, peddle, publicize and advertise yourself – if you want to be available for work, then make yourself available. Plans, progress and direction are all easier to assess if you know your assets.

Help

Generally speaking, there are two types of help: self-help and 'others-help'. How can I, right now, help myself? Self-help is often the best because by generating your own help you empower yourself all the more. Concentrate on the 'helping' and you will not be so consumed by the 'hurting'. How can I help myself, right now, to get help from others? There are all sorts of help-points available for the unemployed, such as careers advice centres, job clubs, employment centres, restart schemes, career development loans, courses for those (particularly women) returning to the job market, and redundancy payment advice. Citizens' Advice Bureaux, local libraries, jobs sections in the press – the sooner you ask for help, the sooner you can benefit from help.

Great!

Strange as it may seem, unemployment might just possibly be the very best thing that ever happened to you! Being out of work gives you the time, space and energy to take a good long look at what you do. Whether you like it or not, unemployment means a new start, and when you contemplate new starts, you might as well also contemplate fresh opportunities, a change in direction and new areas of work. Also, it is highly likely there will come a time in the future when you will wish for all the time you have right now. Why not turn all this time into a positive: explore new interests, renew old contacts, get fit, re-examine new work areas, meet people, pursue some old ideas perhaps, travel to new places – and why not enjoy yourself (within your means)? Things can grate; things can be great! You choose!

Training

The time and space that are freed up by unemployment may offer a fine opportunity for training and development. By brushing up on your old skills and by adding one or two new skills to your collection, you are making a personal investment in your professional future. Any positive investment you make will somewhere along the line yield a positive income of sorts. Unemployment training agencies offer seminars, lecturers and workshops on a variety of subjects including budget control, interview techniques, communication skills, time management and CV presentations. Most of these training opportunities are either free or generously discounted. Your local library or employment centre will be able to assist you further. You can also embark on a course of self-learning, studying books, cassettes and videos as available from your local library. Make the opportunity count.

Presentation

No matter the problem, no matter the place, put on your best face. As Thomas Fuller, M.D., once wrote, 'A good presence is letters of recommendation.' Manage yourself well, keep yourself well and present yourself well. Taking the time to organize and look after the 'outside you' can help to organize and look after the 'inside you'. Present yourself as you would wish to be seen. Whether it's for interviews, meetings, making phone calls, arranging appointments, or writing CVs, job applications or letters, take pride in your presentation. Appearance is a good self-management discipline in that it can inspire mental tidiness, good organization, and, very often, the right response.

Fitness

There is a very high correlation between redundancy/ unemployment and illness. Being out of work and being out of health seem almost to go hand in hand. The major reason for this unfortunate correlation has to do with harmful, stressful reactions to redundancy and unemployment. Most types of work offer at least some physical exercise, at least some mental stimulation and at least some kind of social contact – we can lose all of these things if we do not handle being out of work healthily. Finding work may well be your priority; it should not, however, become your pre-occupation. You must also allow time for leisure, healthy eating, recreation, rest, and whatever else helps to keep you in trim. When things are not going well, it is up to you to keep yourself well. Keep yourself well at all times.

Attitude

There is an old saying that goes, 'The worst type of bankrupt is not the man without money, but the man without meaning and confidence and hope.' Both your attitude and your approach to any perceived personal stress carry a potential far more damaging than the actual stress can ever be. Attitude is a tool, a resource and a skill that can be employed as either a help or a hindrance. You should always be prepared to ask yourself, Is the way I am thinking, right now, helping me to get what I want? The rule is simple: if the answer is 'No', let the thought go.

RETIREMENT STRESS

Retirement is a major life change that can easily perpetuate and provoke a catalogue of personal stresses. The floating fears and hidden assumptions about retiring and growing old are the real villains of the peace: 'nothing more to contribute', 'nothing more to do', 'nothing more to grow for', 'slowing down to a halt', 'going out to graze' and 'nothing new to live for' are just a few of the common insidious messages that can inscribe themselves inside your mind during this time.

Retirement requires readjustment. The readjustment should happen on your terms, not somebody else's. A fundamental problem with retirement is that it is often forced upon people who do not feel like retiring. George Burns, the comedian, once stated, 'Retirement at 65 is ridiculous. When I was 65, I still had pimples'. You may have to retire from work, but that does not mean you have to retire from life. Retirement needn't be a death sentence.

Retirement requires that you re-evaluate and reclassify five key areas in your life. The first key area is *identity*. You may now have a new identity, an identity that is not defined by a workplace label, such as accountant, sales assistant or engineer. Now is the time to wear your original identity of 'you'. The second key area is *time*. You now have time on your hands, more than you might like. Thoughtful, considered time management is vital for your well-being.

The third key area is *direction*. For all of your working life, your direction has probably been planned for you by a boss or by the nature of the work itself. Now it is you who must manage you. Exploring new directions, and the adventure of new horizons – physical, mental and spiritual – are parts of the challenge of retirement. *Purpose* is the fourth key area, and this will develop along with direction in life. Retirement requires that you take time to review and redefine your purpose and direction in life.

The fifth key area is *finances*. Retirement usually heralds a readjustment of financial status. Very often, retirement requires all the skills of a wise accountant. Fortunately, there are groups, associations and organizations who can help you to develop the skills to claim all that is yours, and to enjoy all that is yours. Take time to redefine. You will then be better positioned to embrace your life of retirement with all the vigour and zest you gave to your life of work, and more!

Plan, Prepare and Prioritize

Retirement requires readjustment. Planning for retirement before retirement happens can help to ease the process of readjustment and also placate any perceived or anticipated problems. Essentially put, your approach to retirement and your attitude to retirement will both go a long way towards your enjoyment of retirement. The more you can plan, prepare and prioritize, the better positioned you will be to enjoy the benefits of retirement. The right approach can help you to experience retirement as an opportunity for life and for living, a time of rebirth, renewal and a new beginning.

Positives!

Take one single hour of your life, and list all of the positives you can associate with retirement. Before you can enjoy an opportunity, you must be able to appreciate that the opportunity is there to be enjoyed. Write down, therefore, all of the benefits, the positives and the opportunities of retirement that are there for you to enjoy. Your positives will help you to reorder and to re-evaluate your identity, your time, your direction, your purpose and your finances. Make another list, entitled, 'All that I have wanted to do in the past that I can do now'. Do it, *now*.

Supporters

Throughout every stage of life we pick up supporters to help us on our passage through life. Supporters for retirement and for growing old are there to help you to make the most of this time in your life. There are pre-retirement associations, retirement clubs, and age concern organizations, all of which can help you to advance positively and safely into retirement and old age. There is no need and no reason for solo flights through life. If the support is there, draw upon it for strength, for inspiration and for guidance. A single telephone call might enhance the quality of your life dramatically.

Social Life

A common cause of retirement stress is the fear of or actual experience of loneliness. Often people perceive retirement and growing old as an overwhelming, inevitable tide drifting towards a shore of isolation and aloneness that they are powerless to alter. Effort inspires rewards. The universe only rewards actions! Invest time in maintaining faithful social contacts, and invest time in making new social contacts. Explore societies, lunch clubs, associations, adult education outlets, libraries, Citizen's Advice Bureaux, sports and leisure clubs, and indulge! You have nothing to lose – except, possibly, your loneliness.

Family

Family relationships need never stop growing, developing and improving. Keep contributing to the family. Having something to give, such as yourself, your love and your time, is a foundation for receiving. If applicable, develop a rewarding relationship with your grandchildren. Keep communication open and honest. Talk of your health, your happiness, your fears and your aspirations. Keep as independent as you can, but not isolated. Do not apologize for yourself. Keep giving and you will keep receiving. If you have no family, create a family of friends and social contacts.

Interests

Retirement can offer you the time and space to pursue many of the interests and activities that you may feel have eluded you up until now. Invest effort, energy and enthusiasm in the interests that are affordable and available to you. Exploration, new interests and adventure are by no means exclusive to the young. On the contrary, you may be better positioned now than ever before to appreciate the rewards of hobbies, new horizons and fresh interests. Mental activity prevents retirement from being captivity.

Work

There is no universal law that sayeth 'work is denied the retired'. Many retired people use their experience of work and of life to embark upon a fresh, new and rewarding career late in life. A sudden abrupt halt to work can be very disorientating and can demand widespread readjustment. Retired people sometimes prefer, therefore, to take on part-time work so as to enjoy the best of both worlds. You may also consider contributing yourself, your time and your skills to a local voluntary service. Alternatively, you may wish to work on your house, your car or your garden, for instance. A certain amount of work in the day can be very therapeutic.

Health

Good health is a passport to a happy, active retirement. The more time, care and consideration you invest in your health, the more time you will have to be free to enjoy the benefits of well-being. Poor health is often a result of the misconceptions of old age, such as, 'Old people don't exercise,' 'Old people don't go out' and 'Old people don't do much.' Exercising, eating well, socializing and aiming for happiness are four pointers that will take you a long way towards helping to maintain fitness, health and well-being. Learn to pace and to look after yourself.

Spirituality

Many people only catch up with spiritual interests once the demands of material survival and work performance are satisfied. During the time of retirement there is the opportunity to explore philosophy, religion and spiritual thought. Your experience of the 'how' of life may stand you in good stead for exploring now the 'why' of life. New understandings, philosophical exploration and spiritual knowledge are by no means exclusive to the older generations of a society, but it is true to say that as life progresses more space and time become available for exploring these avenues.

Save your conclusions for after your explorations, not before.

Entertainment

There is no reason why the time of retirement shouldn't be the time of your life. One of the most marvellous stress soothants in life is entertainment. Retirement offers the space, the time and the opportunity to entertain more than perhaps ever before. Plan and pursue entertainments on your own and with friends. The key, always, is to keep contributing so that you keep receiving. Invite friends for a meal. Fear not frolicking and fun! Go out to play! There is truth in the saying, 'I am only as old as I allow myself to be.' Entertain life, and life will entertain you. Retirement need never be dull.

Top 10 Harmful Retirement Stresses

- Boredom – What do I do now?
- Routine
- Loneliness and isolation
- Unclear sense of direction
- Lack of purpose
- Financial considerations
- Time – What do I do with it?
- A changing self-image/identity
- A changing place/value in society
- Lack of self-confidence

BEREAVEMENT STRESS

Is there anything quite so hurtful as loss? We are seldom so sensitive, so uncertain, so despairing, so stressed, as when we are deprived and dispossessed. Readjustment to personal loss is perhaps the toughest test of the course. Loss, be it anticipated or abrupt, leaves a mind, body and heart feeling distinctly bankrupt. Learning to adjust to personal loss can be an excruciating, painful process, yet is not without its own brand of stress.

An experience of loss, or separation, can so easily promote a perceived inability to cope. We experience powerlessness, disorientation, an inner sick feeling of personal distress. To have something snatched, seized, taken away, can leave us empty and torn, wishing, perhaps, that we might never have been born. The world wanders on; we want to stop, but the world wanders on. Gradually, as we reshape, reorder and readjust, so we too will move on, simply, not least because we must.

Within us, one thousand voices will cry, 'But why? The way I feel now, it would be easier to die.' The impulse to live, to continue to receive and to give, is beckoning, strong, and instinctively right; the light of hope will outlive the long, dark night. You can emerge renewed, triumphant and strong. The world wanders on, and you, anew, will rejoin the throng. Things will be different, not as before, but life will present new opportunities, another new door.

Bereavement, readjusting to loss, is a delicate journey of growth. The guidelines set out in Chapter 2 for perceived powerlessness may be relevant for this personal type of stress. So too may the guidelines set out in Chapter 4, which supplies coping strategies for general readjustment and change. Here are few more suggestions that may also be of help for loss, for separation and for saying good-bye.

A Thousand Good-byes

For all the times you said 'hello', you may find you need to say 'good-bye'. Saying good-bye does not need to be rushed. You are not restricted to a single good-bye; you can have more than one. Saying good-bye physically can be altogether different to saying good-bye mentally; and saying good-bye emotionally can be altogether different to saying good-bye spiritually. Practise your good-byes, take time for your good-byes, and say all your good-byes. There need be no final limits to your fond farewells.

Say 'Thank You'

By continuing to say 'thank you' for all the happiness you once shared, you continue to keep that happiness bright and alive. Saying thank you can also help to offset some of the sorrow, disappointment and hurt that you have. Photographs, pictures, memories, gifts and belongings are all prompts that may help you to remember and say thank you. Saying thank you is a reminder not to let the anguish of loss overshadow all that there was, and all that there is. Thank you is a blessing, a healing friend that need never leave.

Together, Still

Your physical relationship together may now be over, but that does not mean to say that your emotional, mental or spiritual relationship is over. To deny a relationship ever existed is as harmful as insisting nothing has changed. Somewhere, however, there is a middle ground where people find they can still relate to deceased loved ones, be it through their emotions, feelings, memories or thoughts, in a way that doesn't deny the reality of the past nor of the present. If it helps, keep relating emotionally, mentally and spiritually to the part of your loved one that is still a part of you.

Tell the Truth

Communicate how you feel, truthfully. When you can, demonstrate how you feel. Express your regrets, talk of your fears, share your loneliness, air your anger, tell of your sadness – let the truth unfold. This needn't be the time to 'behave well', to suppress, to 'put a brave face on it', to deny or to 'put a lid on it'. To communicate, to express and to tell, as and when you can, will help you to adjust and to heal. The only way out is *through*. If you want to say, 'I'm sorry', for instance, try to create the appropriate space, time and company that will help you to apologize. To say how you feel can help to release the pain, and that helps you to heal. Let it out so that you can let it go.

Good Counsel

Sometimes it can help to visit a professional who is trained to help you to work through the crisis of loss. A therapeutic relationship, with a counsellor for instance, will provide a framework for you to acknowledge, confront and deal with the way you now feel. You will be encouraged to help yourself to reshape, reorder and readjust. In groups or one-to-one, you can express yourself, you can share grief with others, you can explore healthy coping strategies, and you can reassess your world, your future and your relationships. CRUSE, a national bereavement counselling service, and RELATE (formerly the Marriage Guidance Counsel), both offer sensitive, strong support (see the Useful Addresses section at the back of this book).

Be Your Own Best Friend

During times of stress, it is essential that you act, work and care for yourself as you would for your own best friend. Too often, a crisis will invoke the critic in us, the judge in us and the jury, all of whom focus on fault, pursue blame, locate weakness and affirm self-failure. To act as your own healer and as your own best friend is wonderful for your own well-being and for the well-being of all who love you. Quality time, rest, sleep, good food, gentle entertainment, time to talk, an attention to your appearance, retreat time, social time – listen to the feelings within you, and aim to take things gently, steadily, kindly, as you would were you caring for your own best friend.

A Time to Heal

The first rule of 'healing bereaving' is that there are no rules. There is no one right way and there is no wrong way. There are no 'should dos', no 'ought tos', or no 'meant tos'. Any separation or loss requires a period of time to reshape, reorder and readjust. It takes time to digest the pain. Time is a healer. The less time you take to work through, the more time you may need to work over, and over and over. So often, the full shock of separation or loss can be delayed over weeks, months, years. Give yourself time. Gently increase day-to-day chores, and give yourself time; gently increase your daily responsibilities, and give yourself time; gently begin to crawl, to walk and to run, and give yourself time.

One Day at a Time

One of the most dangerous reactions to any serious personal stress is to follow the impulse that tells you to cope with everything and everyone well, today. Successful stress control starts with a single day at a time, a single hour at a time and a single task at a time. Take care of the minutes, and the hours will take care of themselves; take care of the hours and the days will take care of themselves, and so on. The more you can focus on now, today, this moment, the less chance your anxiety, fears, sadness and worry have of taking over. Little actions, little tasks and little goals have a wonderful way of taking care of the big actions, the big tasks and the big goals.

Soon you will learn to feel fine, if you take it one day at a time.

Past Experiences

In order to inspire hope, it can help, more than anything, to demonstrate to yourself, 'I can cope.' Identify your past losses. Then, with as much detail as possible, tell yourself or a friend, 1) What was the loss? Date, time, place, etc.? How did you hear of it or find out about it? 2) How did you react to the loss? What were the feelings? What did you suppress? 3) What difference did the loss make to you? How did it affect your relationship with you and with others, both then and now? 4) What helped? How did you help yourself? And what help and support from others did you get? This awareness exercise may, just perhaps, change your view.

Acceptance

Readjustment, coping with loss, begins with acceptance. First, there is the acceptance of facts. Personal loss can be so much more stressful if we persist with 'if only' instead of 'what is'. Second, there is the acceptance of feelings. In other words, loss is a difficult, problematic period in life filled with fragile feelings and personal pains. Accept, therefore, that you need time, space and rest, and balance this with actions, tasks and goals that gradually help you to recover your best. Things cannot be the same as before; now is the dawn of a new time, a new way and a new world order. If you take it gently but surely, you will learn to accept that the future is indeed well worth living for.

6

COMBATTING STRESS-
RELATED ILLNESSES

I can be healthy, happy and well.

SLEEP WELL, LIVE WELL

When we lose the ability to sleep well, even for a single night or two, we tend also to lose the ability to live well. Fatigue and exhaustion bear down upon us, our tolerance levels wane, irritability is easy, inspiration fails us, enthusiasm and interest dry up, concentration becomes nomadic, worry and anxiety reach epidemic proportions, breaks and rest periods are more exhausting than refreshing, and socializing often loses its appeal.

If we go without sleep for even longer periods we wither and dither, we begin to fray at the edges, and our life can, quite simply, begin to fall apart. Our bodies and our minds, cut off from vital nourishment and replenishment, can become severely weakened and disorientated. Coping capacities surrender unconditionally, and harmful, maladaptive coping tactics flourish, such as endless black coffees, working later and longer to catch up, increasing isolation and less delegation, poor time management, higher doses of tranquillizers and insomnia drugs, little or no relaxation, higher alcohol intake, and unhealthy, ir-regular eating habits, all of which serve to exaggerate our condition.

Sleep is a name given to periods of unconsciousness taken by your body-intelligence to heal and repair the wear and tear of cells, tissues, bones, muscles, nerves and organs. It is also a time for your mind to clear its 'internal office', filing the thoughts of the day in their appropriate places. Sleep relaxes you. Sleep allows you to reintegrate and to re-establish essential physical, mental and emotional order and harmony. Sleep refuels, revitalizes and re-energizes you.

Sleep is an active physical and mental condition. It is not, as commonly supposed, a passive, inert, 'doing nothing' state. Knowing this may help you to appreciate better the value of sleep. It can also help to understand that, as with any skill or ability, sleep and its benefits can be controlled and enhanced by your careful preparation and correct practice. Sleeping is a talent; sleeping is a skill.

Insomnia, or sleep deprivation, is becoming an increasingly widespread problem. According to recent medical research, more than two in five people who visit a doctor arrive with a problem which is either caused or aggravated by transient insomnia or chronic insomnia – transient insomnia lasting a few days to a week; chronic insomnia lasting weeks, months, or even years.

Common causes of insomnia include physical pain and discomfort, unpleasant and noisy environments, fear of the dark, fear of death, exhaustion and over-tiredness, asthma, and various drug side-effects. The most common cause of all is a recent or impending stressful event such as bereavement, an interview or test, the need to make a decision, moving house, a son or daughter leaving home, a wedding, financial hardship, or maybe the first day in a new job.

Because insomnia can very often be a presenting symptom of stress, many of the general treatments for stress, such as relaxed breathing, progressive relaxation, meditation, hypnotherapy, autogenics, aromatherapy and music therapy, can all be of help. Whichever one of these exercises or techniques you call upon, you would do well to practise consistently, both daytime and night-time.

Ten Solutions for Sound, Restful Sleep

1. *Relax well before you sleep well.* Take time to wind down and let go. Have a relaxing bath, a warm drink, a light walk, some gentle exercise, or maybe listen to some soothing music, before you sleep.
2. *Only go to bed when you are sleepy.* Listen to your body-clock; not to the clock on your wall. Sleep cannot be forced; it can only be allowed to happen naturally. Save your pyjamas until tiredness persists.
3. *Sleep only in your bed.* Don't be tempted to doze in the bath, to snooze on the sofa, to slump over the dinner table, to become tired-eyed in front of the TV, or to curl up on the rug before the fire. Associate sleep with one place only: your bed.
4. *Save the bed for sleep.* No more midnight snacks, absorbing psychological thrillers, TV films, company reports, crossword puzzles, last cigarettes, or any other work or entertainment that may serve to stimulate, to activate and to awaken you.
5. *Save your sleep for night-time.* If night-time sleep is hard to come by, make sure you cut out the morning lie in, the afternoon siesta, and the evening doze.
6. *Does your bedroom do enough?* How conducive for sleeping are the lighting, the noise levels, the atmosphere, and the bedsprings? Are the sheets fresh and clean? Is the bedroom neat and tidy? Are you warm enough? Do you make sure you leave a window open for fresh air?
7. *Establish a night-time routine.* Prepare for sleep and expect sleep. Folding your clothes, locking the doors, a warm

bath or soothing shower, or light exercise, perhaps, may all play a part in a night-time routine.

8. *Let it happen*. Sleep very often happens in spite of your efforts and attempts. Allow yourself to sleep. Don't try, and don't force it. Be physically still; follow your breath; use a gentle mental affirmation; perform your favourite relaxation, and then allow yourself to drift off.

9. *Get up and try again later*. If you are too anxious about not getting to sleep, the best thing you can do is to get up and to occupy yourself with some light physical and/or mental exercise. Return to bed again when you are ready to allow yourself to sleep.

10. *Rest assured*. Sleep research proves that the insomniac always gets much more sleep in the night than he or she imagines. Also, there is no strict amount of hours you must sleep to be healthy and well. For some, 8 hours is fine, for others, 6 hours, 5 hours or even 4 hours might all be enough. The key is the *quality* of your sleep, not its *quantity*.

Medical drugs for sleeplessness can be very useful in that by knocking you out they help to create space, time and rest between you and your stress. It should be noted, however, that the effects of these synthetic substances tend to be dampening as opposed to liberating. Drugged sleep has been found to be not as relaxing, refreshing and healing as natural sleep. Taking sleeping tablets also carries with it a risk of dependency and withdrawal side-effects. For this reason, in 1988 the Royal College of Psychiatrists advised only inter-mittent use of sleep-inducing drugs, if at all. A commonly acknowledged side-effect of sleeping tablet withdrawal is insomnia!

The art of life and the art of sleep are necessarily bound up with one another. Just as we cannot expect to sleep poorly and live well, we cannot expect to live poorly and sleep well.

Night and day mirror one another, and are, therefore, mutually dependent upon one another for quality and for harmony. If you live as fully as you can this may help you to sleep as fully as you need.

Sleep is an art, and one which is for the most part unappreciated and misunderstood. Preparation for sleep is not about the ten minutes before bedtime. It involves the whole day and our whole life. Like stress, the inability to sleep well is very often a symptom of a lack of inner harmony and a lack of harmony with the world we live in. Our efforts to sleep better must also include, therefore, a concerted attempt to live better – both night and day.

FATIGUE-BUSTERS

This world belongs to the energetic.

Ralph Waldo Emerson

Tired, weary, vulnerable and weepy – stress can so easily sap our inner reserves of strength and energy. Low energy is both a symptom of stress and also a cause of stress. When we feel faint, feeble and fatigued our defences fall, our reserves of inspiration dry up, and we are that much more exposed to the onset of negative, harmful stress. Where there is no energy, there is no armour. Once again, another vicious circle begins as exhaustion leads to stress, stress leads to exhaustion, and so on.

We all of us have experienced the 'energy days' and the 'weary days' of life. The 'energy days' are an inspiration, and often a revelation. We operate well; we are vibrant, positive and alive. There is a rhythm to every action we undertake. Our energy inspires energy. Energy is the ticket to potency, power and potential. With energy we can be creative, we can be practical, we can be inspired, and we can be successful.

Perceived resources outweigh perceived demands.

On a 'weary day', merely getting out of bed requires Herculean efforts. Without fuel to run on, we are left prone and vulnerable. There is no shelter against pressure, no shield with which to defend ourselves against the unexpected or to help us cope creatively with failures or mistakes. Irritation arises easy, anxiety accelerates, tolerance wanes and control falters. Without energy, our self-image deflates, self-criticisms inflate and negatives escalate. Energy is our natural immunity; without it we will fall.

The effects of 'fatigue-failure', 'burn-out' and 'tension drought' have been researched and reported extensively. Exhaustion tends to strike whenever stress leads the way. Therefore, exhaustion contributes to most physical, emotional and mental stress-related dis-eases such as heart disease, high blood-pressure, bodily pain, mental pain, anxiety and worry. Perhaps the most dangerous effect of exhaustion is believed powerlessness, which, in turn, affects believed hopelessness and believed helplessness. Without energy there is nowhere left to go.

Exhaustion can also corrode another important stress-defender, which is perhaps our most effective, natural defender of all, happiness. Happiness and enthusiasm make and use up energy. Zest, vitality and an appetite for life are positive manifestations of creative tension that will usually support health, happiness and harmony. Without happiness it can be very hard to make more happiness. The ability to generate happiness, and energy, is, therefore, a vital skill for successful stress control.

Successful stress control is a product of successful energy control, and vice versa. Failure to be aware of and to control our personal energy levels can cause tremendous harm and upheaval. Yet, in general, we invest little time or effort in looking after our energy. Energy has to be organized, planned, manufactured and managed. Energy management is the basis for self-management and life-management: if you get your energy right, you will be better positioned to get you – your self, your life and your stress – right.

Ten Fatigue-Busters

1. *Low-energy behaviour.* The exhausted are rarely, if ever, truly aware that they are exhausted – until, that is, they fall ill. Exhaustion can blunt self-awareness. Without self-awareness there is little or no scope for self-help, self-kindness or self-control. To be aware of your fatigue warning signals and to identify your low-energy behaviour are essential fatigue-buster skills. Feel for fatigue zones as they register in your body, such as a tight heart, clenched hands and tense shoulders. Watch for emotional and mental fatigue symptoms, such as irritation, anger, making mistakes, being weepy and feeling powerless. Take note of your symptoms so that you can then take control of the causes.

2. *Energy vampires.* Beware of the curse of the energy vampire, for you will be left withered, depleted and stiff! Energy vampires appear in many guises. Your energy vampire could be your early morning 'rush-rush' routine. It may be a certain job, role or responsibility. On the other hand, your energy vampire might take the shape of a person, such as a parent, work colleague, child or partner. More dangerously, your energy vampire might be even closer to home: it might be you and your attitude! Confront it; avoid it: but take control. You must beware in order to take care.

3. *Energy saviours.* Make a conscious note of all of the energy saviours you already employ in your life. A conscious note can inspire appreciation of energy saviours, which, in turn, can multiply their benefits a hundred-fold.

Make another conscious list of all other possible energy saviours that you could benefit from. Energy, like any other commodity, requires a tight budget-controlling exercise from time to time. Be careful how you spend your energy – we have only a limited supply. Invest your energy wisely; save your energy well. Become an energy manager. (See Chapter 3 for Ten 'Portable Rechargers'.)

4. *Pacing*. One of the most important tricks of an efficient energy manager is pacing. Learning to pace yourself throughout your day is a subtle skill that can help to shield you against negative, harmful stress. Constant attention to and awareness of your energy output, your energy input and your energy reserves will help you to create a pitch, a pace and a rhythm that are appropriate and helpful to you. By monitoring your energy, you will be better positioned for managing your energy. The more strategy you employ, the more energy you will enjoy. To win the race, you must set the right pace.

5. *Timing*. The quality of your energy management is determined to a large degree by the quality of your time-management, and vice versa. An effective time-control plan for each day, week, month and year of your life can help you to prioritize your energies, to pace your energies, to delegate your energies and to rest your energies. Like most life-skills, good time-management begins with awareness. With awareness of time-management, you can begin to exert a greater determination, a better discipline and a happier direction in your life. Time and energy mirror one another: by getting one right, you should eventually find they both become right.

6. *A Regular Rest Routine*. Relaxation is a natural, powerful fatigue-buster. Whenever you take the time to relax both fully and deeply, you are allowing the whole of your

being to refuel, to recharge and to re-energize. Formal relaxation techniques such as relaxed breathing, meditation, autogenics or hypnosis can work particularly well. Alternatively, hobbies, interests and leisure pursuits can also be good fatigue-busters. Whenever you take time to relax, you are storing up natural supplies of energy. Without energy, all the time in the world can amount to nothing. Relaxation is an energy saviour.

7. *Exercise.* Sometimes it takes energy to make energy. When you least feel like exercising, that is when you would probably most benefit from taking exercise, particularly if you are suffering from 'TMD' ('Tired Mind Disease'). Aerobics, swimming, yoga, T'ai Chi, calisthenics, jogging, walking and cycling are all powerful potential refreshers, revitalizers and re-energizers. Lifestyle research has shown time and time again that most fatigue victims do not incorporate exercise into their daily routine. Exercise can energize you. Work out your fatigue with regular work-outs.

8. *Sleep.* The quality of your day and the quality of your night are reflections, one of the other. Sleeping patterns are often disrupted and corrupted, therefore, during times of exhaustion and fatigue. To sleep is to heal. By sleeping well, you can allow the whole of your being to recharge well. Restful sleep can energize you, inspire you and uplift you. By working at good sleep you can work out your fatigue. If you sleep well, it can help you to live well. (See the section entitled 'Sleep Well, Live Well' earlier in this chapter.)

9. *Food for Fuel.* There is a simple, ancient saying of yoga, which goes, 'Food energy is life energy.' In other words, food supplies energy for life. What you eat represents energy intake. It follows, therefore, that the quality of what you eat will determine, by and large, the quality of your energy. Energy input must affect energy output.

Too many people resort to 'crash diets', 'dash eating' and 'rash nutrition' during times of exhaustion, all of which only exacerbate exhaustion. By looking after your food, you look after yourself and your energy.

10. *Attitude*. The difference between energy and languor is very often a state of mind. A tired body is often a symptom of a tired mind which, in turn, is often a symptom of a tired attitude. The enthusiast is often endowed with a greater verve and vitality than the defeatist, for example. The same is true for the optimist as opposed to the cynic. Energy begets energy. To change the way you feel you may need to change the way you think. For one day, think of yourself as fatigue-free, full of energy.

EXERCISE

The vital, nourishing role of a regular exercise routine is an essential requirement for a healthy stress-control policy. This is especially true if you occupy a stationary and sedentary position as office-dweller or desk-worker. While we may appear to get away without exercise in the short term, a lack of exercise can certainly lower our stamina, vitality, good health and general performance in the long term.

Apart from keeping us fit and healthy, a regular exercise routine offers the opportunity to socialize, to play, to relax, and to enjoy ourselves and to be happy. Exercise plays an essential part in the formula: work, rest and play. Our health and our balance can be seriously disturbed and upset if we persist with putting exercise and relaxation on a par with 'doing nothing' and with 'wasting time'.

The Ten Essential Benefits
of Exercise

1. *Physically relaxing.* Regular physical exercise can help to disperse muscle tension, to improve circulation, to develop deep and healthy breathing, to tone the nervous system and to keep your whole body poised and relaxed.

2. *Enhances mental relaxation.* Exercise can help you to wind down and to loosen up. Regular exercise is refreshing and refuelling. Regular exercise creates distance and distraction from the stresses and strains of your day. Also, because sensible exercise relaxes your body, your mind will also be favourably influenced.

3. *Increases vitality.* Sensible, regular exercise can help to boost your body's energy by increasing your metabolic rate, by activating your thyroid and adrenal glands, by supporting digestion, and by stimulating your nerves and your muscles.

4. *Promotes excellent mental fitness.* Increased vitality and magnetism from a regular exercise and fitness policy can certainly help you to develop and to sustain cool, calm and clear thought for all occasions.

5. *Supports strength, stamina and suppleness.* Strength, stamina and suppleness, known collectively as the *S-factor*, are the essential cornerstones of a healthy physical, mental and emotional disposition. (See the S-factor Table overleaf.)

6. *Protects from heart disease.* Efficient exercise can strengthen, relax and balance every muscle of your body, including your heart. The Health Education Authority's 'Look After Your Heart' campaign advocates regular exercise as an essential requirement for a healthy heart.

7. *Fosters confidence.* A strong, supple and healthy body can help you to look good and feel good. Positive outward appearance often changes the way you relate to yourself,

The S-factor Table

	Stamina	Suppleness	Strength
Badminton	★★	★★★	★★
Canoeing	★★★	★★	★★★
Climbing Stairs	★★★	★	★★
Cricket	★	★★	★
Cycling (hard)	★★★★	★★	★★★
Dancing (ballroom)	★	★★★	★
Dancing (disco)	★★★	★★★★	★
Digging (garden)	★★★	★★	★★★★
Football	★★★	★★★	★★★
Golf	★	★★	★
Gymnastics	★★	★★★★	★★★
Hill walking	★★★	★	★★
Housework	★	★★	★
Jogging	★★★★	★★	★★
Judo	★★	★★★★	★★
Mowing lawn	★★	★	★★★
Rowing	★★★★	★★	★★★★
Sailing	★	★★	★★
Squash	★★★	★★★	★★
Swimming (hard)	★★★★	★★★★	★★★★
Tennis	★★	★★★	★★
Walking (briskly)	★★	★	★
Weightlifting	★	★	★★★★
Yoga	★	★★★★	★

The 'three S's'

★ No real effect	★★★ Very good effect
★★ Beneficial effect	★★★★ Excellent effect

and often changes the way other people relate to you.

8. *Supports a healthy posture.* A good posture can support relaxation, promote pain relief, enhance positive mental outlook, facilitate relaxed breathing and maintain a healthy heart (see Postural Stress, below).

9. *Airs the lungs.* A good pair of well-exercised lungs is absolutely essential for a strong, poised and healthy mind and body. Let your lungs live well and the whole of you will live well.

10. *Reduces high cholesterol.* High cholesterol can constrain energy, stamina and suppleness, and is also a major cause of heart disease and circulatory disorders. Exercise can be excellent for maintaining the correct levels of cholesterol.

There tend to be two main obstacles to making a regular exercise routine a standard part of our lifestyle. The first is a lack of appreciation and respect for the importance of exercise. The second is a lack of the discipline necessary to keep it going. That is why it is very important to choose an exercise, sport or keep-fit routine which you genuinely enjoy, which makes you feel good, and which you also find easy to slot into your existing daily routine.

The time to start a regular exercise routine is *now*. Begin gently, allowing your strength, suppleness and stamina to build up naturally over the course of a few days, weeks or months. If you ever feel breathless, experience aches and pains, become dizzy, or feel any form of nausea or physical discomfort, you should rest immediately. It is always a good idea to visit your GP for his or her advice before you start (or restart) a regular exercise programme.

Exercise need not be a heavy workout with weights in a body-beautiful, trendy gym. Housework, gardening, mowing the lawn, DIY pursuits, simple stretching, walking the dog, a brisk stroll to the shops and a day in the countryside or at the seaside, for instance, all constitute physical exercise. The important thing to do is to air the body so that it has a chance to stretch, to relax and to tone. This will ensure you build up natural strength and vitality.

'Creating Circles': The CC Exercise Routine

The 'Creating Circles' Routine (or CC Routine, as it has come to be known) has been designed to develop the body's stamina, suppleness and strength, and also to boost body-energy. It is a routine that uses circles (traditional symbols of wholeness and strength) combined with breath control, relaxation, and mental affirmation and concentration.

CC is a therapeutic discipline for all the whole body. Each movement should be accompanied by deep, relaxed breathing, and with a one-word mental affirmation. The four recommended affirmations are, 'relaxed', 'peaceful', 'alive' and 'energized'. You simply pick the one which you would most like to feel, and then repeat it mentally with each inhalation and exhalation.

Your level of concentration is also most important. You should attempt to absorb yourself in the movement, the breath and the affirmation. No other thoughts should enter your mind. Concentration, or mindfulness, has always been an essential part of Eastern exercise disciplines, which the West is now gradually beginning to learn and incorporate.

The CC routine can be performed in its entirety or you can use just certain parts of it selectively. For this reason it can be performed anywhere and at any time, standing or sitting. The selective routine is particularly useful for busy people, office-dwellers, couch potatoes and desk-sitters.

The length of the routine is also up to you. It can last from two minutes, for instance, to a full half-hour. Taking a slow pace, with deep breathing and eyes closed, is a soothing and relaxing experience; using a quicker pace, sharper breathing and open eyes is more energizing and uplifting. The CC routine comes with a guarantee that whatever time and energy you give to it will be returned with interest.

HEAD AND NECK

Sit, or stand, with head, neck, shoulders and spine relaxed and aligned. Begin to create circles with your head and neck by breathing in and lifting your head up and to the right. Exhale as you move your head and neck back and then around to the left, and down again. Put all your body into the movement. Having created a few clockwise circles, then perform a few anti-clockwise circles.

SHOULDERS

Inhale as you raise both shoulders up towards your ears, and then exhale as you push your chest out and move your shoulders down and back. Create more circles by first exhaling as you pull the shoulders down and back, and then, inhaling as you push the shoulders up. Focus particularly on the action of your spine during these movements.

ARMS

Stretch your arms out to the sides. Ensure your elbows, wrist, palms and fingers are firm and fully stretched. Draw small circles with the whole of your arms, at quite a quick pace to begin with. You can slow the pace down as you begin to make the circles bigger and broader. Return again gradually to the smaller, quicker circles. Once again, having performed clockwise circles, you can then perform anti-clockwise circles.

WRISTS AND HANDS

Keeping your arms firmly outstretched, restrict your clockwise and anti-clockwise circles to your wrists and hands. Try to ensure there is as little movement as possible along your arms. As with all these exercises, allow the rhythm of your breathing to follow the movement of your wrists and hands.

CHEST AND STOMACH

Push your arms straight out in front of you. Breathe in as you twist and turn your body as far as you can to the right. Hold the position. Then, breathing out, twist and turn the body over to the left, and hold. After a while you can swing freely from right to left and left to right. Watch your breathing at all times.

HIPS

Place your hands on your hips. Breathe in, move your hips to the left and create full clockwise circles. You can bend your legs to create a fuller sweep. Try to keep your spine, shoulders, neck and head upright, though. Remember to perform anti-clockwise circles with your hips also. Allow your breathing to be deep, slow and even, and to follow the rhythm of your movement.

THIGHS

Balancing on your left leg, bend your right knee slightly and point the toes of your right foot. Push your right leg out to the right and create clockwise circles with the whole leg. Perform the equivalent movement with the left thigh while balancing on your right leg.

LEGS

You can create circles with your legs either standing up, sitting down, or lying flat. If you are standing, you should balance on one leg, keep the other outstretched and perform small to large circles and then back to small circles again, as you did with the arms. If you are lying or sitting down, stick both legs out and perform a similar sequence of clockwise and anti-clockwise circles, moving both legs together in the same direction.

FEET

To exercise the joints of the feet you need to sit or lie down with legs outstretched, and just as you worked with your wrists and hands, you should attempt to create circles both ways with as little movement along your legs as possible. Once again, allow the rhythm of your breathing to follow the movement you create during the exercise.

NO SMOKING!

The first inhalation on a cigarette creates a dramatic rise in blood-pressure, disturbs the electrical activity of your heart, pollutes your lungs, and generally increases your heart's workload. From now on, your heart will now need more oxygen to cope with the extra pressure, but, because of the carbon monoxide inhaled during smoking, the amount of oxygen that gets to the heart will be severely reduced. This aggravates the pressure and burden on the heart, the stress of which can easily lead to serious and fatal heart diseases.

Smokers are faced with a whole catalogue of serious and possibly fatal side-effects that include bronchitis, chronic inflammation of the lungs, mouth and throat cancer, oesophagal cancer, lung cancer, bladder cancer, increased gastric acidity, muscle tremors, heart palpitations, high blood-pressure, strokes, constriction of peripheral blood vessels, nausea, headaches, migraines and very poor breathing patterns.

Inhaling on a cigarette can activate your nervous system and will, thereby, release stress and growth hormones into your bloodstream. Hence, some people equate smoking with arousal, energy and stimulation. On the other hand, inhaling on a cigarette can also lower muscle tension. Hence, some smokers equate smoking with rest, relaxation and calm. These 'false benefits' are short-term, drug-induced side-effects that work against the natural harmony of the body. They are also cancelled out by the long, long list of long-term dangers – premature death being the most obvious one of all.

Smoking is not only a very serious cause of stress for smokers, but also for passive smokers who are forced to inhale tobacco fumes when in the presence of smokers. Medical research has established a number of serious, harmful side-effects of passive smoking. They include headaches, blocked nasal packages, mental discomfort, migraines, coughs, general blocked up feeling all over, and even a risk of lung cancer.

Smoking is also a major source of stress for the friends, relatives and loved ones who see 100,000 people in Great Britain die each year from a premature death because of smoking. On average a person who smokes 20 cigarettes a day shortens his or her life by between five and fifteen years. Furthermore, the cancers and heart diseases that may be caused and aggravated by smoking mean these people must be cared for by loved ones who will have to sacrifice much of their lives and endure much untold stress in their attempts to help.

A successful stop-smoking policy follows three distinct stages: 1) preparing to stop, 2) stopping, and 3) staying stopped. The following guidelines are designed to help support and empower your decision to stop, your motivation for stopping, and your willpower for staying stopped.

Smoke-Busting

1. *Identify a bounty of benefits*. Write down at least 20 benefits of not smoking. The more benefits you can identify, the better positioned you will be to believe that you really

can quit. Keep this 'benefits sheet' about you wherever you go. This simple piece of paper will help you, emotionally and psychologically, to say, 'No butts!' It is estimated that for every cigarette you smoke, you lose approximately 15 minutes of your life. One obvious benefit of not smoking is a longer life. A few more benefits include a healthier life, less worry, reduced tension, more energy, and smelling fresher and cleaner.

2. *Are there any benefits to smoking?* Identify the benefits of smoking, and then identify alternative avenues that can offer enjoyable, health-giving, positive support. Cigarette substitutes, nicotine chewing gum, herbal remedies and dummy cigarettes are available if you really feel you need them. Confidence, relaxation and pleasure need not be confined to cigarette packets only. Try confidence training, practise regular relaxation techniques, pursue recreation and exercise, and enjoy a varied, creative diet.

3. *Plan a day to begin your positive no-smoking policy – and stick to it.* Preparation will help you to prosper. Be kind to yourself – choose a good time in your life to quit; don't do it the day after your dog has died. Prepare yourself physically and psychologically for the changes you will control. Your four cornerstones will be a nourishing, interesting diet, positive recreation, enjoyable exercise and regular relaxation. The organization Quit advise that, 'Thinking about stopping smoking *frightens*. Doing it encourages.'

4. *Identify Supporters.* To be successful you may wish to surround yourself with supporters. Enrol the help of your friends, family and partner. Let your loved ones know what you are trying to do, and why, and show them how they can help you. An enthusiastic and interested doctor can also be a crucial support to you in your campaign to cut out cigarettes. Your doctor can

provide you with all the medical advice, leaflets, addresses and telephone numbers you may need to terminate your tobacco trips. Above all, your doctor can help to ensure you stop smoking safely.

5. *Rearrange your routines.* To save your life, you may need to rearrange your routines. In particular, you must identify the people, the places and the times you associate with smoking. After mealtimes, at pubs, meetings, breaks, evenings out and time with certain friends may all need to be planned for. Identify your friends and 'foes'. Convert the foes who mean most to you, and leave the rest well alone. Create no-smoking zones, such as in your car, bedroom, bathroom, lavatory, kitchen, etc. Schedule no-smoking times, such as mealtimes, meetings, breaks, evenings, etc.

6. *Call in the professionals.* Engage the support of a specialist organization, such as Quitline (see Useful Addresses in this book), which offers telephone counselling, referral to stop-smoking groups and free 'Quit Packs'. Or, engage the support of a recommended professional therapist, such as a hypnotherapist, acupuncturist or counsellor. Once again, your doctor should be able to be of valuable help to you.

7. *Stop.* You may decide to pick a quit-day for stopping altogether. Alternatively, a positive hierarchical, step-by-step, one-by-one approach may help to minimize the stress and strain of stopping. It is possible to distinguish between cigarettes that are 'habit', 'enjoyable' and 'needy'. The 'habit' cigarettes go first, then the 'enjoyable' and then the 'needy'. Create a pace and stick to it, even if it means only giving up one a day. Having reduced your cigarettes at a sensible pace, it will now be easier than ever to quit smoking safely. Your body, your emotions and your mind will be able to cope with a minimum need for readjustment. Choose a day to stop

smoking – and stop. Take a look at your benefits sheet again – from today, the benefits are all yours.

8. *Give up each day – and stay a non-smoker.* Look for all the friends you can find to fuel your courage and conviction. Giving up smoking is only painful if you forget to look at your benefits sheet. Each day, give yourself three clear moments to affirm and to visualize the benefits you believe in. 'I choose not to smoke' – 'I have no desire to smoke' – 'I am a non-smoker.' To stay as a non-smoker you should think as a non-smoker. Reward yourself again and again, and remind yourself, every day, of your personal positive gains.

9. *Reward yourself for being a non-smoker.* A longer life, no smoker's cough, fewer colds, less infections, more money, fresh breath, better stamina and health – you've made one of the best decisions of your life, and you deserve to reward yourself. Celebrate in style. Each day, each week, each month and each year, plan to commemorate your stopping smoking anniversary. Affirm how good it is to be a non-smoker. Let the long-term benefits take away the short-term pain.

10. *'Non-Smoker Shares' – watch your financial dividends grow!* Smokers watch their money go up in smoke, every single day. Keep your newfound savings in an account where you can watch the interest accumulate. Invest it so as to enrich your life. Profit from the savings you make as a permanent non-smoker.

Giving up smoking is one of the best contributions you can make to your overall effort to control stress. All of the guidelines written in this section are supported by Quit and the Health Education Authority. They can be supplemented by other techniques such as hypnotherapy, acupuncture, massage, confidence training, herbal treatments and a regular relaxation programme. Whatever help you decide to call

Assessing Your Annual Smoking Bill

1 a day = 365 per year
10 a day = 3650 per year
15 a day = 5475 per year
20 a day = 7300 per year
30 a day = 10,950 per year
40 a day = 14,600 per year

Number of cigarettes a day	Cost per day	Cost per week	Cost per year
	.	.	.

upon, you can be your greatest friend if you believe and remember that giving up smoking is not about punishment and sacrifice; it is about liberation, better health, and a longer life.

POSTURAL STRESS

A poor posture, with a tilting head, a wilting chin, shoulders falling forward and a collapsed chest, is not only a common symptom of stress, but a common cause of it also. It stands to reason, therefore, that an improved posture is a helpful, practical technique for healthy stress control.

Postural stress can cause any number of problems for the physical body, including a weakened spine, slipped discs, backache and bodily pain, poor breathing, high blood-pressure, heart strain and chronic muscle tension. When the body is held in balance it works in balance and according to its natural capacity. Imbalance creates discomfort and illness.

Your mind can also be adversely affected by postural stress. Whenever we feel we have failed, whenever we feel lost and lonely, and whenever we feel down and out, depleted and disorientated, worried and uncertain, fearful or depressed, the body very often reacts by closing in on itself. The mind associates a memory of how we felt with every different body posture we assume. Therefore, whatever body statement or body expression we use, this promotes a mental message and influence upon us and upon the people we meet.

Exercises for a Perfect Posture

The following set of exercises for a better posture can be performed as a full routine once a day, or individually at any time throughout the day. Apart from these exercises it is also good to train yourself to make a conscious note of the effects of each of the postures you commonly assume. If you sit in a chair for long periods at a time, for instance, try to sit upright and away from the back-rest; and whenever you are out walking, make a conscious effort to walk tall, with your head, neck and spine aligned and your chest out.

HEAD AND NECK

1. Press your chin in to your chest. Then, slowly tilt your head back so that it rests on your shoulders and your chin is pointing straight up to the ceiling. Hold this position. Perform it three times.
2. Tilt your head to the right and rest your face on your right shoulder, and hold. Then, tilt your head to the left and rest your face on your left shoulder, and hold. Perform this three times.

SHOULDERS

Push both shoulders upwards and attempt to get them to touch your ears. Then push them backwards and down, pushing your chest up and out as you do so. Do this three times.

ARMS

Perform a windmill action with both arms, swinging them first clockwise and then anti-clockwise, and pushing your chest out firmly each time again as your arms swing back.

CHEST

With your arms at your sides, breathe in, filling the top of the lungs and the chest area. Take your arms up and out in front of you and over your head, crossing them before your chest. Be sure to open up your chest as your arms move upwards and outwards. Perform this exercise three times.

STOMACH AND SIDES

1. With your arms at your sides, breathe in and lift them out to the sides and upwards so that your palms meet and press together over your head. Hold this position for at least 30 seconds, and be sure to stretch your entire body fully.
2. Stretch your arms out fully at either side. Then, keeping your arms rigid, stretch them back so that your shoulders are pulled back and your chest is stretched out. Hold the position again for at least 30 seconds.
3. Stand with your legs slightly apart. Raise your arms up and over your head as you breathe in. Then, as you exhale, bend forward, taking your head towards your knees and your hands towards your feet. Hold the position for a count of three, and then, very slowly, come up again, ensuring that you lead with your chest out and your shoulders pulled right back. Perform this three times.

TAKING TRANQUILLIZERS

The power of pills has played a prominent part in the progress of the modern physician. Treatment via tablets, especially tranquillizers, seems to be so smooth, so short and so speedy, and therefore so satisfactory, that the modern-day doctor is in danger of becoming more of puppet prescriber and less of a whole physician. Indeed, the average pattern of prescribing by a modern doctor has been estimated to cost approximately £75,000 per year, and rising.

Benzodiazepines is the name given to the most common set of 'minor tranquillizers' and 'sleeping tablets'. Included in this set is diazepam, which is more commonly known as Valium, and lorazepam, which is perhaps still better known as Ativan. Those who witnessed the introduction of Valium and Ativan in the 1950s and 1960s met with a mass-marketing campaign that published promise after promise and described tranquillizers as 'pills for paradise' and as 'nirvana for nerves'. The promises soon stopped; the prescriptions still soared.

The benefits of benzodiazepines have since been revised, revalued and reassessed. As a result, doctors and patients alike are having to be re-educated. Benzodiazepines, or 'minor tranquillizers' are, essentially, muscle-relaxing drugs. They can sedate your muscle system, numb your nerves, calm you down, alleviate anxiety, wind down worry, send you to sleep, switch off symptoms of stress, and generally, thereby, help you to cope – providing, that is, the prescription is appropriate and the period of prescribing is proper.

Doctors in Britain have a drugs bible, entitled the *British National Formulary* (or BNF), which gives guidelines for prescribing drugs, including minor tranquillizers. Until very recent times, prescriptions of minor tranquillizers were indiscriminate and their period of prescribing was almost indefinite. Valium and Ativan were as common as chocolate buttons. Anyone could have them, anytime, anywhere, and for anything. Once prescribed, all you had to do was to ask for more.

Today, the BNF recommends a very different pattern of prescribing. To quote from section 4.1.2.:

> *Although there is a tendency to prescribe these drugs to almost anyone with stress-related symptoms, unhappiness, or minor physical disease, their use in many situations in unjustified. In particular, they should not be used to treat depression, phobic or obsessional states, or chronic psychosis. In bereavement, psychological adjustment may be inhibited by benzodiazepines.*

The recommended period of prescribing has also been dramatically reduced. To quote from the same section of the

BNF, 'treatment should be limited to the lowest possible dose for the shortest possible time.' In Britain, the Committee on Safety of Medicines, 1988, recommended that minor tranquillizers should be prescribed for a period of no longer than two to four weeks. And the Royal College of Psychiatrists, 1988, recommended that sleeping tablets should only be taken intermittently and for no more than three consecutive nights.

Short-term benefits can deteriorate into long-term dangers if the recommended periods of prescribing are not observed. The most serious side-effects are addiction, dependency and withdrawal complications. Other long-term side-effects can be nausea, headaches, sadness, numbness, depression, a sense of insecurity, insomnia, dwindling sexual desire, fatigue, no motivation, poor co-ordination, and a general sense of lifelessness.

The most important tenet with regard to minor tranquillizers is that pills cannot persuade your problems to go away. Tranquillizers suppress symptoms; they do not empower, liberate or rouse your resources. This is why, for instance, tranquillizers are not recommended for loss or bereavement, during which it is absolutely essential that you stop suppression and learn expression. Tranquillizers will give you your space, and this can at times be a lifeline; they cannot, however, give you your solutions.

Come Off It!

1. *Consult your GP.* No attempt should be made to withdraw from tranquillizers without first consulting your GP, who will be able to arm you with the assurance, advice, addresses and answers you may be looking for. Your GP will be able to steer you through a safe and secure passage. He or she might be able to put you in

touch with a local Tranquillizer Withdrawal Service as your next port of call. Alternatively, you can contact CITA, the Council for Involuntary Tranquillizer Addiction (see the Useful Addresses section of this book).

2. *Tranquillizer Withdrawal Services*. These are free and confidential services designed especially for each individual to explore a variety of powerful, effective coping strategies other than pills. Emphasis is on a gradual, step-by-step withdrawal, at a pace that is suitable to each individual. There is no force, only support. This very safe approach ensures that the individual is always in control of his or her reduction. The address of your local Tranquillizer Withdrawal Service contact can be given to you via your GP, Health Promotion Unit, Social Services, Citizens' Advice Bureaux, or from your local telephone directory.

3. *Positive preparations*. Pick a positive time in your life, and not the middle of a life crisis, to begin your withdrawal programme. Physically, mentally and emotionally prepare yourself to begin, and this beginning will be sound. The very first step to take is to stabilize your tablet-taking. Take your dosage at a regular time each day, and not haphazardly. This is the foundation for a firm and flourishing success. Remember, stopping tranquillizers suddenly is dangerous.

4. *Be your own best friend*. Withdrawal is all about readjustment, and readjustment takes time. Concern yourself not so much with the speed of your success, but more with the security of your success. Be kind to yourself. Put away any impatience, criticisms and frustration. Do not demand too much of yourself. Today you are crawling; tomorrow you will walk; and in the future you will run again.

5. *Establish your 'support zones'*. Your support zones are

friends and family members, GPs and counsellors, who will be there to support and to help you along the way. Communicate freely with your allies. Educate them. Let them know what it is you are going through. Teach them to allow you to express yourself and to release your thoughts and feelings. Be as honest as possible. The sooner you do this, the sooner the whole thing will be over.

6. *Create your own 'success systems'.* Establish the essential benefits of giving up your tranquillizers. The more you know about the benefits, the more you will know how to motivate yourself. Relate to these benefits each day, and allow them to inspire you along the way. Allow yourself to be as creative, as resourceful and as cunning as possible. Mobilize all your efforts and always keep focused on the final success.

7. *Adopt alternative coping strategies.* Empower yourself with relaxation skills, with moments of gentle meditation, with counselling, with hypnotherapy, with relaxed breathing or with autogenics. Explore herbal, biochemical, aromatic and homoeopathic substitutes for tranquillizers. Attend any local self-help groups for stress management, anxiety management or assertion training, for instance. Enjoy exercise, play, recreation and quality time with your family and friends. Do not tie your coping capacity only to tranquillizers.

8. *Nourishment.* Quality food intake is an essential support for you during your withdrawal programme. The foods you feed yourself will feed you with vital strength, energy, resources and reserve. A variety of fresh, natural foods is the foundation for a therapeutic diet. Reduce your intake of junk foods, slow down on sugar and salt, cut down on caffeine, avoid alcohol, stabilize your smoking, and stick to fresh, fresh, fresh. See Chapter 7, on Diet and Nutrition, for further advice.

9. *Which tranquillizer do I need least?* You may be taking more than one kind of tranquillizer and do not know which to cut down on first. Seek professional advice. Do not attempt to cut down on all of your dosages at once. The common route is to reduce each one in turn, or to come off one and then the other. Keep looking and keep listening. The greater your store of self-knowledge, the greater your chance of successful self-control.

10. *Measure for measure.* The BNF suggests that a gradual, step-by-step approach is the safest and most secure road to success. It states that when you are planning your first reduction, reduce only one type of tablet, and do so by not more than one eighth of your daily dosage. Make a reduction no more than once every fortnight. The smaller the reduction, the smaller the reaction. The length of time of withdrawal varies from person to person. An average guide of one month per one year of usage is usually quoted. Once again, professional advice is the safest path for positive, personal advance.

HEADACHES AND MIGRAINES

When your head hurts, all of you hurts. Whether it is the tedium of a temporary tension headache or the momentous misery of migraine, it is life that becomes the headache when your head is hobbling with aches, pains and hurts. Even the slightest head-hurt renders the Herculean hamstrung, helpless and handicapped. Quite simply, when your head is out of harmony, the whole of you hears it, the whole of you feels it and the whole of you suffers it.

Headaches leave their hallmark. There is the 'bottle opener', where you might experience a tight band of pressure around the top of the head. There is the 'onion grater', when your nerves feel peeled, raw and on edge. There is the 'bread 'rolling pin', when your head sounds with a bang. There is the 'oven grill', where your head feels horrible and hot. And there is the 'kitchen scales', which wraps your head with all the weight of the world.

Nine out of ten headaches are tension headaches, also known as psychogenic headaches. These headaches have an insidious, temporary nature. In other words, they enter and exit in a short space of time without any formal kind of announcement. Tension headaches are usually the result of sustained stretching or continued contraction of the muscles of the neck, shoulders and forehead, such as the trapezius, sterno mastoid and frontalis muscles. These muscles must relax before the pain can retreat.

Migraine is commonly characterized by recurrent attacks of headache and head tension. Many types of migraine have been formally identified; very few certain causes of migraine have been satisfactorily clarified. A classic migraine comes complete with visual, sensory or speech disturbances. Other types of migraine can provoke other conditions, such as cluster headaches – which can commonly continue for a course of days, weeks and even months – and facial migraine, which is characterized by facial pain. Migraines commonly make for misery.

Tension headaches and migraines may be caused by any number of physical, emotional or mental villains. Physical villains include VDU screens, television sets, loud hi-fi equipment, neighbourhood noise, clenching the teeth, eye strain, sinus trouble, menopause and menstruation, food allergies, caffeine, alcohol, high blood-pressure, low blood-sugar, poor posture, or hyperventilation, for instance. Emotional or mental villains include stress, tension, pressure, fatigue, exhaustion, sadness, upset, confusion, indecision, procrastination, concentration, fear, guilt, or anxiety, for instance.

Very occasionally, a headache can be hiding a more serious

and sinister sickness. It is, therefore, very important that you be humble enough to take your head along for a professional check-up. This is particularly true if, for instance, the headache is persistent, painful, aggravated by mild movement, or if your head hurts when you sneeze, yawn, cough or eat. If there is vomiting, then also you should consult your doctor; if there is eye strain, you should consult an optician; and if there is toothache or jawache, then you would be wise to visit a dentist.

Hints for Healing the Head

1. *Rest, retreat and relaxation.* To continue to hurry along with the hustle and bustle when your head hurts will only invite worse to come. Your muscles must relax. Most relaxation techniques aim directly to relax your muscles. Progressive relaxation, meditation and autogenics are three popular relaxation methods. Relaxed breathing can be very effective, and can also be useful for times when you must persist in spite of your aching head. A regular relaxation routine can help to prevent the recurring pain of headaches and migraine. (See Chapter 3 on relaxation)

2. *High-tech.* Biofeedback monitoring can measure muscle stress and relaxation. By measuring your relaxation performance with biofeedback, you can begin to relax, to release and let go of muscle tensions at will. Electroacupuncture attends to individual pressure points around your head, your neck and all over your body. Electroacupuncture is fast gaining a reputation for providing rapid relief and recovery. TENS is another piece of electrical nerve-stimulation technology, now available on the British NHS, that works by blocking pain signals that are sent to the brain. Magnet therapy

is one more high-tech remedy for horrible headaches.

3. *Herbal healing.* Painkillers are often the most pertinent option for pain repression. You can, however, opt for herbal remedies which are thought to release pain rather than to repress it. Modern medical research has revealed that feverfew can often heal an ache or pain in the head. Other herbal healers may include chamomile, rosemary, or lime blossom. Rescue Remedy, from the Bach Flower Remedy range, is also widely recommended by headache and migraine sufferers. (See the section on Herbal Medicine in Chapter 8.)

4. *Scents, oils and aromas.* Lavender lends gentle support and soothing to a sore head. You can place a single drop of lavender oil on the tip of each index finger and then gently press and massage your temples. Or, at night-time, you can place one or two drops on your pillow. Other aromatic oils you may like to try are peppermint and pine for a refreshing pick-me-up, or chamomile and rose for rest and relaxation. Many headache and migraine sufferers claim that the luxury of aromatic oils can very often lift away oppressive aches and tensions. (See the section on Aromatherapy in Chapter 8.)

5. *Biochemical Salts.* The biochemical range of tissue salts offers several soothing and relaxing alternatives. Ferr. Phos., or phosphate of iron, is most often recommended for tension headaches that exert a pressure upon the skull. Kali. Phos., or potassium phosphate, is thought to be good for nurturing nervous headaches and for alleviating anxiety headaches. And Nat. Mur., or sodium chloride, is encouraged for heavy headaches that accompany emotional events and emotional symptoms.

6. *Hypnotherapy.* Modern medical research has found that hypnotherapy can be particularly helpful for healing headaches and for managing with migraines. By suggesting, implanting and affirming positive ideas while

your mind, brain and body relax, hypnotherapy aims to heal the causes of your aches and pains. Hypnotherapy is also a marvellous preventive medicine. It concentrates on the causes that send out the symptoms.

7. *Hot and cold.* A warm bath, a hot water bottle, a comforting compress, a warm flannel, or a warm drink can all work well to rest and to relax the muscles around your head, neck and shoulders. Alternatively, you might find that cold compresses and cold flannels do the trick. Herbal teas often heal a hurt head. Chamomile, peppermint and lime are all very good. Alternatively, something as simple as a cold, refreshing mineral water can move muscle tensions in moments.

8. *Massage, movement and music.* Massaging the temples, squeezing gently at the base of the neck, resting your palms upon closed eyes, and pressing your fingertips on the sides of your head above the eyes can all work well. Having another person do this for you may be even better. Stretching a little, walking for a while and breathing in fresh air can also help. And listening to music, perhaps while you move or massage, can also help to relax the mind and heal the head.

9. *Diets.* Headaches and migraines can sometimes be caused by food sensitivity and food allergy. Also, headaches can be linked to low blood-sugar levels. Careful choice and consideration is the first essential step for cure. Your tolerance to sugar-rich foods, caffeine drinks, convenience foods, dairy products, food additives and wheats may have to be carefully checked. There is also such a thing as a hunger headache. Regular, nutritious meals will help to keep you well. It is thought that as many as 10 per cent of all migraines are caused by poor diet.

10. *Prevention.* By playing detective you can gain a greater self-knowledge so as to assess and to identify the

situations, the feelings, the actions, the people and the times that may provoke your headaches and migraines. Also, a regular course of acupuncture, cranio-sacral osteopathy or other complementary therapy can help you to build up a greater resource of resistance against aches and pains. Prevention is a much more pain-free path.

High Blood-Pressure

Hypertension, or high blood-pressure, is one of the most prevalent chronic ailments affecting the health of the Western world today. This 'silent sickness' most often stirs slowly over a period of several years without any significant symptoms. And yet, this sickness can have severe, life-threatening side-effects such as, stroke, thrombosis and angina. Stress can often accentuate the advance of this serious ailment.

Blood-pressure is measured most often in the brachial artery of the arm, using a biomonitoring instrument called a sphygmomanometer. Blood-pressure pushes your blood through the circulation canals of your body. Without blood-pressure, your body could not be fed with the fuel of renewed, oxygen-rich blood. Pressure is, therefore, important. To be more specific, it is the amount of this pressure that is most important. Too much or too little pressure may promote problems.

Blood-pressure measurement looks for an appropriate harmony between two types of pressure, the systolic pressure and the diastolic pressure. The systolic pressure, or active pressure, measures the upper point of pressure as the heart's ventricles contract and push out blood. The diastolic pressure, or resting pressure, measures the lower point of pressure as the blood flows evenly along the artery. It is the balance of these two pressures that helps to promote a positive blood-pressure performance.

There are two types of hypertension. Essential hypertension describes a raise in blood-pressure caused by an impairment or blockage in the arteries. The term arteriosclerosis describes hardening of the inside walls of the arteries, which can promote hypertension. Essential hypertension can be hereditary. There is also a definite correlation between hypertension and overweight. In each individual circumstance, there tends to be, however, no one specific cause of essential hypertension.

Secondary hypertension describes high blood-pressure as an effect or symptom caused by an illness or foreign drug, for instance. Tobacco, steroids for asthma, the contraceptive pill, kidney malfunction and certain hormone replacement programmes can cause secondary hypertension.

A common fundamental cause of either type of high blood-pressure is pressure. Any prolonged or repeated physical pressure, mental pressure or emotional pressure can promote high blood-pressure. Therefore, a successful stress control programme that strengthens you with coping strategies for tension, pressure, anxiety, nervousness or anger can help to heal hypertension. The pressures of stress and the pressures of blood can correspond.

Healing Hints for Hypertension

1. *See your doctor regularly.* Make regular appointments with your doctor so as to monitor your blood-pressure. A regular appointment can be once a month, once every six months or once a year. Decide with your doctor how often you should have a check-up. Your doctor should also be able to advise effective self-help coping skills, other than drugs, that can help your heart.

Blood Pressure Table

Systolic/Diastolic	Reading
90< over 50<	Hypotension
130 over 70	Normal Range
140> over 90>	Borderline
160> over 100>	Hypertension

Diagnosis of hypertension depends upon
a number of individual variables, i.e. diet,
weight, life event stresses and ageing.
For a professional blood pressure check,
contact your doctor.

2. *Breathe easy*. Hypertension can so easily be exacerbated by uneven, irregular, shallow breathing patterns. Conversely, an even, regular and deep breathing pattern has been found to support the function of the heart. A simple, consistent routine of relaxed breathing, performed perhaps three times a day for about five minutes or so, can be a marvellous medicine for your heart.

3. *Relaxing remedies*. Blood-pressure responds to relaxation. Thousands and thousands of modern medical research trials have recommended regular rest and relaxation as a marvellous recipe for the heart. Meditation, autogenics, hypnotherapy and progressive relaxation can all help. Trials using music therapy, creative visualization and remedial movement have also been very positive. The harmony of rest relaxes the heart.

4. *Fun, play and recreation*. Gentle, enjoyable exercise can enable your blood-pressure to be even and healthy. Recreation for fun, for play, for entertainment and as part of socializing is a happy way to stay happy and well. Punishing routines are only punishing. They are unnecessary and unwise. Consult your doctor for a Fitness Assessment Test, if you are at all concerned or unsure about what amount and what type of exercise would be both enjoyable and healthy for you.

5. *Yoga power*. Yoga, with its creative combinations of deep breathing, stretching and resting, can be particularly beneficial for beating high blood-pressure. Yoga seeks to support the suppleness of your body by balancing the lungs, calming the nerves, and relaxing the muscles, all of which can only help to serve your heart. A regular yoga routine is often recommended by health care professionals.

6. *Complementary help*. Massage, reflexology, Shiatsu, Alexander technique, acupuncture, hypnotherapy, herbal healing, aromatherapy and colour therapy, for

instance, have all recorded successes for stress relief and hypertension control. A full course of any complementary therapy will aim not only to benefit your heart but the whole of you. Remember, complementary medicines work best in combination with orthodox medicines.

7. *Weight control.* The more you weigh the harder your heart has to work. Hypertension is often caused by overweight. The more you weigh, the more your heart has to put up with. Sensible weight control will help to control your hypertension. Medical research has proved time and time again that blood-pressure levels out when the extra pounds are done away with. Heavy meals and big blow-outs can also seriously hinder the performance of your heart.

8. *Diet.* Caffeine creates and stimulates an almost immediate rise in blood-pressure. Caffeine consumption – from coffee, cola, tea and chocolate – must, therefore, be carefully controlled. Too much salt and not enough potassium are also thought to set blood-pressure levels soaring. Natural, fresh foods are usually high in potassium and low in sodium, whereas processed, preserved and canned foods are often high in sodium and low in potassium. Put no salt on the dinner table; use unsalted butter; eat unsalted bread; and beware salted snacks, peanuts and crisps. Vegetarians have been found to have generally lower blood-pressure than meat-eaters. One reason for this is that vegetarians consume less fats. High-cholesterol foods and sugar-rich foods should also be carefully controlled.

9. *Smoking and alcohol.* If you have hypertension, the bad news is that smoking and your alcohol consumption have to be cut down. The good news is that you will be alive to invest and to enjoy all of your savings! Smoking pollutes and clogs your entire system, making it harder for your heart to perform well. Giving up smoking is

often the only sensible solution. Alcohol taken in moderate quantities can be OK and may even be quite healthy. Consult your doctor for professional advice.

10. *Pace, rhythm and pitch.* Healthy day-to-day living is the most magnificent magic of all for helping to mend the heart. Make each day a recipe for rich and rewarding balance. Attend to your work, to your rest, to your fun and to your play. Add style to your lifestyle. Embrace the quality of life as well as all the quantities. Of all the healers there are, happiness is the most effective of all. The proper pace of life, the right rhythm and the correct personal pitch will help to secure the harmony of your heart.

PREMENSTRUAL SYNDROME

Once a month, twelve times a year, a woman's biological system moves house! Her automatic renewal service removes, rearranges, drains, cleans, polishes and alters her entire body balance so as to affect a new order and a new harmony. Just as soon as she is settled in again, her automatic renewal service arrives and the 'For Sale' boards go up again. Meanwhile, the woman must continue to smile, be courteous, be calm, cope, care for others, work, shop, cook, iron and generally act as if 'nothing unusual is happening'.

'Nothing unusual is happening' has been a traditional response from a male-dominated medical profession to Premenstrual Syndrome, or PMS. Until very recently, PMS was dismissed by doctors as an 'imaginary illness', a 'woman's problem' and as 'monthly madness'. Menstruation was all in the mind. Doctors would not hesitate, therefore, to prescribe tranquillizers, sedatives and anti-depressants, to advise a hysterectomy, or even to recommend a psychiatric assessment for this 'mental malady'.

PMS refers to a measurable condition of physical,

hormonal imbalance that can also trigger a corresponding emotional and mental imbalance. An accepted accurate definition of PMS is: 'the recurrence of symptoms before menstruation, with complete absence of symptoms after menstruation'. Today, there are many in the medical profession who are eager to make amends for their misdeeds and their misdemeanours. PMS is achieving a new, elevated status from 'imaginary illness' to a real and serious condition.

Symptoms of PMS can begin to stir at any time during the two weeks before menstruation. Premenstrual tension, or PMT, is one very common symptom. Other symptoms can include depression and sadness, feeling low, low self-esteem, low sex drive, tearfulness, powerlessness, forgetfulness, fatigue, feelings of emptiness, clumsiness, and a general despair and dissatisfaction with life. Symptoms can also include increased irritability, high anxiety, panic attacks, accelerated anger, impatience and intolerance, mood swings and mood changes.

Particular physical symptoms may include headaches, backaches, muscle tension, fluid retention, bloating and swelling, food cravings, perspiration, acne and allergies, a feeling of stomach vacuum, breast enlargement and breast tenderness. PMS symptoms can be made more severe by menstrual cramps, heavy periods (menorrhagia), painful periods (dysmenorrhoea) and even, very occasionally, by absence of periods (amenorrhoea). You will know if any of these symptoms are related to PMS if you notice that they are relieved once your period actually begins.

Menstruation can often be made more difficult to manage because of uncontrolled personal stress. You may have already found that your monthly cycle can cause you stress and can make your existing stresses worse. Successful stress control is, therefore, essential for soothing the symptoms of PMS. Professional help, support and advice are more readily available to you now than ever before.

PMS is a medical problem and should be treated by physicians. Doctors, Well-Woman Clinics, Health Promotion Centres, specific national and local PMS organizations and groups, and certain complementary medicine professionals represent an ever-increasing network of care and support. A number of safe, self-help suggestion that are commonly recommended for coping and controlling PMS are set out for you below.

Self-Help Medicine for PMS

1. *Education*. Create a chart to record the onset, the intensity and the duration of any suspected PMS symptoms. Remember that PMS symptoms can begin to stir at any time from ovulation to the full flow of menstruation, and that PMS symptoms should begin to ease and to fade as menstruation progresses. It is wise, therefore, to work with a daily chart for the whole of each cycle. By charting your life in this manner, you create a conscious record of self-knowledge. If there is a regular pattern to your symptoms, then it will be easier for you and for your health professionals to create a suitable plan for successful PMS control. The more you understand about yourself, the more you will be able to help yourself.

2. *Communication*. Communicate with the people whom you most want to communicate with. Educate your partner, your mother, your father, your child, etc. If you are seeing your doctor, let your loved ones know. If you are on a special diet, explain why. Communication is risky, but rewarding. Not everyone will want to listen and not everyone will be able to understand. The chance to express what you are feeling, to a close friend, for instance, can so often help to enhance your capacity to

cope. Communication may be awkward at first, but once achieved it can help to know that you have both understanding and support.

3. *Compensation*. To carry on as normal is a worthy but often unrewarding gesture. It can also be decidedly self-defeating. By keeping a daily chart of your cyclical progress you can cater for any adjustments and compensations that you might need to make. PMS is not, of itself, a mental or emotional weakness. If you do not care for yourself, however, you can be overcome by symptoms of mental or emotional weakness. Learning to compensate can mean giving yourself extra sleep, taking more time to rest, strengthening your diet with wholesome, fresh foods, avoiding excessive demands or confrontations before and during menstruation, and waiting until after menstruation to make important decisions.

4. *Nourishment*. A fully nourishing diet can help to alleviate and to control many PMS symptoms. What you eat and the way you eat can help you to cope. For instance, reduce your intake of stimulants such as caffeine, salt and sugar, tobacco and alcohol. The things that you might instinctively grab for are often the things your body ends up paying more for. Your body is cleansing itself. Therefore, feed your body with fresh foods, with green vegetables, with fruits and with salads. Also, cut down on dairy products and purchase the 'high in polyunsaturated fats' products. PMS sufferers are now advised to eat three main meals a day – breakfast, lunch and dinner – with three 'top-up' meals interspersed. All meals should contain high-fibre complex carbohydrates to maintain the healthy blood-sugar levels essential for PMS control.

5. *Movement*. A gentle exercise routine can help to soothe, stretch and massage the body before, during and after

menstrual discharge. Rigorous exercise is not recommended, though it can sometimes 'sweat out' any symptoms of emotional irritability and anger. On the whole, subtle systems of movement, such as yoga, T'ai Chi and gentle dance can help to enhance strength, stamina and suppleness. Taking a regular walk, spending time in the garden, a visit to the countryside or local parks, or playing a sport can be very therapeutic during times when the tension of premenstrual stress runs high.

6. *Breathe*. A restful, regular and relaxed breath, down deep in the abdominal and diaphragm region, helps to deliver harmony and balance to these areas. Deep breathing has been found in yoga trials and in medical respiration research to relax the menstrual regions of the body. It soothes nerves, it releases muscle tension, it clears and strengthens circulation, it helps digestion, and it can speed up sluggish menstrual discharge. Deep breathing can help you to cope with and to control many of the manifestation of PMS, such as anxiety, worry, panic, fatigue and sleeplessness. In ancient times, yoga breathing was described as 'the internal remedy'.

7. *Relaxation*. Personal space and time are priorities for PMS sufferers. One way to create this space and time is adopt a regular relaxation routine so as to rest, relax and release your tiredness, you tearfulness, your tension and any other symptoms you may experience. Gentle meditation, relaxation music, creative art, sewing and embroidery, massage and aromatherapy, therapeutic touching, exchanging hugs with someone you love, hypnotherapy and autogenic relaxation can all be helpful and healing. Rest and relaxation help your system to recover, recuperate and restore. Rest is the natural remedy.

8. *Alternatives*. Many people have found comfort, cure and

Your Menstrual Chart

On this chart mark the days of menstruation with an 'M' and
the days of each of your three most important symptoms
with an appropriate symbol, e.g.:

H = headache
W = water retention
B = breast tenderness
D = depression
I = irritability
A = asthma attack
P = panic attack

or invent symbols for your three priority symptoms, using
large or small letters according to the severity.

Name						Year					
Jan	Feb	Mar	Apr	May	Jun	Jul	Aug	Sep	Oct	Nov	Dec
1											
2											
3											
4											
5											
6											
7											
8											
9											
10											
11											
12											
13											
14											
15											
16											
17											
18											
19											
20											
21											
22											
23											
24											
25											
26											
27											
28											
29											
30											
31											

relief in the complementary arts. The natural healing sciences of massage, reflexology and Shiatsu, for instance, can help to harmonize the upheaval of PMS. In aromatherapy, clary sage is especially recommended. You can add clary sage to a bath, to your night clothes, to your pillow, or you can create a clary sage compress to soothe your abdomen. In herbal medicine, chamomile, balm and peppermint have all been found to have helpful properties for PMS symptoms. Chamomile tea as a substitute for caffeine-full coffee is sensible for PMS sufferers. Evening Primrose Oil is also thought to be exceptionally good. The biochemical salts Mag. Phos. (Magnesium Phosphate) and Kali Phos., (Potassium Phosphate) are predominantly prescribed for PMS. Whatever choices you make, the only accurate way to measure success is to keep on keeping your personal menstrual chart.

PAIN RELIEF

Whether it's a twinge, a nip or a pinch, a wince, a flinch or a quiver, there is nothing quite so miserable as the malady of physical pain. The punishing effects of physical pain, particularly prolonged pain, can leave a person feeling down, dismal, disconsolate and debilitated. Pain is a purgatory, and uncontrolled stresses serve only to increase this sentence. Relief, release and recovery often require regular relaxation, careful pacing, and above all, successful stress control.

Because pain receptors are prevalent throughout the whole of your physical body, the whole of you is sensitive to sensations of ache, itch and sharp pain. There are also, therefore, many, many types of pain. Body zones particularly prone to pain include the heart, the lower back, the spine, the neck, the head and the eyes (see Headaches and

Migraines, above). Pain from other parts of the body can also be 'referred' to these zones.

The action of physical pain still holds many mysteries for the modern physician. Pain has a chemical dimension, a biological dimension, an emotional dimension, and even, at times, an imaginary dimension. Intensity of pain, duration of pain, location of pain and the manner in which a pain will choose to manifest itself affect no two people in exactly the same way. There are still so many undiscovered variables as to the pang and the prick of personal, physical pain.

Medical research trials have demonstrated quite clearly that there is a precise relationship between physical pain and the pressure of stress. Subjective reports pinpoint that physical, mental and emotional stresses can make sensations of physical pain more severe. Happiness, for instance, can help to heal a pain quicker than sadness can. A positive patient perspective is, for example, a greater healer than angry, frustrated, indignant behaviour. Successful stress control can only help successful pain control. Many of the methods and coping strategies outlined in the Stress Buster programme are also, therefore, natural pain-busters.

The medical marketplace is full of back rests, orthopaedic beds, pelvic support chairs, pain plasters, orthopaedic insoles, health support belts, medical corsets, mechanical massage couches, posture performers and pain-relieving drugs. Your doctor is, of course, your first port of call for pain relief. He or she can then put you in touch with any number of national and local pain clinics and pain organizations (see the Useful Addresses section of this book). Always ask for any professional recommendations before making a personal choice of any pain product. This will help to protect you from the pain of disappointment!

Pain-Relief Pointers

1. *Relaxation and release.* Modern medical research reveals that a regular relaxation routine can help to promote positive pain relief. Most relaxation techniques concentrate on calming the nervous system and on soothing muscle tension. Because the torment of pain can be made worse by muscle tension and nervous stress, relaxation is a very practical coping strategy. As well as adopting a daily relaxation routine, it is also very important to divide the activities of your day equally between work, rest and play. The art of pacing is about enjoying a break rather than needing a break. It helps you to plan and to organize daily and weekly activity schedules that will not provoke or inflame your pain. Progress by pacing provides safe and proper pain relief.

2. *Biofeedback.* Biofeedback instruments can measure an inner, biological response to tension, relaxation, stress and pain. Because pain is such a subjective, personal experience, a medical professional will sometimes use biofeedback to achieve an objective, non-personal measurement. One person's tedium is another person's trauma. Combining relaxation with biofeedback monitors, which measure muscle tension (EMG) or nerve tension (ESR), for instance, can help to improve relaxation response – and thereby reduce pain. (See the section on High-tech therapy, above.)

3. *The needles and pins of acupuncture.* Acupuncture is an ancient healing system patiently awaiting modern medical approval. Using acupuncture for pain relief was among the very first orthodox medical trials, the results of which were very favourable indeed. Acupuncture was found to release endorphins, the body's natural pain-killing chemicals, from the brain. Today, acupuncture is an accepted anaesthetic treatment that is being practised

in more and more operating theatres within the NHS in Great Britain. Acupuncture can affect pain relief.

4. *Electroacupuncture.* Electroacupuncture is one of the most exciting prospects of recent medical research. Like traditional acupuncture and acupressure, electro-acupuncture uses predetermined points on the body to promote healing for pain relief. The term electro-acupuncture, or EA, describes the application of a very low-frequency electrical impulse that is put into these predetermined points. The current flow is approximately 20 micro-amps (20 millionths of an amp), which is well below the threshold of sensory perception. Rapid and long-lasting pain relief is one of many clinically assessed responses to EA treatment. EA has no serious or harmful side-effects.

5. *TENS.* The acronym TENS stands for transcutaneous electro nerve stimulation. The primary therapeutic benefit of TENS is pain relief. Like acupuncture and electroacupuncture, TENS encourages a flow of endorphins, the body's natural pain relief agent. TENS instruments create a current flow of approximately 50 milliamps, the intensity of which blocks pain signals from passing into the brain by either tiring peripheral nerves or by shutting down pain fibre passageways. TENS units are available for use on the NHS in Great Britain. Not everyone benefits from TENS, but those who do may rely upon it on a day-to-day basis to affect temporary pain relief.

6. *Massage and manipulation.* Many former pain sufferers recommend a course of one or other of the complementary medicines. Massage, reflexology, Shiatsu and acupressure are acknowledged pain relievers. Acupuncture has a large body of orthodox medical research and a tradition of four thousand years and more to support its case. Osteopathy and chiropractic are also

accepted by modern medicine and by many private health plans as an appropriate treatment for pain. An offshoot of osteopathy, called cranial-sacral osteopathy, is also gaining medical recognition for its ability to promote positive pain relief. Yoga, T'ai Chi and Alexander Technique each has its supporters who testify to safe and satisfactory personal pain relief.

7. *Hot and cold*. Healing the hurt of pain with heat is a time-honoured technique. Hot water bottles, a portable electric heating pad, therapeutic baths, warm showers, saunas and hot compresses, placed near to the pain zone but not directly on it, may all serve to rest and to soothe muscle tension and nerve strain. Careful attention to what clothes you wear can also help to keep in and to regulate your body warmth. Alternatively, your pain may pacify using a cold compress, a portable ice pack, or by having a cool shower regularly. Exploration and experimentation may help to ease your excruciating pains.

8. *Posture and pose*. The way you sit, the way you lie down, the way you get up and the way you walk can have either a helpful or harmful effect on your pain. Portable back supports for chairs are a marvellous tool for both preventing and curing back pain. Orthopaedic mattresses or, alternatively, a solid wooden board placed under your existing mattress, are also widely recommended. Lifting places the greatest amount of pressure on your muscle and nerve systems. You should take every care, therefore, not to stress and to strain yourself when you stand. The way you stand and the way you walk should basically be, relaxed, upright and well aligned. A collapsed, slouched posture can add to the pressure of your pain.

9. *Attitudes and attributes*. The sensation of personal pain is an entirely subjective experience, complicated by emotion, attitude and outlook. Pain without perspective

is truly punishing; a positive personal approach to pain can help to pale your pain. A tense, stiff and anxious attitude speeds adversity; a relaxed, accepting approach can help your pain to ease. To fight pain is often to invite pain; to relax your pain helps speed recovery. Recent research into laughter medicine has discovered that laughter and a positive outlook can help to release endorphins, the body's natural pain tranquillizers. Hypnotherapy, autogenics and creative visualization can work well with thought to promote pain tolerance. Take an attitude that will work alongside your pain and not against it. Your attitude is your first aid.

10. *Drugs.* Your doctor is armed with a store of analgesics for rapid pain arrest. Aspirin, for instance, is a non-narcotic analgesic which is also anti-inflammatory. Your doctor or chemist will recommend the appropriate drug for your personal pain disorder. There are also natural pain-relief remedies you may wish to work with. In aromatherapy, lavender is often lauded for its pain-relieving properties. Apply lavender to a compress, to your bath water, to a corset or girdle, or to your pillow at night. In herbal healing, balm has been found to benefit pains, aches and tensions. Feverfew works well for headaches and migraines. Biochemical salts also offer specific salts for specific situations. Hunt around your local health food shops for more helpful healing hints.

ELECTRO-STRESS

Humanity has created, in modern times, an environmental soup of unnatural electromagnetic radiations which appears to be growing thicker and thicker with each passing day. Indeed, it is only now that we are beginning to invest any significant amounts of time, energy and money in exploring and assessing what possible effects and consequences the balance of this 'soup' may be having upon our own balance of harmony and health – and on the balance of our very survival.

The radiations that are emitted by common household goods, such as microwaves, televisions, radios, stereos, computers, telephones, cars, electric cookers, electric blankets and many other modern-day conveniences may be invisible to the naked eye, but that does not mean to say they are therefore without effect. As Rodney Girdlestone, a respected expert on the effects of electromagnetism and founder of the Natural Therapeutics organization, wrote in a challenging article for the healing journal, *Caduceus*,

> *It is now accepted that electromagnetic fields can interfere with radio and TV reception or can affect the operation of computers. Surely it is not fanciful to suggest that the human body may also be susceptible and that external fields may upset the even more delicate balance of biological functions, including the immune system.*
> 'Are You Building in a Safe Place?', *Caduceus*, Summer 1989, pp. 12–14.

Aside from the household goods, there are also the numerous TV satellites, towering electricity pylons, broadcasting transmitting and receiving stations, international telecommunication centres, industrial generating plants and the latest radar technology, all of which contribute their own ingredients to this unnatural soup. Maybe your feelings of depression, powerlessness and apparent apathy are a reaction not to life but to a nearby electricity pylon?

Insomnia, fatigue, depression, muscle tension, migraines and even miscarriages, stillbirths, various birth defects, cot deaths, post-viral fatigue syndrome and other immune system-related diseases have all been verified by modern researchers as capable of being caused or aggravated by electro-stress. Invisible electro-stress can have a visible effect, on you.

You are a natural, electrical lifeform, now living in an unnatural electromagnetic atmosphere of radiation that has a definite impact and influence on the quality of your health, the quality of your stress control and the quality of your life. Although some of us are more susceptible to electro-stress than others, all of us are influenced somehow and in some way.

It may well be that your personal stress is linked in some way to electro-stress, and that you should, therefore, do all you can to protect yourself against this electrical insult. Electro-stress detection and protection equipment that is now available includes computer VDU shields, low-emission TV sets, shielded cables and bio-cables, pulsors, specialist crystals, air ionizers and NT demand switches – electronic devices that can be wired into mains circuits to clear electromagnetic discharge.

Electro-stress is just one aspect of a broader environmental stress generated by humanity's lack of respect and knowledge of Mother Nature. The water you drink can sometimes be a dangerous cocktail of lead, aluminium, fluorides, chemical wastes and other alien assortments. The foods you eat can be a potential environmental stress. A simple-looking product may in reality be an exotic recipe of additives, artificial colourings, preservatives, chemical fertilizers, fungicides, pesticides and herbicides, all of which may be harmful to you. Even the air, the sun and the rain are not quite what they used to be.

Successful stress control must now address these new types of unnatural man-made stresses. Your environment may well be having a damaging and debilitating effect on your natural mind/body defences. Electro-stress therapists, allergy therapists, naturopaths, acupuncturists and a host of other complementary therapists, as well as your doctor, may be able to advise you further if you are in any doubt about the effect your environment may be having on your health, harmony and happiness.

7

DIET AND NUTRITION

I can eat well and be well.

*Let your food be your medicine; let your medicine
be your food.*
Hippocrates, Father of Medicine

Just as the performance of a car's engine depends upon
sensible fuel management, so too the performance of your
body-engine and your mind-engine depends upon sensible
food management. Food choice, food quality, food eating
patterns and your attitude to foods are all very important for
your health, happiness and wholeness. It is the foods of your
life that are the fuels of your life. No engine, mechanical or
biological, can run well, travel far or go the distance without
the right type and the right amount of fuel intake.

Food management can support your capacity to cope well
with stress because food nourishment affects the vital
function of every important organ in your body, including
your heart, lungs and brain. Foods can facilitate fitness,
enhance energy, promote positive performance, nourish
nerves, feed muscles, improve circulation, balance breathing
and support immune system functioning. During moments
of stress it is essential that your body and your mind receive
a sufficient supply of strength and support to see the strain
through.

Foods can also provide a powerful, plentiful form of

emotional nutrition and sustenance. A choice of foods together with the actual act of eating can provide, for instance, a sense of personal comfort, deep relaxation, quiet consolation, pleasure and enjoyment, company, a sense of control, distance, escape and recreation. Food can change the way you feel. As the writer and commentator Aldous Huxley once observed, 'A man may be a pessimistic determinist before lunch and an optimistic believer in the will's freedom after it.'

Sadly, many people often allow a regular, healthy eating pattern to collapse during times of emotional stress, sadness and strain. This form of food abuse tends to deplete the resources, energy and strength necessary for successful stress control. Typical eating patterns may include either comfort overeating or obsessive under-eating. Choice is generally mood-orientated, impulsive and dictated by convenience; there is no time to consider health, balance or nourishment. The message is simple: Eat well, be well.

STRESS AND YOUR STOMACH

The sensitive linings of your stomach area often succumb to the insidious actions and effects of prolonged or repeated stress. During the stress response we will often notice and experience that our stomach is alive with 'aches', 'cramps', 'knots' and 'butterflies'. Common phrases and idioms of our everyday language include, 'My stomach has gone all queasy,' 'My stomach is churning,' or, 'My stomach feels stuck.'

During short-term stress, your body's intelligence will mobilize only the most essential systems of your body in an attempt to guarantee survival. The 'fight or flight' response is tantamount to a 'live or die' alarm. Because the digestive system is not deemed essential for immediate survival, the body's digestion processes are usually slowed down or are allowed to pause completely until the perceived stress is judged to have passed.

During long-term stress or frequent, repeated bouts of stress, however, your digestion system manufactures large amounts of acids produced in response to the orders conveyed by your stress hormones. This disturbs the homoeostasis or balance between acid and alkaline in your stomach. If there is no food to absorb the excess acid it will attack and burn the linings of your stomach.

Indigestion and dyspepsia, heartburn, gastritis (inflammation of the stomach), gastric ulcers, duodenal ulcers, peptic ulcers, excessive and erratic bowel and bladder movements, minor incontinence, nausea and stomach cramps are all stress-related illnesses and symptoms linked to the abdominal area. These symptoms and illnesses can become aggravators and causes of stress, especially if proper nourishment is neglected. Foods are the foundations for the fullness of your health.

STRESS-AGGRAVATING FOODS

Each and every food that you eat has its own specific character and distinctive personality which can promote a set of specific effects and influences on the healthy functioning of your mind and body. Depending on the intrinsic composition and essential attributes of the foods you choose to eat, you will find that your diet can either help or hinder, support or obstruct your coping capacities for successful stress control.

The foods that hinder your natural coping capacity are stress-aggravating foods. They are also sometimes called 'mood foods', because of the profound effects they can have on your physical, mental and emotional equilibrium. It is very important to ensure that you either cut out or cut down on these foods if you wish to allow your mind and your body to function more closely to their optimum levels and peak capacities.

Sugar

Sugar is a rich source of 'empty calories'. In other words, sugar contains none of the essential nutrients such as protein, fibre, minerals or vitamins. On average, each person in Great Britain purchases a one-pound bag of sugar each week, and eats almost the equivalent of a two-pound bag of sugar during the course of the week.

Sugar is perhaps the most common food additive there is. Types of sugar include glucose, dextrose, fructose, sucrose and maltose. These are found in many sweet foods such as honey, syrup and molasses, and in many savoury foods such as sauces, pickles, pastries and soups. It would be wrong to say sugar is bad; rather, it is our use and consumption of sugar which is very often bad.

The action of sugar promotes an instant, short-term surge of energy throughout your body. When, however, you eat too much sugar, your adrenal glands can become overworked and exhausted, thereby depleting your body of its natural strength and relaxation and encouraging you to be poorly focused, irritable, lacking in concentration and generally depressed. High sugar intake can also put stress on the insulin-producing glands of the body, thereby precipitating 'burn-out' and possibly bringing on diabetes. Other common problems linked with high sugar intake include tooth decay, overweight, a possible link with hyperglycaemia, and mood swings from hyperactivity to lethargy.

Poor weight control is often a source of stress in that it may promote a lack of self-confidence, low self-esteem and little or no self-respect. Excess weight and obesity are certainly an extra pressure and potential stress on your body, which needs to work extra hard to perform its natural daily functions. The weight of your body can also add extra pressure, tension and load to the weight of your mind.

Ten Tips for Cutting Down on Sugar Intake

1. Replace sugary desserts with fresh fruits
2. Substitute sugary snacks with fresh fruits or fresh vegetables
3. Try unsweetened natural juices
4. Develop discretion in the supermarkets between sugar-rich, sugar-coated and sugar-free foods
5. Leave out sugar in coffees and teas
6. Try mixed fruit herbal tea for natural sweetness
7. Look for the 'sugar-free' labels on cereals
8. Halve the sugar content in homemade recipes
9. Drop junk foods
10. Read tin labels – tinned foods are often packed with sugars

Salt

Salt is a natural preservative found in many, many foods. The body needs salt. The precise amount necessary is somewhere between 1 gram and 3 grams per day. Unfortunately, though, the average person in Great Britain is a salt over-doser to the tune of over 10 grams per day.

This excess salt intake may have a number of harmful side-effects which in many ways mimic the stress response. Too much salt can promote high blood-pressure, aggravate premenstrual syndrome, stimulate and deplete your adrenal glands, stimulate and drain your nervous system, and tense and strain your muscular system. Too much salt may also promote emotional irritability, edginess, uptightness and general instability.

Ten Tips to Reduce Salt Intake

1. Leave the salt pot in the cupboard when you're cooking
2. Leave the salt pot in the cupboard when at the dinner table
3. Remember, it's the first salted peanut, popcorn or crisp that starts an avalanche of salt craving
4. Replace salty snacks with fresh fruit and vegetable snacks
5. Look out for the 'no added salt' labels on the tins in the supermarkets
6. Replace normal salt with 'low-sodium' salts or *Bio-Salt*
7. Halve the salt content in cookery recipes
8. Reduce your intake of 'high salt content' condiments, such as olives, pickles, sauces, mustards, stock cubes, etc.
9. Rinse meats, fish and tinned vegetables to wash away their excess preservative salt content before cooking
10. Use alternative herbs and spices to flavour your foods

Fats

Fats in diet must be carefully controlled. Eating too many fats can lead to excess weight and obesity. It can also create extra stress and pressure for the heart, which can in turn lead to many types of heart disease, including strokes and heart attacks. There are essentially two groups of fats, the saturated fats and unsaturated fats.

Saturated fats can be found in milk, cheese, butter, animal fat, vegetable fats, coconut oil, palm oil, hard margarines, biscuits, cakes, desserts, sauces and sweets.

The group of unsaturated fats includes a special type of fat called polyunsaturated fats, found in sunflower oil, corn oil, soya oil, some soft margarines, nuts, and certain fish oils such as those from trout, mackerel and herring. These polyunsaturated fats do not raise cholesterol levels in the same way as do saturated fats. They are also thought to help to restore and repair the day-to-day wear and tear of body cells.

Ten Guidelines for Healthy Fat Intake

1. Always discriminate between the saturated and the polyunsaturated fats
2. Replace full-fat milk with semi-skimmed or skimmed milk
3. Look out for the 'low fat' and 'polyunsaturated' labels on dairy products, margarines, etc.
4. Buy lean cuts of meat, cut the fat off before you cook, and beware of supermarket mince!
5. Try natural unprocessed yoghurts instead of salad creams or mayonnaise
6. Put away the frying pan – grill, oven, bake or steam
7. The marvellous baked potato! – The healthy alternative to chips, crisps and french fries (provided, of course, you don't smother it in butter and cheese!)
8. Go vegetarian – try pulses, beans and vegetables
9. Substitute poultry for red meat meals
10. Replace meats with fish – particularly white fish, which has only a minimal fat content

Additives

Additives have been found in certain cases to cause and to aggravate stress. Food manufacturers rely on a cocktail of some 3,500 different additives to prepare and to preserve foods for consumers. Some are quite natural; others are based on natural products; and then there are those others which have been invented and created by food scientists.

Preservatives, anti-oxidants, emulsifiers and stabilizers, colours, flavour enhancers and sweeteners, anti-caking agents and raising agents are all types of additives, all of which have found their way into foods over the last few decades, courtesy of poor consumer awareness. Some of these additives have since been found to be disturbing and harmful to our physical and mental constitution.

Thanks to the power of the media, and to the rising power of consumer choice, many food products now boast a 'no preservative, flavourings or colouring' label. There are also a number of good publications that have been created to help you to make an informed choice. The Ministry of Agriculture, Fisheries and Food have published *Food Additives, the Balanced Approach*, which lists all the major additives in use. It can be obtained on request (see Useful Addresses section of this book).

Caffeine

Caffeine is the professional impressionist among foods in that it can produce reactions in your mind and your body almost identical to the initial surge of energy and arousal that happens during the stress response. Caffeine can activate your adrenal glands, increase blood-pressure, stimulate your heart, light up your nervous system, and feed the muscles of your body. The mind can also switch on and become alert and ready.

Too much caffeine, particularly if taken to revive a flagging effort, can have harmful side-effects in much the same way as too much arousal can. These disturbing effects include exhaustion, lethargy, nervousness, emotional instability, poor mental control, headaches, migraines and palpitations. Using caffeine for energy is a bit like running your mind and your body on a false energy with no natural reserves to back it up. Failure and breakdown can happen to you without a moment's notice.

You can reduce your caffeine intake by reducing the amount of coffee, tea and cola you drink, by reducing the strength of these drinks, and by replacing them with caffeine-free or herbal substitutes. Some decaffeinated coffees can be quite good, but with some brands the decaffeination process uses substances that may be just as harmful and disturbing as caffeine.

Alcohol

Alcohol is a gentle stimulant for some and a pleasant relaxant for others. A glass of wine, a pint of lager, a tipple of sherry or a smooth malt whisky can often round the day off quite nicely. Problems hover on the horizon, however, when you find yourself resorting to one of these delights in order to *begin* the day well!

When taken in excess, alcohol can become a poison that damages the organs of your body, drains your body of its essential nutrients, pollutes the mind and thereby hinders mental performance, enhances any emotional instability, further develops obesity and, most serious of all, encourages dependence.

Alcohol intake, particularly during times of stress, should be avoided. Alcohol is no answer to the problem of stress. It will give you a kick or a boost for a moment or two, but the price you pay for that fleeting, transitory experience may be impaired judgement, poor-quality thinking, unbearable emotional sensitivity, poor-quality work and the onset of further fatigue, exacerbated exhaustion and drowsy depression.

STRESS-HELPFUL FOODS

Certain vitamins, minerals, essential amino and fatty acids and natural foods have been found to be excellent for helping mind and body control stress successfully. Indeed, many foods and supplements are now marketed solely or primarily as recommended stress supports.

It must be emphasized that the following list of items represents only a general introduction to a complex, specialist and often very controversial subject. Perhaps the best general advice that can be given is that all the stress-helpful foods are supplied in a natural, varied and well-balanced diet. Stress-helpful foods are by no means only those that come in the form of pills, potions or other packeted substances.

VITAMIN B$_6$

A deficiency of vitamin B$_6$ can be a cause of physical and mental tiredness and is also linked to anaemia. B$_6$ may be of help for stress and exhaustion, for premenstrual syndrome, for morning sickness during pregnancy, for anxiety and worry, and as a supplement to assist in offsetting the side-effects of antibiotics and other biomedical drugs. Natural sources of B$_6$ can be found in fish, most fresh vegetables, dairy products, pulses and whole-grain cereals.

BREWERS' YEAST

This is a good source of all the B vitamins, with the exception of vitamin B$_{12}$. It is considered by many to be an excellent natural tonic for tiredness and exhaustion. It is also thought to be good for times of irritability and general emotional instability, such as during premenstrual syndrome.

VITAMIN C

According to many expert nutritionists, a deficiency of vitamin C is a dangerous and widespread problem in the modern world. The main reason most commonly identified for this deficiency is the high levels of stress in our modern lifestyle, which dampen and suppress the body's production and absorption of vitamin C. The deficiency has been connected to scurvy, lethargy and fatigue, a weakened and less effective immune system, recurrent colds and influenza, and degenerative diseases such as arthritis and arterio-sclerosis. Alcohol and cigarettes are also thought to inhibit the action of vitamin C. Natural sources of vitamin C include fresh citrus fruits and fresh vegetables.

IRON

Iron deficiency commonly manifests symptoms of fatigue and exhaustion, anaemia, and moods of powerlessness and depression. Iron absorption can become deficient when not enough vitamin C is taken into your body. Signs of deficiency include brittle nails, pale complexion and continual ulcers in your mouth. Natural sources of iron can be found in pulses, beans, grains, fish, poultry, meat, molasses and, in small quantities, spinach, potatoes and peas.

ZINC

Zinc deficiency is a common sign of stress which is also a common additional cause of stress. Zinc is essential for so many natural processes of your body. Deficiency can cause deterioration of the immune function, poor wound healing, temporary impotence, stomach problems, poor appetite, fatigue, lack of concentration and a lack of emotional control, as well as general symptoms of mental stress. Natural sources of zinc can be found in seafoods, diary products, meat, ginger root, oysters, soya beans and some varieties of nuts.

IODINE

This is linked to the healthy functioning of your thyroid gland, which helps to govern the metabolic rate of your body. Iodine deficiency can, therefore, sometimes cause exhaustion, while increased iodine intake can be a natural stimulant and tonic. Natural sources of iodine are kelp, seaweed, seafoods, spinach and green peppers. It is also possible to buy iodized salt.

CALCIUM

Calcium is very important for the growth and structure of your body. It is essential for healthy bones, for ache-free joints, for teeth, for nerves, for cell structure, for muscles and for effective blood clotting. Shortage of calcium is sometimes linked with a shortage of vitamin D. Natural sources of calcium include dairy products, pulses, apples and cabbage. Many dairy products are now enhanced with calcium and are advertised as calcium-fortified foods.

GINSENG

Ginseng has been called the root of heaven and the herb of eternal life. It can be found in certain parts of the world including Korea, China and North America, and has been acclaimed for centuries as a natural revitalizing and strengthening agent, useful for many forms of physical and mental stress. Ginseng is an acclaimed 'harmony herb' that is thought to rebalance the *milieu interieur*, thereby increasing the body's resistance to infection, restoring homoeostasis and enhancing adjustment to stress. It is now commonly available at most health food shops.

EVENING PRIMROSE OIL

This oil has a pure, high and natural level of the anti-stress agent called Gamma Linolenic Acid (GLA). GLA is understood to be essential for feeding, supporting and nurturing essential body cycles, such as cell regeneration and the menstrual cycle, as well as fostering immunity, heart-pressure harmony and nervous-system balance. The degenerating effect of stress is thought to inhibit GLA production; it is believed, therefore, that Evening Primrose Oil offers an excellent opportunity during times of stress for recharging, renewing and replenishing the reserves that support regular, healthy body function. Many nutritionists now believe that Oil of Javanicus is an even more potent, plentiful and pure source of GLA than Evening Primrose Oil.

SELENIUM

This has been hailed as an essential healing trace element that is vital for protecting and maintaining the health and harmony of our cellular structures. It is considered to be an anti-oxidant, an anti-polluting agent and an immune-system strengthener. Recent medical research is beginning to unveil the importance of this trace element. Surveys in the USA, Sweden, the Netherlands, Denmark and Finland, for instance, have all linked high instances of heart disease to low- selenium climates. One result of this research is that the government of Finland has made it law to add selenium to farming fertilizers. Nutritionists advise that selenium supplements are best taken together with vitamin E.

ROYAL JELLY

This substance is produced by worker bees as a special banquet for the queen bee. It is thought to enhance and support the immune system, strengthen the adrenal glands, and promote the functioning of the mind. Along with ginseng it is often described as a wonder food that can help to promote peak performance and a natural harmony in both body and mind.

MOLASSES

Another food often hailed as a wonder food, for molasses contains a number of mineral elements such as calcium and iron, and some B vitamins. Blackstrap molasses is the variety recommended most often – a dark black treacly substance, available from most health food shops.

CHLORELLA

This tiny green natural micro-algae is cultivated in the freshwaters of the Orient. Described as 'Gem of the Orient', Chlorella is acclaimed the most potent nutritional whole-food made by Mother Earth. Chlorella is considered a natural health-building substance, packed with proteins, some 20 vitamins and minerals, numerous amino and nucleic acids, zinc, selenium, iodine, iron, calcium, vitamin E, vitamin C, essential fatty acids and more. For depletion through stress, this natural food is recommended as being especially healing and good.

A STRESS-FRIENDLY DIET

The international book market has suffered acute indigestion in recent years with its many hundreds of new food and diet bestsellers piling onto the shelves each month. Some of these books claim to have discovered the universal elixir; others advertise the one food we all of us must never go without. Some claim to have established proof that a certain food or substance will miraculously energize you; others say that a particular combination of foods and meals will give you the IQ of a genius. There are even books that claim there are certain foods you can stuff yourself with all day long and actually lose weight in the process!

This acute 'book indigestion' will undoubtedly become chronic as more and more books appear on the shelves of your local bookshops. Some of these publications will be enlightening and transforming, others may be interesting and useful, and then there will be those which should perhaps be transferred onto the fiction shelves!

In the meantime, there are some simple and essential guidelines that should play a part in all our diets. They amount to little more than common sense, but without doubt they represent a most effective way of energizing, healing and supporting your mind and your body in their bid to perform to their natural, optimum and peak levels.

EAT FRESH FOODS

Many of the essential nutrients in foods are killed when cooked in high temperatures. Eating fresh fruits, vegetables and breads can help us to get the very best of nature's lifeforce. *Raw Energy* (Thorsons, 1987), by Leslie and Susannah Kenton, gathers many scientific reports from Europe and around the world which confirm the many benefits of fresh food as opposed to over-cooked foods. It is a very worthwhile read.

EAT REGULAR MEALS

An adequate meal three times a day is of much greater benefit than a single blow out. Also, resist the temptation to skip meals on a regular basis. Eating regularly is, of course, vital for energizing your mind and body. Biofeedback surveys have found that mealtimes can also provide therapeutic time for rest and relaxation: eating offers a time to detach yourself from the day, to slow down and wind down, to rest and relax, to create your own space perhaps, or maybe to socialize with pleasant, agreeable company. Try to use mealtimes as positively as possible in these ways.

EAT SLOWLY

Appreciate and enjoy mealtimes. Chew the food so as to absorb fully its taste, texture and energy. Eating is like meditation. The more attention, care and time you give to eating, chewing and swallowing, the better the foods will be digested. Being purposefully slow at mealtimes can help you to, for instance, break away, detach and distance yourself from the furious, unrelenting pace of a normal stressful day.

RESIST THE TEMPTATION TO OVEREAT

Stressed people very often like to overeat because overeating exhausts the body and shuts down the mind. Very often we will fall asleep after a heavy meal; this is, however, a poor substitute for relaxation. Indeed, we have not so much relaxed as passed out! Eating too much amounts to one more pressure and stress for your body, which actually has to use up almost as much energy as it receives in an effort to digest the foods taken in.

EAT A VARIETY OF FOODS

Variety provides interest, enjoyment and balanced, adequate nutrition. Carbohydrates consist mainly of sugars and starches. They supply over half the energy you receive from your diet. Proteins are great energy-givers. They also provide the materials for creating and repairing cells, tissues and organs. Fats are a valuable supply of energy for long-term storage. They all have their place and they all find their place in a varied and well-balanced diet.

THE ACID/ALKALINE BALANCE

The homoeostasis or natural harmony of the body requires there to be a balance between acids and alkalis in the foods we eat. Acid is formed from food rich in protein; alkaline is formed from fruits and vegetables. The normal ph of the blood is 7.4, anything below is acidic; anything above is alkaline. There are many systems in your body which operate to keep this balance accurate. A well-balanced and varied diet certainly helps. An upset in balance can irritate your mind and perhaps lead to excess gastric acidity.

FLUIDS

Fluids are essential for cleansing the body. When you consider that most of your body is water, you can begin to appreciate that a fresh and plentiful supply of water can help you to perform at your best. The only time when you should be careful how much you drink should be at mealtimes, because too much fluid can sometimes water down the digestive agents in your stomach.

SNACKS

These can be a great source of pleasure and enjoyment, and also provide quick energy for the mind and body. Providing your weight is normal, there is no need to give up snacks altogether, but you should perhaps make them a treat rather than a daily occurrence. In particular, you should make sure they do not take the place of square meals.

FIBRE

Fibre has become a cornerstone of most modern diet plans. Most foods rich in fibre usually have many additional vitamins and minerals as well. Fibre is also thought by many nutrition experts to improve the digestion and metabolizing of food. Cereals, beans, pulses, wholemeal bread, vegetables and fruits are also natural sources of fibre, as is bran.

BALANCE, BALANCE AND MORE BALANCE

If you supply your body with a balanced diet, and you are in good health, you can trust your body to process your foods in its natural and accustomed way so as to heal, to nourish and to strengthen you day by day, every day, to the very best of its ability.

THE 7-DAY 'STRESS-BUSTER' DIET

The 7-day 'Stress-buster' diet offers a practical guideline for sensible, healthy eating during times of personal stress and strain. The recommendations of the diet are inspired by four basic goals: 1) healthy choices, 2) variety, 3) regular eating, and 4) personal enjoyment. Any diet that fulfils these four essential goals is a valuable personal resource of strength, energy and coping for times of excessive demand and dilemma. Eating well supports coping well.

If you make healthy choices, you create a more healthy chance of coping well: healthy choices will increase your resources of nourishment, energy and strength, which are vital for coping with the demands of stress, strain and effort.

You will get all of the nourishment you require if you ensure a healthy variety of foods; a healthy variety will ensure you do not miss out on any of the vitamins, minerals, proteins and carbohydrates that are so essential for healthy being and healthy coping.

Regularly eating small meals is much preferable to one big meal. Eating too much too quickly promotes stress on the body and fatigue for the mind. Regular eating will ensure you have a steady supply of healthy energy for coping.

Perhaps the most essential ingredient of a truly healthy diet is personal enjoyment. If you take the time to relish your food, to savour its taste and perhaps, to enjoy your company, then mealtimes can be moments of comfort, retreat, detachment and pleasure, the experience of which can help to fortify you for coping.

Aim to make healthy food management a priority in your life for just seven consecutive days, and the theory of healthy eating will transform itself into a hatful of practical, tangible healthy benefits for you to enjoy. There is truth in the ancient idea that you are only as good as your food. Eating well and coping well complement one another very well indeed.

MONDAY TO SUNDAY

Breakfast

A glass of water, preferably mineral water.

One bowl of low-sugar muesli, with skimmed milk or soya milk. You can create your own muesli, using any bran, wheat and oat base with an assortment of mixed nuts and fruits, fresh or dried.

One glass of fruit juice, or a small bowl of grapefruit, pineapple, apple or orange segments.

Wholewheat or granary toast – marmite, honey or any other 'healthy choice' spread.

A cup of herbal tea, e.g. peppermint, chamomile, cherry or mixed fruit, for instance.

MONDAY TO SUNDAY

Mid-morning and mid-afternoon snacks

Choose from:

Cereal health bars, unsweetened biscuits, wholemeal crisp breads, fruit health bars, wholemeal scones, wholemeal muffins, fresh fruits, herbal teas and health drinks.

MONDAY

Lunch

Wholemeal salad sandwiches. Enjoy a small spread of butter/margarine on your bread.

Fruit, e.g. apple, banana or pear.

A health drink, e.g. orange juice

Dinner

Steamed white fish or salmon with steamed
vegetables: e.g. cauliflower, potato and carrots.
Cheese, biscuits and celery. Try vegetarian cheese.
A glass of your favourite wine.

TUESDAY

Lunch

Wholemeal tuna salad baguette. Vegetarians may
like to try vegetarian pâté.
Wholemeal scone, with a 'healthy choice' jam or
marmalade, low in sugar.
A health drink, e.g. carbonated apple juice.

Dinner

Homemade vegetable soup or meat broth.
Baked potato with a filling of your choice, e.g.
broccoli and cheese.
Natural Greek yoghurt with fruit or tofu with
fruit.
A glass of your favourite wine or a glass of perry.

WEDNESDAY

Lunch

Wholemeal pitta bread with humous, taramasalata
or tzatszki dip.
Melon.
A health drink, e.g. pineapple juice.

Dinner

Homemade pizza with a selection of enjoyable toppings, e.g. pineapple, olives, anchovies, tomatoes, cheese, tuna, mushrooms or ham.

Wholemeal garlic bread, made with a light spread of butter or margarine and freshly chopped garlic (not garlic powder).

Fruit salad.

A spritz mix: white wine and tonic water.

THURSDAY

Lunch

Wholemeal cheese salad baps. Vegetarians may like to try vegetarian cheese.

Dundee cake.

Health drink, e.g. grapefruit juice.

Dinner

Chili, made with meat or kidney beans, served on a bed of wholemeal rice or bulba wheat.

Fromage frais with fruits.

Carbonated juice, e.g. pear juice, grape juice or apple juice.

FRIDAY

Lunch

Vegetable or meat samosa or spring rolls.

Muesli biscuit bar and fruit.

A health drink, e.g. tropical fruit juice.

Dinner

Steamed sweetcorn cobs.

Wholemeal spaghetti bolognaise, meat or vegetarian variety. Steam all your vegetables.

Baked apple, currants, cinnamon and single cream.

SATURDAY

Lunch

Hamburgers or tofu burgers with low-fat oven chips and steamed vegetables.

Peaches and ice cream.

A health drink, e.g. citrus fruit juice.

Dinner

Chicken, chickpea or vegetable curry. Steam all vegetables. Serve with wholemeal rice and breads.

Enjoy a favourite dessert, and also a favoured after-dinner drink.

SUNDAY

Lunch

Sunday poultry roast or a nut roast, served with roast potatoes and steamed vegetables, e.g. broccoli, sprouts, carrots and turnips.

A fruit crumble, served on its own or with single cream or ice cream.

A health drink, e.g. mango juice

Dinner

Baked potato with a healthy choice filling, e.g.
baked beans, cottage cheese, prawns or sweetcorn.
Serve with a side salad.

Cheese, biscuits and celery.

Mineral water.

8

NATURALLY
DOES IT

I can learn to look after myself.

MUSIC THERAPY

The man that hath no music in himself,
Nor is not mov'd with concord of sweet sounds,
Is fit for treasons, stratagems, and spoils.
Shakespeare, *The Merchant of Venice* V. i. 83–5

Music has been acknowledged throughout the ages by many medical, healing and spiritual traditions as a potent healing force. It has been described many times as 'the art that can calm the agitations of the soul'. Today there are many, many practising psychologists, biologists, physiologists, psychiatrists and surgeons who share this conviction and who incorporate music in their healing work.

Music was so revered in ancient times it was considered as the speech of angels, as the movement of celestial bodies, as expressions of the universe, and as a direct communication with the very gods themselves. The word 'music' originates from words used to describe the feminine, sustaining and healing principles of the universe. Today we use expressions in our everyday language such as 'music to my ears', 'playing my song', 'in tune', 'a musical quality' and 'feels sound', all of which convey a sense of pleasure and satisfaction, agreement and harmony.

Music has always been with us. Indeed it would be hard to think of a world without music. Even without instruments we would still hear the wind singing, water tinkling, fire crackling, the songs of bird and animals. Christian hymns, national anthems, Gregorian chants, Buddhist mantra, Native American chants, symphonies, concertos, requiems, choral pieces, operas, ballads, country music and rock and pop have all been lauded for their healing, pacifying and liberating qualities, touching the very essence of our being, stimulating our self-healing mechanisms, and thereby allowing strength and harmony to be restored.

A piece of music is a compilation of, among other things, tone, rhythm, rest, pitch and vibration. The human body is also composed of these things. Modern science has confirmed what those who practised the ancient therapeutic arts always believed to be true, that the human body vibrates and sings at cell-level, and that this vibration is either held together or torn apart by the quality of tone, rhythm and rest that you experience in your life.

Here, once again, we are reminded of the words of Aristotle: 'Health is harmony; dis-ease is discord.'

Stress is a type of music. So too are anger, peace, rage, love, jealousy, contentment and all other emotional expressions of delight or discord. We all know, sense and feel if we are 'out of step', or 'in tune' with the world. The control of rhythm and harmony in life is essential then, because, as the expression goes, 'in life we make our own music'.

Musical Relaxation

To prepare for musical relaxation you should follow a similar procedure to that for normal relaxation. Find a space which is as quiet as possible so as to ensure you will not be disturbed.

Either lie down in a comfortable position or sit upright with your head, neck and spine well aligned. Loosen any tight clothing, and then, when you are comfortable, close your eyes.

Begin by tuning into silence. Allow yourself to settle naturally, so that you can become aware of a still, silent space within you.

Next, tune in to the rhythm of your breathing. Feel for flow, duration, pace and harmony. Follow the rise and fall of your stomach as you breathe in and out.

When you are truly settled, put on your choice of music (it should not matter if you have to get up). As the music begins, try to breathe into the music, allowing yourself to absorb completely the entire melody.

The deeper you breathe, the deeper you will relax; and the deeper you relax, the deeper you will breathe. Continue to breathe fully and in tune for the complete duration of your chosen music.

Ensure you retain your relaxation and composure after the music has finished, allowing yourself to return to a normal waking state, nice and gently.

Music can either raise or lower your blood-pressure. It can either quicken or reduce your heart rate. Music can affect your respiration, your digestion, your muscle tension and your nervous equilibrium. Above all, it can affect your moods, your thoughts, your feelings, your every gesture. It can delve down so deep inside that it can soothe, pacify, calm and heal the tensions which so often tie us up and eat us up.

Music can be a perfect remedy for stress if you will let it work for you. It is a nonverbal, universal form of communication which takes us beyond words, which carries us away from our own limited world and transports us to a place where we can open up to the greater world of the whole. It replaces the moment with the eternal. We can then breathe easier, think more clearly, feel consoled, rest more fully, experience fresh hope, and replace worn out ambition with fresh endeavour.

Music is like an ointment for the soul which can also invigorate, uplift, strengthen, encourage and enhance our resolve to make the most of ourselves. Athletes, performers, politicians, generals and campaigners have often openly admitted they benefit from music. Successful clinical tests have also been conducted where people who suffer from depression and other forms of under-arousal have been prescribed lively pieces of classical music and rock 'n roll to charge them up and help them get out of themselves for a time.

Music can be used for catharsis. It was no coincidence that in ancient Greece the theatres were built next to the healing temples. Patients were actively encouraged to listen to music as part of their rehabilitation programmes. The music they listened to was, like the plays they saw, a clever mix of comedy and tragedy which would often take an audience through the whole gamut of emotions.

The sedative effect of music, so effective at consoling and at easing pain and grief, has also long been recognized and worked with in therapeutic settings. The Italian surgeon, Gaetano Zappalau, has operated on several thousands of patients using only local anaesthetic and selected doses of hypnotic mood music played throughout. On certain occasions he has dispensed with his surgical tools altogether and prescribed only music for certain conditions.

Once you connect to a piece of music it can soon become your own personal anthem which can be made to work for you in any number of ways. By making a piece of music a personal companion, you have a friend for life, an inspiration, a battery of strength, a retreat and a trustworthy counsel committed to helping you to create the reality you wish for and deserve.

AROMATHERAPY

The therapeutic properties of scents and aromas was first put to a positive purpose some 4,000 years ago in the ancient civilizations of China, Phoenicia, Egypt and India. In those days of long ago, the medicine priests of the healing temples deliberately employed 'fragrance medicine' to help to restore health and to prevent illness. Scents and aromas were given another use and purpose by these medicine priests, who employed fragrances in places of worship to help to still the mind, to raise consciousness and to effect a spiritual enlightenment and healing.

The healers and medicine priests of these times would collect and press the finest flowers in all the land so as to extract drops of essential oil, sometimes called the 'honey of the flowers'. These drops were so highly concentrated that, for instance, a sizable basket of some 40 rosebuds would be needed to extract one pure drop of essential rose oil.

The scents and aromas of these flowers were found to have such a profound affect on the skin, tissues and organs of the human body, as well as on the mental and emotional equilibrium of mind, that they were later described as 'original hormones of mother nature', capable of effecting a return to balance, health and harmony even in the most apparently severe conditions.

The therapeutic effects of these highly concentrated oils can be classified thus: some soothe, relax and calm; and others stimulate, energize and rejuvenate. Depending, therefore, upon whether you have an illness or stress that is the result of over-arousal or under-arousal, you may wish to use an essential oil that stimulates you or an oil that soothes you, an essential oil that refreshes you or an oil that relaxes you, an essential oil that helps to uplift you or an oil that helps you to unwind.

For example, in the case of exhaustion and fatigue, you may

wish to use an essential oil such as chamomile, which massages your nerves, relaxes muscle tension, stabilizes blood-pressure, promotes deep respiration, cleanses your skin, eases pain and generally calms your mind; or you may wish to use an essential oil such as lemon, which improves poor circulation, warms cool body temperature, stimulates the metabolism and clears, uplifts and energizes your mind.

The past 100 years, and in particular the last three decades, have witnessed a renaissance in fragrance medicine, or *aromatherapy* as it is more commonly known. There are now well-established aromatherapy colleges, federations and organizations which can supply lists of hundreds of trained aromatherapists throughout Great Britain. There are also innumerable suppliers of essential oils throughout the country. Boots, Culpeppers and The Body Shop are three high-street shops which stock their own brands of essential oils.

Aromatherapy is truly the most luxurious of natural treatments and remedies. It can be used on its own or combined with other natural therapies such as massage, Shiatsu, acupressure, music therapy or colour healing. A most significant reason for the success of aromatherapy in recent years has been its undoubted ability to help relieve and alleviate the increasingly evident detrimental effects of stress and tension.

Professional aromatherapists often encourage their clients to use home treatments to supplement their therapy. It is not necessary then to be well-versed in biology, anatomy and psychophysiology to benefit from aromatic oils. Indeed, some people have found they don't even need the oils: their imagination and sense of smell are so well developed they can just create the smell for themselves from memory and receive the benefits that way.

Essential oils can be used either individually or in blends, and can be prepared and applied using a number of different methods. You can use essential oils to create your own massage solution, for instance, by adding between 15 and 25 drops of oil to 50 ml of a vegetable 'carrier oil' such as almond oil, sunflower oil or olive oil.

You can use 6 to 10 drops of essential oil as a bath oil to be used instead of your normal salts and bubbles. A footbath oil made with several drops of essential oil can also be very therapeutic. Herbal teas can be fortified with one or two drops of orange, lemon, lemongrass, rose, fennel or chamomile, for instance. You can now buy natural room fresheners in the form of a ceramic oil burner which uses a night-light to heat up and release vapour from a few drops of essential oil. An alternative to this is to put a couple of drops on your radiator. There are even car fresheners now available to help keep you poised at the wheel.

Compresses for sprains, bruises and muscle relaxation can be made by rinsing a cloth in a bowl of hot water with two or three drops of essential oil in it, and then placing the cloth over the affected area. This is particularly soothing for the face. Inhalants are useful for general mood therapy and for stresses such as headaches, anxiety, migraines, fatigue and influenza. You can add essential oils to a basin of hot water or put them on your pillow or handkerchief.

Perfumes can be made using essential oils. Add between 4 and 6 drops to every 5 ml of vegetable carrier oil and apply as a normal perfume. Oils can also be applied 'neat' to external pain spots, burns, stings and sores. Lavender oil is particularly recommended for neat applications. It is perhaps the most versatile of all essential oils, being very good for skin healing, stress control, tension relief and general aches and pains.

The list of home treatment suggestions overleaf shows remedies which have proved most effective for relieving and alleviating conditions generally thought to be caused or aggravated by stress.

Stress Condition	Bath Oil	Massage Oil (50 ml)
Hypertension	4 drops lavender 4 drops ylang-ylang	10 drops lavender 10 drops ylang-ylang
Nervous tension	2 drops bergamot 4 drops marjoram 2 drops sandalwood	8 drops bergamot 4 drops marjoram 4 drops neroli
Exhaustion	4 drops clary sage 4 drops bergamot 2 drops ylang-ylang	8 drops clary sage 8 drops bergamot 4 drops ylang-ylang
Muscle Tension	4 drops lavender 2 drops geranium 2 drops sandalwood	8 drops lavender 4 drops geranium 8 drops sandalwood
Insomnia	2 drops chamomile 4 drops juniper 4 drops neroli	10 drops lavender 6 drops ylang-ylang
PMS	5 drops clary sage 5 drops lavender	25 drops clary sage (rub on abdomen)
Headaches	6-10 drops lavender	Massage temples with a drop of lavender

MASSAGE THERAPY

Touching is an instinctive, universal language we all use, either consciously or unconsciously, to express and convey the way we feel about ourselves and about one another. It can mean many, many things to us, such as intimacy and closeness, trust and acceptance, approval, caring, friendship, understanding, empathy and, above all perhaps, love.

Touching is a natural, therapeutic tool, again used either consciously or unconsciously to relax, soothe, stimulate, uplift and heal ourselves and others. When a child grazes his knee, when a friend needs consoling, when our body aches and we have injured ourselves, or when we see a poor defenceless animal hurt or crying, our first reaction is to touch. Very often the simple act of touching will of itself be enough to alleviate the discomfort and unhappiness.

Massage is sometimes described as therapeutic touch. As a medicine and natural remedy for stress, massage is one of the oldest forms of healing known to humanity. It is not unreasonable to assume that the very first time a caveman produced the 'fight or flight' response (during a stressful encounter with a dinosaur perhaps!), he was later comforted and healed by the touch of a cavewoman.

A professional masseur or masseuse understands that your mind and body are interconnected, the quality and performance of one affecting the quality and performance of the other. Your mind and body are seen, therefore, as mirrors of one another. During the course of a normal day, your body will often soak up and reflect the stress and tension perceived and experienced by your mind, and your mind will often soak up and reflect the stress and tension accumulated by your body.

Finger-Tapping Exercise

Tap your skull lightly with all of your fingers for two to three minutes, working from the top of the crown of your head, down around the sides and around your ears, and around the back of your neck. This is an ancient massage exercise which has been found to be most helpful for stimulating mental concentration, arousal and performance.

By working on your body, a masseur or masseuse aims to create an environment that can prepare for and promote harmony of the mind. This is because the body is in many ways a natural extension of the mind. Therefore, a massage that soothes and relaxes your body will also have a soothing and relaxing effect on your mind; and a massage that stimulates, tones and invigorates your body will also clear, energize and uplift your mind.

A well-performed massage will have a beneficial,

therapeutic benefit for the whole person. It can either soothe or stimulate your muscular system, your nervous system, your circulatory system, your cardiovascular system, your cells and tissues, your glands and your organs. Massage can also balance and harmonize your respiration, your digestion and your metabolism.

Common physical benefits of massage include help for pain relief, muscle tension, cramps, high blood-pressure, hyper-ventilation, strained nerves, overactive or underactive organs and glands, fatigue and lethargy, body aches, headaches, migraines, heart disease, arthritis and poor circulation.

Chinese Facial Massage

Rub both your palms together vigorously until they begin to feel hot with friction. Then place both palms over your face and rub the warmth into your skin. Begin on your forehead, and slide down gently over your eyes, over your cheeks, along your jaws and down to your throat. You can enhance this exercise my imagining your skin filling with white light, with energy and with lifeforce. You may find this to be both relaxing and refreshing.

Massage is as much a psychotherapy as it is a physical therapy. It can, therefore, help a person to relax out of many mental and emotional dis-eases and dis-orders such as anxiety, worry, fear, guilt, poor self-worth, depression and anger. For many people massage is a heavenly moment which somehow seems to slot everything perfectly into place. It is in many cases a perfect remedy to stress.

The different techniques of massage use the full expression of the hands and of touch, and are very important for creating the desired effect. For instance, kneading uses the heel and palm of the hand to delve deep into knots of tension along, in particular, the back of the body and up by the shoulders. Chopping uses the outer edge of the hand to work on fleshy parts of the body.

Gliding is a common technique used for working along the complete length of a muscle. *Pressing* the hand over a muscle can either create a release of tension or a gentle pressure and stimulation. *Cupping* uses the hand in a cupped position, which is then used to tap the body. Other techniques include vibration, circular pressure and friction.

Each technique will either soothe or stimulate the body depending on the pressure, length of stroke, depth of touch and general rhythm of each movement. For instance, a short, sharp, flat stroke may invigorate you; while a long, smooth, gentle stroke may be more relaxing.

Many people make a weekly or fortnightly appointment with a masseur or masseuse for the purpose of a general relaxation therapy, a stress-relief session or even as a stress-prevention measure. Sometimes professional masseurs or masseuses will supplement their treatments with aroma-therapy oils, music and sound, colour healing, and also with other similar techniques such as reflexology, Shiatsu, and acupressure. Everyone should have a professional massage at least once in their lives.

Tired Eye Massage

Whenever you feel tired it is often the eyes, and in particular the muscles behind the eyes, that feel the most strain. When you experience tired eyes, place either the pads of your fingers or the heal of your hands over both eyes and gently press for a few moments as you breathe in and out, deeply, slowly and evenly. Do this for one minute, and then gently open your eyes to the world again.

It is perfectly easy and very satisfying to perform do-it-yourself massage or to have a partner or friend do it for you. Headaches, cramps, stiff shoulders, body aches, muscle tension, a tired mind and frail emotions are all common symptoms of stress that can be alleviated by simple massage and touch. Body massages can be beautiful moments for rest, relaxation and healing.

The sterno mastoid muscles of the neck, the trapezius and deltoid muscles along the shoulders, the frontalis muscles of the forehead, and the muscles of the arms and upper back are all exceptionally grateful for the therapeutic properties of touch. Between them these muscles soak up most of the stress and tension of the body. Attention to these areas alone can provide tremendous relief and upliftment if you and/or a partner ever decide to use 'DIY massage'.

HERBAL MEDICINE

Even in the green herb have I given you all things.
Genesis 9: 3

The healing power of ancient, Earth-old herbs provides us with an abundance of powerful, natural antidotes and cures for many of the common modern-day manifestations of stress such as nerve strain, muscle tension, aches and pains, high blood-pressure, anxiety, fatigue, depression and general mental irritation and imbalance.

Herbal remedies were held in especially high regard by the fathers of modern medicine. Every ancient, successful and enduring healing tradition has, without exception, discovered that herbs can help to influence and to restore a person's inner balance and self-harmony. Indeed, it has only been in the last hundred years (and more specifically the last 40 years) that natural herbal medicines have been eclipsed by the synthetic drugs cultivated, grown and harvested in new high-tech science laboratories.

Herbal medicines never lost their healing power, it was we who lost our understanding and appreciation of them. Today, herbs are enjoying a resurgence and are being used more and more to supplement and to complement modern drug therapy, mainly because, unlike many tranquillizers and anti-depressants, for example, herbs do not encourage dependency, there is little or no evidence of any severe withdrawal symptoms, serious side-effects are virtually nil and the substances are entirely natural.

Herbalists also believe that their preparations can be used to tackle the *cause* of illness, unlike modern drugs which, they believe, deal merely with symptoms. Furthermore, they argue that modern drugs create false cures because they work by the suppression of illness, whereas herbal remedies are designed to help to liberate and to stimulate the self-healing mechanism, thereby restoring harmony and balance to the whole person. There is also evidence to suggest that herbal remedies are better absorbed by the body than are chemical substitutes used in modern drug therapy.

A professional herbalist will prepare and prescribe herbal remedies in a number of different forms, such as infusions, decoctions, loose teas, suppositories, inhalants, lotions, tinctures, tablets and pills. Many of these preparations are available for home treatments and can now be bought from chemists, health shops and a number of national suppliers of herbal products.

CHAMOMILE

Chamomile has a profoundly relaxing effect on your mind and body. It is an excellent nerve-sedative, muscle-relaxant and mind-soother. It is also a good cleanser, thought to be excellent for premenstrual syndrome. Loose chamomile tea, first and last thing each day, is a wonderful support for your entire system.

PEPPERMINT

This is often very good for unsettled stomachs. It relieves indigestion, flatulence, constipation and nausea, while also helping to balance over-acidity. Peppermint is also a wonderful tonic to help clear and freshen a fatigued and exhausted mind. Peppermint is beneficial for colds and influenza. A peppermint and chamomile tea is thought to be particularly good for head tensions and migraines.

VALERIAN

Valerian is sometimes called 'nature's heal all'. The name valerian comes from the Latin word *valere*, which means 'to be whole'. Valerian is often prescribed as a general remedy for counteracting the physical effects of stress. It is thought to be very good for insomnia, anxiety and nervousness.

LIME FLOWERS

These are thought to be therapeutic for nervous irritability, a racing mind, hysteria and general over-arousal and hyperactivity. They are also good for insomnia, high blood-pressure and for soothing muscles and nerves. The cleansing effect of lime flowers is also well known.

LAVENDER

This uplifts and rejuvenates a tired mind. Exhaustion, fatigue, tension and tiredness all dissolve with the influence of lavender.

VERVAIN

Vervain is a natural nerve tonic which helps to heal depression, depletion and powerlessness. Known sometimes as 'the divine herb of grace', its influence on the mind is generally liberating and uplifting. Excellent for you first thing in the morning.

BORAGE

This restores strength and clarity to a flagging mind. It is good for migraine and headaches, and also for depression, dejection and sadness.

BALM

Balm helps to cool, calm and collect the nerves of your body, and can also help to restore the order and harmony of your mind. It heals the stomach, harmonizes the mind, and assures deep, restful sleep. It is a marvellous cleanser which may promote copious perspiration.

ION THERAPY

Every expression of nature is created and supported by a universal dance of order and harmony. Even the air we breathe has its own unique harmony. First there is the gaseous harmony of nitrogen, oxygen, argon, carbon dioxide and many smaller proportions of other gases, together with variable amounts of water vapour. Then there is the electrical harmony, for the air around us is composed of a large number of electrically neutral gas molecules and also a smaller number of electrically positive and electrically negative molecules. These splendid gaseous and electrical harmonies of the air support all life upon our planet, including you.

Modern science has found that the harmony between the electrically negative and electrically positive molecules in the air varies according to location, and that the arrangement and harmony of these molecules has a profound affect and bearing on our own harmony and well-being. In particular, it has been found that a depletion in electrically negative molecules, called negative ions, can seriously hinder your health, impede your general performance and leave you vulnerable to stress.

Negative ions are natural cleansing agents that help to control the quality of the air around you, keeping it fresh, charged and alive. A full supply of negative ions in the air can help you to feel fresh, alert, invigorated, happy and optimistic, and generally can enhance your health and well-being. On the other hand, too many positive ions can make you feel tired and irritable, heavy and jaded, and generally depleted and worn through.

While modern scientific methods confirm that serious negative ion depletion can be harmful to the human condition, it has also identified humans as the major cause of negative ion depletion. For example, in a wholly natural environment, such as near a waterfall, running stream, forest, hilltop, or mountain range, the number of negative ions in the air can be as many as 40,000 per cubic centimetre. This compares with as little as 40 per cubic centimetre in man-made environments, such as in an office or home located in an affluent and effluent busy city dwelling – filled with its TV sets, computers, telephones, fluorescent lighting and air-conditioning systems, and submerged and drowning in urban smog, industrial waste and numerous other polluting agents.

Many illnesses and symptoms of stress are thought to be caused or aggravated by negative ion depletion. These include hay fever, bronchitis, catarrh, influenza, asthma, migraines, depression, fatigue, exhaustion and anxiety. Mood swings, emotional fragility and poor mental performance have also been linked to negative ion depletion. 'Weather-sensitive people', whose performance seems to be linked to the quality of the weather, may also find they suffer from negative ion depletion (see the section on Light Therapy, below).

Increasing your exposure to negative ions during stressful times can have a practical, therapeutic effect. One solution is to buy an ionizer, which is designed to pump out negative ions. Ionizers have been found to be effective in helping to clean the air of smoke, dust, bacteria and pollen. They can also have a very profound effect on your mental disposition, helping you to feel happier, freer, more optimistic and more positive. Most health shops now stock ionizers. There are many brands which differ in power and effectiveness, so choose wisely and be careful not to opt just for the cheapest.

Natural solutions to the problem include spending time in places where negative ions are rich and prolific, such as by a waterfall or a river, in a green forest, at the seaside, in a nice stretch of countryside, a park, or on the village green, or on a mountain range or hilltop. While you are there, if you take the time to perform relaxed breathing, meditation or any other enjoyable relaxation practice, the benefits to you will increase a hundred-fold.

TEMPERATURE THERAPY

Temperature can alter the balance of your moods, your thoughts, your feelings and your general well-being. An awareness of body temperature and of room temperature can, therefore, be a very useful antidote to stress, and a useful aid for relaxation.

The extremities of the body, such as your hands and your feet, can become very cold during the stress response. This is because your circulation often decides to concentrate blood on those organs and systems that best help to prepare for 'fight or flight'. A tense, stressful and demanding day can often, therefore, leave you feeling uncomfortably cold, tingly or numb, particularly around the hands and feet.

Uncomfortably cold body temperatures are often a cause as well as a symptom of stress. Feeling the cold can cause your muscles to tense and to tighten throughout your whole body. Coldness can put your nerves on ice, inhibit deep and healthy breathing, force uncomfortable and unhealthy postures, put pressure on the circulation and the heart, and may leave you generally unable to relax, release and let go.

Chronic stress can sometimes lead to a circulatory disorder known as Reynaud's disease. Common symptoms of

Reynaud's disease include severe sensations of pins and needles, constantly cold hands and feet, a bluish, pale complexion, persistent muscle tension and nervous exhaustion. Many people live with these symptoms for much of their lives, unaware that the symptoms are manifestations of a potentially serious lack of harmony.

When the body feels cold, the mind feels cold also. As a result, your thinking can become tense, rigid and frozen. Concentration may also be difficult, as all your efforts and energies are either distracted by or dealing with counteracting the coldness. You may, therefore, feel less well disposed and charitable to others. In other words, you may fail to be warm to people, to their presence and to their ideas. Everything becomes an effort, a problem, or a nuisance, and all because you feel so generally uncomfortable.

Many of the most popular relaxation techniques and traditions, such as meditation, creative visualization, breath therapy, hypnotherapy and autogenics, use exercises that are designed to promote feelings of warmth throughout your entire body. This increased warmth is the result of a conscious and direct control of your circulation system, and can help very much to soothe, to comfort and to relax your body, thereby restoring a happier health and harmony.

Feeling too warm can also create stress, particularly mental and emotional stress. A stifling or muggy warmth can leave you feeling sluggish, heavy, drowsy, tired and even a little irritable. You may feel low and lethargic, lack motivation and willpower, be unable to concentrate well, fail to muster any creative or inspired thought, and you may experience gloomy, depressed and pessimistic tendencies.

Opening up a window or turning the heating down whenever you feel too warm are simple, obvious remedies that can help to wake you up and to stir up the lifeforce within you. They can also help to invigorate you, enliven you and generally freshen you up. Your concentration, energy, will, drive, determination, optimism and creativity may all be restored in a matter of moments.

Either way, a slight variation in body temperature or room temperature can create dramatic changes in your own inner harmony and balance. Our appreciation and understanding of the effects of temperature for health and for performance is by and large restricted to the files of our unconscious minds. We describe people as 'cold-(or warm-) hearted', 'warm and relaxed' and 'hot and bothered', for instance, but we often fail to see that these metaphors may have basis in fact. Making this connection may be an invaluable aid for helping you to control your own inner harmony and even your temper.

LIGHT THERAPY

The majority of us spend the most of our daytimes indoors, investing large amounts of time either leaning over a desk, bending over a kitchen sink or glued in front of a television. Indeed, many days can pass before we decide to expose ourselves to a few moments of natural daylight and sun-energy. In the winter months, the commuter, for instance, goes to work too early and arrives home too late to know what his or her front garden looks like. Such a way of life is characteristic of modern living, and brings with it certain new modern-day stresses, such as a lack of true, natural daylight.

The lighting we rely upon from incandescent bulbs and fluorescent tubing is more of a dim orange-yellow colour than natural daylight. Because we adapt and cope so well, we sometimes forget to register just how yellow and orange the lighting in our homes and our offices really is. Take a look, now, with a fresh pair of eyes, at a bulb in your home or office and remind yourself just how yellow and dim it is.

One of the most serious consequences of living with

artificial light is that some of us are particularly susceptible to a form of stress called SAD, which stands for Seasonally Affected Depression or Seasonally Affected Disorder. SAD is a type of depression prevalent in the long, dark winter months, when the levels of natural daylight and natural sun-energy are naturally low. Although certain people are more susceptible to SAD than others, we are, all of us, affected by SAD to some degree.

Light is a most vital source of natural nourishment. The genius of your mind and your body has designed and evolved a system which allows light to be absorbed not only by your eyes but also by your skin and by the whole of your being. The amount of light you receive and the quality of that light support the healthy functioning of your cells, glands and organs, all of which, in turn, help to promote and to secure the harmony and balance of your mind, body and spirit.

Depression, fatigue, lethargy, exhaustion, anxiety, migraines, unbearable tension headaches, and a general sense of depletion and powerlessness may all be aggravated by a lack of natural daylight. We should all make a point, then, of ensuring we step outside each day for a few moments at least for a top-up of natural sun-energy and daylight.

Ancient healers understood the importance of natural light. They worshipped the sun as a god whose rays of light carried powers of healing and rejuvenation. Patients who were fit enough were taken out to pick their own medicinal herbs, not because the doctors were lazy, but so that the patients could enjoy the fresh air, the daylight and the sun-energy. Also, the architecture of ancient Greek and Asian healing temples, for instance, was often designed to allow as much light as possible to flood in and fill every area.

Modern science has come up with its own solution to a lack of natural light, called full-spectrum lighting. The Philips Daylight Blue bulb and Sungro-light bulbs are two examples of full-spectrum lighting which have been designed to filter out the excess yellows and oranges of normal light bulbs so as to produce a whiter, cleaner and more natural light which more closely resembles daylight.

Research has shown – particularly in Scandinavia and in other countries of Europe – that many people who have converted to this full-spectrum lighting have felt generally much better for it. We should always remember that no matter how sophisticated and independent we think we are, we are supported by and dependent upon the simple laws and natural grace of Mother Nature. Failure to acknowledge and to live by these laws leads to many forms of stress.

COLOUR-FULL LIVING

Colour consciousness is a search, an adventure. It is losing ourselves to find ourselves again. It is the most beautiful thing we will ever do in our lives.
Lilla Bek and Annie Wilson, *What Colour are You?*

It is the energy that we call light, and the many expressions of light that we call colour, that breathe life into the world and that enrich and enhance the quality of life. Many of the well-established and respected medical traditions of our world have long recognized and worked with the therapeutic properties of light and colour. The medicine chiefs of the Native Americans, the acupuncturists of the Orient, the Yogis of India, and the herbal specialists of Tibet are but a few examples. They all believed, quite simply, that a world devoid of colour would be a world devoid of life.

The research and practice of many modern psychologists, and also modern colour healers, confirm a recent renewed interest in the healing potential of light and of colour. The Luscher colour test, for example, is a well-known modern psychological test that uses colour choice to identify and to diagnose personality traits. There are several versions of the test, one of which involves choosing eight colours. The order of choice and the colours chosen are the two clues as to the predominant mood and harmonies (or dissonances) of a person.

The marketeers and the world of advertising have also been quick to investigate and to utilize the pleasing power of light and colour to help influence and manipulate the moods of their potential customers. It is now commonly accepted that the success of a product depends for the most part on the colour and the arrangement of colours found on the packaging, and not necessarily on what is contained inside. Colours attract interest; interest attracts desire.

Interior designers, textile and clothing manufacturers, political parties, environmentalists, charities, medical associations, hospital administrators, prison administrators and large multi-national and industrial groups are also conscious more than ever of the important, influential role of colour in helping to further their own particular causes or aims.

Each colour of the rainbow is an expression and mani-festation of light. What makes each one different is its individual rate of vibration. The retina within our eye can only see light and colours within a wavelength range, or spectrum, of about 410 nanometers (nm) to about 770 nm. Red, for example, has the longest wavelength – between 630 nm and 770 nm – and therefore has the heaviest and slowest rate of vibration in the spectrum. Violet has the shortest wavelength – between 410 nm and 440 nm – and therefore has the quickest rate of vibration in the spectrum.

We do not just experience light and colours with our eyes, but 'see' them with our whole body. Physicists and biologists have confirmed what ancient medicine always knew to be true, that all forms of matter, including the human body, are essentially vibration. Therefore, each time a person meets a different colour it is as if two great seas of vibration mingle and merge, each influencing the other. And because the whole body reacts to the vibration of a colour, the cells, tissues, glands and organs of the body are all affected in some way.

The specific therapeutic benefit and value of a colour upon a person is governed by certain conditions. These are:

- the colour's saturation and purity,
- its brightness and shade,
- the amounts of the colour we see and experience around us,
- the length of time we are exposed to a particular colour,
- the number of times we are exposed to a particular colour,
- the quality of our attentiveness and concentration, and
- the quality of our relaxation.

Red, for instance, is claimed by colour healers to cleanse the blood, build up red corpuscles, and help to stimulate a sluggish mental alacrity. Orange activates the adrenal glands and can be particularly useful for certain forms of stress. Green stimulates the pituitary and thymus endocrine glands. Blue boosts metabolism and helps alleviate insomnia and exhaustion. Violet is claimed to be very good for assuaging migraines and headaches.

Every day of your life you make creative choices of colour. A conscious consideration of and appreciation for the therapeutic properties of colour can help to 'colour' your day in so many ways. Colours can calm, pacify and relax; they can energize, activate and invigorate. Colours are comforting, consoling and pleasing. They can heal, uplift, restore and balance. Colours speak, to those who are ready to listen.

Colour and Personality

We are attracted to colours either because they represent how we see ourselves or because they possess something we need.

RED

An active, hot and dynamic energy. Outgoing, extroverted and social. A colour for the competitive and ambitious. Essentially a physical colour. Indicates someone with a strong physical will, leadership and magnetism; a hard worker and a self-motivator.

ORANGE

Extroverted, energetic and magnetic. Orange stimulates the adrenal glands, and 'orange people' love to play sports and generally keep themselves aroused. Orange shares many of the qualities of red, coupled with intuitive and sensitive emotional qualities. People who love orange also love food!

YELLOW

Intelligent, discriminates well, evaluates well and learns quickly. Has a good grasp of fundamentals and a concrete knowledge of many subjects. Happy, optimistic, well-disciplined and can always bounce back. Likes to entertain and always enjoys good stimulation.

GREEN

A colour of harmony, order and balance. A person who is at peace with him- or herself and with others and the environment. Practical and creative; loyal and faithful; makes time to work and time to play. Much better at group and family situations than are red, orange or yellow people. Obvious links to nature and the natural life.

BLUE

A communicator, particularly through speech. Links well with people. A cool colour. Calm and assured. Appreciates balance and order. A creative flair also. Essentially, a reliable colour with enough freedom to express unique and individual talents.

VIOLET

Linked to creativity and to healing. A calm, pacifying and comforting ray. An appreciation for beauty, art, creativity and also music. A person who is interested more in the philosophy of life than in a day-to-day wage. Excellent intuition, imagination and sixth-sense.

WHITE

Represents purity, cleanliness and also perfection. A tidy, orderly and neat person. As the highest expression of colour (pure white light being the combination of all the other colours in the spectrum), it points to realization, essence, and complete integration. A desire to hold ranks with the elite.

Colour Association and Bias

Colour association and colour bias are two other important factors that can influence the potential effects of colour upon a person. If we associate green with the car we had a crash in, or with the horrible foods we were always forced to eat when we were young, then maybe we won't allow the therapeutic properties of green to work for us. And if we have a bias against the colour violet (often a very therapeutic colour for stress sufferers) then it is unlikely that we will allow violet to help us soothe and alleviate our stress. Very often the reason we are biased about a colour has to do with some kind of inner stress.

There are, generally speaking, two underlying reasons why we may be attracted to a colour. The first is that we may feel, consciously or unconsciously, we 'need' the colour to create balance or harmony within ourselves. The second is that we use the colour, again consciously or unconsciously, to accentuate an already existing imbalance. It is very important that you try to assess the motive and reasoning behind every colour choice you make.

Colour consciousness is one more route to the goal of greater self-knowledge. The better equipped we are with this essential knowledge, the easier we will find it is to be kinder to ourselves, to control and to manage ourselves, and to discover and to realize our true, innate potential and happiness. Colour-full living can improve our capacity to cope.

YOGA THERAPY

The word 'yoga' is derived from the ancient Asian language called Sanskrit. It serves both as a name and aim of a particular way of life, and means 'union', 'peace', or 'inner harmony'. Yoga has been practised in the East for over 6,000 years as a physical, psychological and philosophical discipline, but it has only been over the last three or four decades that yoga has begun to enjoy popular acclaim in the West, where it is now widely recommended and used by many members of the medical profession and general public.

The effectiveness of yoga as an antidote and cure for physical and mental stress is based on the astonishing intuitive knowledge of the yogis of ancient times who taught anatomy, physiology and psychology. Throughout the centuries a number of different branches of yoga have been devised so as to accommodate a variety of approaches and techniques for treating illness, for maintaining health and for developing the human potential. Although the approaches and techniques are all different, they are dedicated to the same original aim, of union and wholeness through inner harmony and control.

PRANAYAMA YOGA

This identifies poor breath control as the principal cause of illness and stress. The yogic art and science of breathing is now a popular study and practice in the West – its relevance as a health aid has increased especially since the advent of widespread cases of hyperventilation syndrome (breathing that is too rapid and shallow) throughout the West.

RAJA YOGA

This method states that poor mind control is the underlying cause of all illness and stress symptoms. Concentration, contemplation and meditation exercises are prescribed so as to help restore strength, agility, a positive outlook and immunity to negative and unhealthy thought-patterns. Western psychotherapists and psychologists now commonly use and teach Raja yoga techniques in their work.

BHAKTI YOGA

This theory describes stress as a symptom of a lack of love for the world as a whole, for the people in our lives and, in particular, for ourselves. The route to harmony and wholeness requires unconditional love, respect and reverence for all life, everywhere, including for ourselves.

KARMA YOGA

This is the study and practice of work, action and behaviour in the world. It involves an understanding of the Law of Cause and Effect, the Law of Like attracts Like, and all other laws which if properly understood can be manipulated for positive effect. Failure to understand these laws is a most common cause of stress and illness.

GNANI YOGA

Gnani yoga is the study of knowledge and wisdom, particularly self-knowledge and self-wisdom. The words of the Greek philosopher, Pythagoras, 'There is no illness, only ignorance', sum up the principal belief of this approach to balance and order. With self-knowledge we can attain self-control, and thereby experience self-realization.

Hatha Yoga

This is undoubtedly the most popular of all the yogas to come to the West. It is a branch of yoga which seeks union, harmony and wholeness for the entire being through physical exercise. Although each of the different branches of yoga are separate in theory, they are, in truth, interconnected and united in practice. Hatha yoga is, therefore, a therapeutic multi-discipline which may combine the breath control of Pranayama yoga, the mental agility of Raja yoga, the discipline of Karma yoga, and the reverence and awareness of both Bhakti yoga and Gnani yoga, to help prevent and relieve the causes and symptoms of dis-order and dis-ease.

The exercises of Hatha yoga are called *asanas*, or postures or holds. Like Western exercise disciplines, each asana is based on a stretch; unlike Western exercise disciplines, though, the body is held immobile for a certain period of time once the hold has been achieved, during which the student concentrates the mind, relaxes the body and performs deep, rhythmic breathing, all of which can help to enhance the benefits particular to each hold.

TEN PRINCIPAL BENEFITS OF A HATHA YOGA SESSION

1. *A relaxed body and tranquil mind*. A Hatha yogi learns to balance effort and ease, and thereby strengthens both the ability to relax and to perform well. A well-exercised mind and body promote a well-relaxed mind and body.

2. *Vitality.* Profound relaxation together with well-controlled movement has a precise effect on the muscles, nerves, organs and endocrine glands of your body, all of which help you to enhance and to regulate your body's energy systems. Your mind can enjoy the benefits of being calm, clear and alert.

3. *Suppleness.* Regular yoga exercise keeps your mind and body supple, flexible, well poised, and better able to cope with the demands and pressures of life. One reason for this is the profound degree of relaxation you can achieve.

4. *Better breath control.* Every Hatha yoga asana requires deep, relaxed, rhythmic and well-co-ordinated breath control. The energy of the air, referred to as *prana*, is the energy that creates and supports every manifestation of life within you and around you.

5. *Improved mental performance.* Yoga can help strengthen concentration, develop creativity, improve perception, support problem-solving and decision-making, enhance mental relaxation, and help sustain mental vitality and vigour. Many business experts make it their business to practise yoga.

6. *Greater emotional stability.* So many Western psychotherapists have been impressed with the emotionally therapeutic benefits of yoga that they now use yoga techniques in their work. The harmony of yoga works throughout the whole of you. A calm body and calm mind inspire calm emotions.

7. *Internal massage.* The combination of movement, relaxation and deep breathing helps to create a form of internal massage action. In particular, the organs of your chest and abdomen region are carefully and thoroughly soothed and stimulated.

8. *Improved health.* Allergies, asthma, pain, anxiety, arthritis, migraine, insomnia, poor posture, high blood-pressure, digestive illnesses, endocrine deficiencies and

lung infections are just a few of the conditions that medical research has found benefit from yoga.

9. *Weight control.* Although yoga has none of the pain and exhaustion of many modern exercise methods, it is acknowledged as one of the most healthy and effective methods of realistic, long-term weight control.

10. *Youthfulness.* Yoga has often been acclaimed for its remarkable effect on the ageing process. The secret appears to be linked to the complete and utter emphasis on the exercise and relaxation of the spine – described as the axis of life by ancient yogis. A glowing and healthy complexion, bright eyes, supple and smooth skin, and physical and mental poise are among the well-documented benefits of yoga.

Hatha yoga concentrates on the whole person. Every position has been designed, therefore, to exercise and to relax specific muscle groups, to soothe and to tone certain nerves, to develop and to improve body circulation, to stimulate and to massage vital internal organs, and to regulate and to control particular endocrine glands. This emphasis on the whole person, rather than on specific symptoms of illness, is the main reason, say its exponents, why yoga can be so effective at achieving health, harmony and wholeness for you.

Hatha Yoga Exercise Routine

Hatha yoga should be performed in loose clothing and at least two hours after eating. The following routine should be performed in sequence so that the benefits specific to each asana can complement one another. Each asana should be held for approximately ten seconds at first, and performed for a total of three times. Each asana should also be practised with full attention and awareness, and accompanied by a long, deep and even breathing pattern.

HANDS-TO-FEET ASANA

Stand upright, hands at your sides, with your head, neck, shoulders and spine aligned. Inhale and stretch your arms over your head. Exhale and bend forward at the waist, taking your hands to your feet and tucking your head as far as possible towards your knees. Hold this position and breathe freely. Ensure your legs are not bent at the knees.

This asana encourages blood to flow and to feed your brain, your scalp and your facial tissues. It extends and flexes your spine, tightens and firms your stomach, aids digestion, strengthens your knees and stretches your leg muscles.

TRIANGLE ASANA

Stand upright with your feet 2 to 3 ft (60 to 90 cm) apart. Stretch your arms out to your sides, shoulder height, palms facing down. Inhale and turn your right foot out 90 degrees and your left foot in 45 degrees. As you exhale, bend over and down towards your right foot, keeping both your arms outstretched to the sides. Touch your right ankle or knee with your right hand, and point your left hand upright towards the ceiling, palm facing forward. Hold and breathe freely. Repeat on the left-hand side.

This asana exercises your hips, manipulates your back muscles, massages your spine, tones your nervous system, strengthens the sides of your body, encourages good posture, expands your chest and tones your abdominal organs.

TREE ASANA

Stand upright with your feet together. Balance on your right foot. Inhale as you grasp your left foot with your left hand and tuck it into your left buttock. At the same time, stretch your right hand up towards the ceiling. Breathe freely. Ensure your knees are touching, that your right arm rests against your right ear, and that your right palm is facing forward. Repeat with your right foot.

This asana stretches your spine and strengthens your back, improves posture, exercises your legs, tones your stomach, encourages physical and mental balance and acts as a harmonizer for your mind and your emotions.

THE SPINAL ROCK

Lie down on the floor on your back with your arms to the side. Inhale as you tuck your knees in over your stomach, and then clasp them with both hands. Tuck your head up to your knees and begin to rock gently, breathing out as you rock back and breathing in as you rock forward. Perform this for 30 seconds. *Do not perform this exercise if you have a bad back.*

This is not strictly an asana. It helps, though, to massage your spine, tone your nervous system, loosen up your back muscles, exercise your stomach and abdominal organs, aid digestion, strengthen your lungs and stretch and exercise your neck.

HEAD-TO-KNEE ASANA I

Sit with your buttocks resting on your heels and your knees together. Breathe in and stretch your arms up above your head. Breathe out as you bend forward, resting your forehead on the ground before your knees. Your arms should swing back as you bend forward so that your hands settle next to your feet.

This asana promotes deep and profound relaxation. It encourages a flow of blood to your head, lengthens your spine, soothes your nervous system, massages your abdominal organs and creates rest for your neck.

HEAD-TO-KNEE ASANA II

Lie down on the floor on your back. Raise and stretch your arms over your head. As you inhale, tuck your chin into your chest, bringing your arms and back up off the floor. Exhale as you reach forward, taking your head towards your knees and your hands towards your feet. Breathe freely as you hold this asana. Ensure your legs are fully stretched and not bent at the knees.

This particular asana is a most wonderful hold in that it exercises just about every muscle in your body. It also strengthens your spine, tones your nervous system, opens up your back, strengthens your knees and legs, firms your waistline and massages all the organs of your abdominal region.

COBRA ASANA

Lie down on the floor on your front with your hands resting either side of your face, palms down. As you breathe in, push your chin and forehead away from your body, up, and then back. As you do this arch your back and straighten your arms so that your chest rises from the floor. The position should resemble that of a cobra about to strike. Hold your breath for as long as you hold the asana. Breathe out as you return to the starting position. Ensure that your forehead points towards the ceiling, and that the small of your back is well stretched. You must be particularly careful with this asana if you have a weak back or impaired spine.

The Cobra asana is excellent for improving posture. It also stimulates your thyroid and adrenal glands, quickens metabolism, boosts vital energy, exercises your spine, tones your nervous system, strengthens your lower back and firms your stomach.

MOUNTAIN ASANA

Sit cross-legged on the floor with your hands beside your knees, palms facing upwards. As you breathe in, raise your arms up and allow your palms to meet over the top of your head. Breathe freely while you hold the asana. Ensure that your arms, elbows, wrists and fingers are held firm and straight at all times.

The Mountain asana opens out your chest, pins your shoulders back, helps make your spine supple, firms your stomach, strengthens your neck, tones your arm muscles and improves posture.

CORPSE ASANA

A good yoga routine should begin and end with your body feeling relaxed. Lie down on your back, with arms resting at your sides. Consciously work through the body, breathing through any tension so as to ensure both body and mind are settled and at peace. You will then be refreshed and relaxed and ready to get on with your day.

THE POWER OF PRAYER

Prayer is the most powerful form of energy one can generate. The influence on the human mind and body is as demonstrable as that of the secreting of glands. Prayer is a force as real as terrestrial gravity. It supplies us with a flow of sustaining power in our daily lives.

Alexis Carrel, French biologist and Nobel Prize Winner

One of the most fascinating medical explorations of the potential therapeutic powers of prayer was conducted by Dr Randy Byrd, a San Francisco cardiologist and former Assistant Professor of Medicine at the University of California. The results of his double-blind randomized study were published in *The Medical Tribune* in the US on January 8th, 1986: 393 coronary care unit patients at San Francisco General Hospital were arranged into a group of 192 patients who were prayed for by members of various prayer groups, and a group of 201 patients who were not prayed for. The prayer groups were Protestant, Catholic and Jewish organizations operating in different locations throughout the whole of the US. Both groups of patients were comparable in terms of age and the severity of their medical conditions.

The results showed that the subjects who were prayed for suffered fewer complications in three ways: only 3 required antibiotics, compared to 16 of the control group; only 6 suffered pulmonary edema (inflammation and excessive fluids around heart and lungs), compared to 18 of those who were not the objects of prayer; and none of those prayed for required intubation (insertion of a tube into hollow organs, such as the trachea, as a method of treatment) compared to 12 of the others, who did require intubation.

This report is only one of more than 150 controlled medical trials which have demonstrated the effects of the power of prayer on stimulating growth and altering the chemical balance of water, enzymes, cells *in vitro*, yeasts, bacteria, plants, animals and humans. Prayer would seem, therefore, to be a direct communication with God, or at the very least a natural and most powerful form of positive thinking, affirmation, therapy and healing which is subject, like any other action, to the Law of Cause and Effect and the Law of Attraction. Perhaps it is both!

The anthropologist, philosopher, theologian, psychologist and layperson all fail to agree on a common definition of prayer. This is perhaps not too surprising when one considers the inestimable number of methods and techniques of prayer, which include spiritual healing, confession, bene-diction, invocation, text prayer, inspirational prayer, arrow prayers (made up on the spur of the moment in times of immediate need), meditation, mudra (signs made with the hands during prayer), hymns, song and dance.

The often acknowledged 'affirmation power' of prayer makes praying a very powerful psychological act. There is certainly no shortage of testimonies to the power of prayer in life. Here are three powerful, irrevocable attestations:

The spectacle of a nation praying is more awe-inspiring than the explosion of an atomic bomb. The force of prayer is greater than any possible combination of man-controlled powers, because prayer is man's greatest means of trapping the infinite resources of God.

Herbert Hoover, 31st President of the United States

Let the Divine Mind flow through your own mind, and you will be happier. I have found the greatest power in the world in the power of prayer. There is no shadow of doubt of that. I speak from my own experience.

Cecil B. DeMille, American film director

And Samuel Taylor Coleridge, British poet and philosopher, once described prayer as, 'the very highest energy of which the mind is capable'.

A prayer is a bit like a battery: it needs to be charged regularly before it can begin to discharge energy to you. Like all affirmations, the power of prayer is conditioned by the power and conviction of our performance. Certainly the more you use a prayer the more it begins to resonate within you, the more it means to you, the more you believe in it and the more, therefore, it can then begin to work for you.

While you should not rule out instant return from your prayers, it is sensible to expect that it is a disciplined, attentive and consistent approach that works most often. We should not make the mistake of Huckleberry Finn, who, in a passage from *The Adventures of Huckleberry Finn*, tells us,

Miss Watson she took me in the closet and prayed, but nothing come of it. She told me to pray every day, and whatever I asked for I would get it. But it warn't so. I tried it. Once I got a fish-line, but no hooks. It warn't any good to me without hooks. I tried for the hooks three or four times, but somehow I couldn't make it work. By and by,

*one day, I asked Miss Watson to try for me, but she said
I was a fool. She never told me why, and I couldn't make
it out no way.*

The prayer of St Francis of Assisi is a beautifully worded
exposition which is as much a healing teaching as it is a
healing exercise. Each line is a powerful mental and spiritual
affirmation particularly helpful to the stressed and confused
mind.

Lord make me an instrument of thy peace;
Where there is hate that I may bring love,
Where there is offence that I may bring pardon,
Where there is discord that I may bring union,
Where there is error that I may bring truth,
Where there is doubt that I may bring faith,
Where there is despair that I may bring hope,
Where there is darkness that I may bring light,
Where there is sadness that I may bring joy:

O Master, make me not so much to be consoled as to console;
Not so much to be loved as to love;
Not so much to be understood as to understand;
For it is in giving that one receives;
It is in self-forgetfulness that one finds;
It is in pardoning that one is pardoned;
It is in dying that one finds eternal life.

Prayer can perhaps be described as a spiritual psychology – a
psychology that allows the person who prays to escape the
clutches of the limited, often confusing world of ego, and
thereby to enter for a time the spiritual retreat of the soul.
Once bathed in this light, a person receives healing. Clarity
of mind, profound peace, intimate awareness, less anxiety,
belief in oneself, high creativity, abundant energy, inspir-

ation, love, the courage to continue – these are just some of the reported benefits of a heart-felt prayer.

PET FACILITATED THERAPY

Animals deal in only two types of relationships, the no-frills relationship and the no-conditions relationship. The no-frills relationship makes for a very refreshing change because it happens without any of the sophisticated deceit, innuendo and general confusion found in many human relationships. With a cat, for instance, the relationship is most direct, and you know exactly where you stand. There is no doubt whatsoever. If you are out of order, you will know about it. If the food is good, you will be informed of it. If the fire is out, only then will your cat tolerate sitting on your lap.

The no-conditions relationship is based upon seven simple, lovely words: 'I love you because you are you.' Dogs are often adept at this type of relationship. They are obedient for the sake of obedience, they forgive, they forget, they are not judgemental, and they very often show amazing tolerance. As the novelist George Eliot once wrote, 'Animals are such agreeable friends – they ask no questions, they pass no criticisms.'

Whatever the type of relationship, perhaps the main reason why animals can be such a great source of joy to us is that, whether they believe it or not, they need us. Being needed often helps us to respond at our best. We can afford to laugh, to play and to enjoy their company because we know where we stand and we know most often what they are thinking (or at least feel that we do). A relationship with an animal holds little or none of the threats of a human relationship. The rewards may not be as great as those in a human relationship, but then, there are many who would refute even this.

Animals often specialize in relationships of touch. Of all

the human senses, touch is often the most isolated, deprived and under-nourished. To touch, to stroke, to hold and to play with another living being, animal or human, can be a truly healing, uplifting and regenerating experience. As Tennessee Williams once wrote, 'Devils can be driven out of the heart by the touch of a hand on a hand.' Animals teach us that touch is a truly universal language which, when practised, can help us to heal.

The healers of ancient Greece, Rome, Babylon, Persia and Tibet all purposely employed animals in their healing temples to help stimulate and encourage the healing process of their patients. The animals were put there to supply, exchange and facilitate love. Even many thousands of years ago, medicine was under no illusion that love is one of the greatest healing forces in the universe.

Today, animals are being introduced into the hospital wards, for example at Warwickshire County Hospital. The doctors and nurses have been surprised and greatly encouraged by what they have witnessed there. A rheumatic old lady, for instance, will spring to life when a little terrier dog appears. A confused and forgetful old man will suddenly display tremendous recall when he talks of a budgie, and a frightened and lonely child will open up and reach out when he or she touches, talks and plays with a cat on the ward. What is truly fascinating is that the animal will very often show an understanding of exactly why he or she is there. Animals heal!

Perhaps the most romantic of all the animal healers is the dolphin, who for thousands and thousands of years has displayed amazing powers of communication with and love for humans. Dr Horace Dobbs has devoted his life to studying dolphins. His work has been the focus of a number of television documentaries, radio programmes, books and magazine features. One important part of his work he called 'Operation Sunflower'. He took people with different experiences of depression to Dingle Bay in Ireland to meet and to play with a wild dolphin called Dorad. The results were nothing short of life-transforming.

One person who visited Dorad described her experience of healing and transformation in a very moving account published by the healing journal *Caduceus*. She wrote:

Dorad approached me from behind and below. Slowly and gently he nudged my feet, then my knees, then my stomach, and then he swam up to within six inches of my face. Turning to the side to look into my face with one eye he then gazed deliberately into my eyes. There was nowhere to hide. This wild creature was looking not at my body nor even at my expression, but right at the pain in my soul. I am sure now that a wild dolphin in the icy waters of Dingle Bay located my anguish as no human being could.

No matter how much I try to assess the experience of meeting a dolphin in his natural, wild, free state, I cannot define where the importance of it lay. Sometimes I think that the significance which I felt as this beautiful creature chose to swim with me was precisely that: because he was free in the sea; for him to be with me was obviously from choice. I could not do anything impressive or interesting to warrant his attention, yet there was something about me which was apparently worth his time. My sense of self-esteem was so low that to suddenly feel special, and especially without doing anything to earn it, was a poignant and very powerful moment.

Meeting Dorad was the first step on the way to a recovery which I now feel capable and sure of making. Of course I still get depressed from time to time. I would by lying if I did not admit that occasionally a low feels interminable, but those around me know that I can be happy. To be reminded of my time underwater in an environment without words, but one shared by that joyful, free creature, is enough to ease me back to a position from which I can continue to make an effort. Dorad taught me how to look at and truly face my pain. The experience was one of mutual and unconditional love and trust which perhaps only another intelligent species like the dolphin can provide. We must be humble enough to learn.

LOVE THERAPY

In the final analysis we must love in order not to fall ill.
Sigmund Freud

The important medicinal role love plays in combating stress, disease and illness is becoming better appreciated and is implemented more and more often by health professionals and patients alike. The pioneering work of love as healer, as portrayed in modern classics such as *Being Loving is Being Healthy* (Fowler & Co., 1987) by the healer and counsellor, Paul Lambillion, *Love is Letting Go of Fear* (Celestial Arts, 1979) by the American psychiatrist, Gerald G. Jampolsky, and *Love, Medicine and Miracles* (Rider, 1986) and *Peace, Love and Healing* (Rider, 1989) by the American surgeon, Bernie Siegel, have all made a valuable impact on the modern developments of medicine and health care.

So many of the common manifestations of stress in our world either originate from or are aggravated by a lack of appreciation, value and love, both for others and for ourselves. Often, it is the lack of self-love which is the most damaging and most profoundly serious malady. Can we truly love another if we have not yet learned to love ourselves? Creative, loving relationships help a person to evolve, to express and to experience a greater sense of completion, of wholeness and of individual fulfilment. Love is connection; love is the provider.

On the days when we can accept ourselves for who we are, when we feel reasonably good and confident about ourselves and when we are happy and at peace within, the day-to-day stresses assume their true proportions and are often relatively easy to deal with. Self-acceptance and self-worth, understanding and forgiveness, trust and a freedom from fear, and all those other things that add up to contentment and fulfilment, are so much easier to attain when we can live easily with ourselves.

THE PHILOSOPHY OF LOVE MEDICINE

1. *Love is the energy of life.* Rather than an emotion, a feeling, or a sickness, love is best defined as a universal lifeforce, available in abundance to all who reach out and to all who reach in. A world without love is impossible to imagine. Without love, perhaps there could be no life. Or, if there were life, it would hardly be worth living. As Robert Browning once wrote, 'Take away love and our earth is a tomb.'

2. *Love is a healer.* Love is the energy that holds the cells of our physical body together. It is also the most pure and most worthy expression of positive thinking, which is itself a healer. 'Love cures people – both the ones who give it and the ones who receive it,' wrote Carl Menninger.

3. *Love is unconditional.* Illness and stress are often the result of desires – a desire to own, to possess, to control and to have. Love is the exact opposite of desire. Love is unconditional. With love there is complete commitment, but no ties, no bonds and no limitation. Love is the Creator and love sets you free.

4. *Love is wisdom.* To understand is to love. Understanding yourself is fundamental to your health. Self-knowledge and self-awareness are the prerequisites for health and

harmony. Once again, the words of Pythagoras, 'There is no illness, only ignorance,' hold true.

5. *Love is union, love is harmony.* The use of love as a psychotherapeutic aid is essential, because, as the French philosopher Teilhard de Chardin wrote, 'Only love can bring individual beings to their perfect completion as individuals, because only love takes possession of them and unites them by what lies deepest within them.'

6. *Love is its own reward.* Love is such a powerful medicine because, like all things, it is subject to the wonderful, universal law of Cause and Effect, or, as Sir Issac Newton put it, the Laws of Action and Reaction are equal and opposite. In other words, love creates love; love receives love; and love facilitates love.

7. *What you love is what you are.* Or, as Johann Goethe said of love, 'We are shaped and fashioned by what we love.' Love is what you become; love is the power of generation and growth. Love shapes, forms and moulds you; love evolves, finishes and completes you.

8. *Illness is a teacher.* All illness, adversity, pain and grief are best treated not as punishments or tragedies but as lessons. They are lessons in self-understanding and in self-love. When the lesson is learned, or, at least accepted, you are left stronger, more complete, more whole and more healthy than before.

9. *Love is the lesson.* All forms of stress and illness are lessons in love. They are consequential symptoms of an absence or lack of love, either for yourself, for others or from others. See your stress, now, through a lens of love, and of understanding, and watch and be open for any new perceptions and for any new truth.

10. *You are love.* You are created by love, you are supported by love, and you are evolving through love. If you do your very best to live by love, love will live with you. This is the greatest truth of the philosophy of Love Medicine.

The quality of your relationship with the world will only be as good as the quality of your relationship with yourself. This is perhaps the essence of stress management. And if we are to love the world we must learn first to love ourselves. This involves, perhaps, learning to be patient and forgiving to ourselves, to accept and to appreciate ourselves, to value who we are as much as what we do, to enjoy and celebrate living for the sake of living and, above all, to understand and know ourselves well. Stress management begins with the lack of love and is complete only when there is a fullness of love.

USEFUL ADDRESSES

Stress Centres

'Stress Busters'
The Happiness Project
Elms Court
Chapel Way
Botley
Oxford OX2 9LP
Tel: 01865 244414
Fax: 01865 248825
Email: hello@happiness.co.uk
Website: www.happiness.co.uk

Care Assist Group Ltd
Wheatfield Way
Hinkley
Leics LE10 1YG
Tel: 0121 233-0202

Centre for Stress Management
156 Westcombe Hill
London SE3 7DH
Tel: 0181 853-1122

International Stress Management
　　Association
Division of Psychology
Southbank University
103 Borough Road
London SE1 0AA
Tel: 07000 780430
Fax: 01992 426673
Email: stress@isma.org.uk
Referral system for stress practitioners.

Stress Management Training
　　Institute (incorporating
　　Relaxation for Living)
Foxhills
30 Victoria Avenue
Shanklin
Isle of Wight PO37 6LS
Tel: 01983 868166

L.I.F.E. Foundation
Mind, Body, Heart Technology
Maristowe House
Dover Street
Bilston
West Midlands WV14 6AL
Tel: 01902 409164
*Courses on laughter, joy, healing
and holistic health.*

The Relaxation Room
41a Norfolk Road
Brighton BN1 3AB
Tel: 01273 321110

Stress Relief Programme
Comic Relief
74 New Oxford Street
London WC1A 1EF
Tel: 0171 436-1122
Fax: 0171 436-1541
Email: red@comicrelief.org.uk

Complementary Therapies

The British Holistic Medical
  Association
Rowland Thomas House
Royal Shrewsbury Hospital South
Shrewsbury
Shropshire SY3 8XF
Tel: 01743 261155

Institute for Complementary
  Medicine
PO Box 194
London SE16 1QZ
Tel: 0171 237-5165
*For a full register of
complementary therapists.*

Council for Complementary and
  Alternative Medicine
179 Gloucester Place
London NW1 6DX
Tel: 0171 724-9103
Fax: 0171 724-5330

Holistic Nurses Association
Royal Shrewsbury Hospital South
Mytton Oak Road
Shrewsbury
Shropshire SY3 8XF
Tel: 01743 242466

Acupuncture

British Acupuncture Association
  and Register
34 Alderney Street
London SW1V 4EU
Tel: 0171 834-1012

Aromatherapy

International Federation of
  Aromatherapists
Stamford House
2–4 Chiswick High Road
London W4 1TH
Tel: 0181 742-2605

International Society of
  Professional Aromatherapists
82 Ashby Road
Hinckley
Leics LE10 1SN
Tel: 01455 637987
Fax: 01455 890956

Bach Flower Therapy

Dr Bach Centre
Mount Vernon
Sotwell
Wallingford OX10 0PZ
Tel: 01491 834678

Biofeedback

Biomonitors Ltd
2 Old Garden Court
Mount Pleasant
St Albans
Herts AL3 4RQ
Tel/fax: 01727 833882

Chiropractic

The British Chiropractic
  Association
Blagrave House
17 Blagrave Street
Reading RG1 1QB
Tel: 0118 950-5950

McTimoney Chiropractic
  Association
21 High Street
Eynsham
Oxon OX8 1HE
Tel: 01865 880974

Herbalism

The National Institute of Medical
  Herbalists
56 Longbrook Street
Exeter EX4 6AH
Tel: 01392 426022

Homeopathy

British Homeopathic Association
27a Devonshire Street
London W1N 1RJ
Tel: 0171 935-2163

Hypnotherapy

National College of Hypnosis and
  Psychotherapy
12 Cross Street
Nelson
Lancs BB9 7EN
Tel: 01282 699378

Laughter Medicine

The Happiness Project
Elms Court
Botley
Oxford OX2 9LP
Tel: 01865 244414
Fax: 01865 248825

Massage

British Massage Therapy Council
Greenbank House
65a Adelphi Street
Preston PR1 7BH
Tel: 01772 881063

Osteopathy

British Osteopathic Association
8–10 Boston Place
London NW1 6QH
Tel: 0171 262-1128

Relaxation Music

New World Music Ltd
The Barn
Becks Green Common
St Andrew
Beccles NR34 8NB
Tel: 01986 781682

Yoga

The British Wheel of Yoga
1 Hamilton Place
Boston Road
Sleaford
Lincs NG34 7ES

Yoga for Health Foundation
Ickwell Bury
Nr Biggleswade
Beds SG18 9EF
Tel: 01767 627271

Relationship Stress

Asian Family Counselling Service
74 The Avenue
London W13 8LB
Tel: 0181 997-5749
Offers professional counselling and assistance.

Carers National Association
20–25 Glasshouse Yard
London EC1A 4JS
Tel: 0171 490-8818

CRUSE
Cruse House
126 Sheen Road
Richmond
Surrey TW9 1UR
Tel: 0181 940-4818
Bereavement care.

Family Welfare Association
501 Kingsland Road
Dalston
London E8 4AU
Tel: 0171 254-6251

Gingerbread
16–17 Clarkenwell Close
London EC1R 0AA
Tel: 0171 336-8183
Advice line: 0171 336-8184
Help for single parents.

Home Start UK
2 Salisbury Road
Leicester LE7 7QR
Tel: 0116 233-9955
Fax: 0116 233-0232

National Association of Widows
54–57 Allison Street
Digbeth
Birmingham B5 5TH
Tel: 0121 643-8348

National Council for One-Parent
    Families
255 Kentish Town Road
London NW5 2LX
Tel: 0171 267-1361

National Stepfamily Association
Chapel House
18 Hatton Place
London EC1N 8RU
Tel: 0171 209-2460
Helpline: 0990 168388

Parent Helpline
Endway House
Endway
Hadleigh
Essex SS7 2AN
Tel: 01702 559900
*Formerly OPUS – Organization
for Parents Under Stress. Look up
Parent Helpline in your local
telephone directory for the branch
nearest you.*

RELATE National
Herbert Gray College
Little Church Street
Rugby
Warwicks CV21 3AP
Tel: 01788 573241
*Formerly the Marriage Guidance
Council. Look up RELATE in your
local telephone directory.*

Women's Aid Federation England
PO Box 391
Bristol
BS99 7WS
Tel: 0117 944-4411

Child Stress

Childline
Freepost 1111
Nottingham NG1 1BR
Freephone 0800 1111

The Children's Society
Edward Rudolf House
Margery Street
London WC1X 0JL
Tel: 0171 837-4299
Fax: 0171 837-0211

Christian Lewis Trust
Child Care Centre
62 Walter Road
Swansea SA1 4PT
Tel: 01792 480500
Fax: 01792 480700
Caring for children with cancer.

Kidscape
152 Buckingham Palace Road
London SW1W 9TR
Helpline: 0171 730-3300 Mon
     and Wed

NSPCC
67 Saffron Hill
London EC1N 8RS
Helpline: 0800 800500 24hrs

PROteen
Ben Renshaw
Suite 11
2 St Quintin Ave
London W10 6NU
Tel: 0181 964-2624
*Personal/social skills for young
people, and workshops on '100%
Happiness'.*

Health

Health Education Authority
Trevelyan House
30 Great Peter Street
London SW1P 2HW
Tel: 0171 222-5300

English Sports Council
16 Upper Woburn Place
London WC1H 0QP
Tel: 0171 273-1500

AIDS

National AIDS Helpline
PO Box 5000
Glasgow G12 8BR
Helpline: 0800 567123 24hrs

Alcoholism

Alcohol Concern
Waterbridge House
32–36 Loman Street
London SE1 0EE
Tel: 0171 928-7377
Information/referral service.

Alcoholics Anonymous
PO Box 1 Stonebow House
Stonebow
York YO1 2NJ
Tel: 01904 644026

Aquarius
White House
6th Floor
111 New Street
Birmingham B2 4EU
Tel: 0121 632-4727
Charity giving counselling relating to alcohol/drug problems.

Cancer

Bristol Cancer Help Centre
Grove House
Cornwallis Grove
Clifton
Bristol BS8 4PG
Tel: 0117 980-9500

Cancerlink
11–21 Northdown Street
London N1 9BN
Tel: Freefone 0800 132905

Diet and Nutrition

The British Nutrition Foundation
52–54 High Holburn
London WC1V 6RQ
Tel: 0171 404-6504

Eating Disorders Association
Sackville Place
44 Magdalen Street
Norwich NR3 1JU
Helpline: 01603 621414
Youth Helpline: 01603 765050

Institute of Optimum Nutrition
12–13 Blade Court
Deodar Road
Putney
London SW15 2NU
Tel: 0181 877-9993

Ministry of Agriculture, Fisheries
   and Food (MAFF)
Helpline: 0645 335577
Publications: 0645 556000
MAFF Publications
London SE99 7TP

Weight Watchers
Check your local telephone directory for nearest branch.

Disabilities

DIAL UK
Park Lodge
St Catherine's Hospital
Tickhill Road
Doncaster DN4 8QN
Tel: 01302 310123

Disabled Living Foundation
380–384 Harrow Road
London W9 2HU
Tel: 0171 289-6111

Drug Addiction

CITA (The Council for
  Involuntary Tranquillizer
  Addiction)
Cavendish House
Brighton Road
Waterloo
Liverpool L22 5NG

Families Anonymous
Unit 37
DRCA
Charlotte Despard Avenue
London SW11 5JE
Tel: 0171 498-4680

TASHA (Tranquillizer and
  Anxiety Self-Help Association)
  Foundation
R Block
West Middlesex Hospital
Twickenham Road
Isleworth TW7 6AF
Tel: 0181 569-9933

Westminster Drug Project
470 Harrow Road
London W9 3RU
Tel: 0171 286-3339
*Advice, information and
counselling on drug-related
problems.*

Smoking

Quit
Helping Smokers to Quit
Victory House
170 Tottenham Court Road
London W1P 0HA
Tel: 0171 388-5775
Quitline: 0171 487-3000

Stress-related Disorders

Asthma

National Asthma Campaign
Providence House
Providence Place
London N1 0NT
Tel: 0171 226-2260
Asthma Helpline: 0345 010203
  (9am–7pm weekdays)

Bodily Pain

National Back Pain Association
16 Elmtree Road
Teddington
Middlesex TW11 8ST
Tel: 0181 977-5474

Diabetes

British Diabetic Association
10 Queen Anne Street
London W1M 0BD
Tel: 0171 323-1531

Heart Disease

British Heart Foundation
14 Fitzhardinge Street
London W1H 4DH
Tel: 0171 935-0185

Chest, Heart and Stroke Scotland
65 North Castle Street
Edinburgh EH2 3LT
Tel: 0131 225-6963

The Coronary Prevention Group
42 Store Street
London WC1E 7DB
Tel: 0171 580-1070

M.E.

M.E. Association
Stanhope House
High Street
Stanford-Le-Hope
Essex SS17 0HA
Tel: 01375 642466

Migraine

British Migraine Association
178a High Road
Byfleet
West Byfleet
Surrey KT14 7ED
Tel: 01932 352468

Migraine Trust
45 Great Ormond Street
London WC1N 3HZ
Tel: 0171 831-4818

PMS

National Association of
  Premenstrual Syndrome
PO Box 72
Sevenoaks
Kent TN13 1XQ
Tel: 01732 741709 (for
  information)

Skin Disorders

National Eczema Society
163 Eversholt Street
London NW1 1BU
Tel: 0171 388-4097

The Psoriasis Association
Milton House
7 Milton Street
Northampton NN2 7JG
Tel: 01604 711129

Life-event Stress

Age Concern
Astral House
1268 London Road
London SW16 4ER
Tel: 0181 679-8000
*Or look up Age Concern in your
local telephone directory.*

Help The Aged
St James's Walk
London EC1R 0BE
Helpline: 0800 289404

National Association of Victims
  Support Schemes
Cranmer House
39 Brixton Road
London SW9 6DZ
Tel: 0171 735-9166
Helpline: 0845 30 30 900

Shelter
88 Old Street
London EC1V 9HU
Tel: 0171 253-0202
Helpline: 0800 446441

The National Childbirth Trust
Alexandra House
Oldham Terrace
London W3 6NH
Tel: 0181 992-8637

Counselling Services

The British Association of
  Counselling
1 Regent Place
Rugby
Warwickshire CV21 2PJ
Tel: 01788 678328 (information
  service)

British Association of
  Psychotherapy
37 Mapesbury Road
London NW2 4HJ
Tel: 0181 452-9823

MIND (National Association for
  Mental Health)
Granta House
15–19 Broadway
Stratford
London E15 4BQ
Tel: 0181 519-2122

Samaritans
10 The Grove
Slough
Berks SL1 1QP
Tel: 01753 532713
*Or look up Samaritans in your
local telephone directory.*

Saneline
199–205 Old Marylebone Road
London NW1 5QP
Helpline: 0345 678000

LAUGHTER, THE BEST MEDICINE

The healing properties of laughter, joy and happiness have been celebrated in the most ancient cultures, including Greece, Egypt, India, China, Africa and South America. Today, modern medicine is once again recognizing the healing power of joy and how it can alleviate stress, depression and illness.

In *Laughter, The Best Medicine* Robert Holden explores how laughter is one of our most valuable and basic human needs, and presents over 50 of his most popular prescriptions to help you:

- Feel good again
- Strengthen confidence
- Stimulate creativity
- Create new beginnings
- Release your fun side
- Profit from fun at work
- Enjoy loving relationships

'Read this book. Open to the healing effects of laughter and love and full life will follow.'

Dr Bernie Siegel, author of *Love, Medicine and Miracles*

STOP THINKING, START LIVING

'Happy people understand, either instinctively or because they have been taught, that the name of the game is to enjoy life rather than think about it. If you are constantly analysing or keeping score of your life, you will always be able to find fault in whatever you are doing.'

Revolutionary in its simplicity and accessible to all, *Stop Thinking, Start Living* offers profound short-term, common-sense methods that allow you to let go of negativity and tap into your natural state of wellbeing.

In this indispensable handbook, Richard Carlson demonstrates how we can change everything in our lives – earn more money, meet new friends, get a new job – yet still feel dissatisfied. Happiness, he says, is not 'out there' but within, a state of mind that is independent of circumstance: 'If you begin to see that your thoughts are not the real thing – they're just thoughts and as thoughts they can't hurt you – your entire life will begin to change *today*.'

Carlson's step-by-step guide explains:

- how your thoughts determine how you feel
- why thinking about problems only makes them worse
- that thoughts come and go – you are free to choose at any moment which to hold on to and which to let go of
- straightforward methods for conquering depression
- how to dismiss negative thoughts and discover inner peace
- how to overcome lifelong pessimism and start really living

Richard Carlson PhD is a stress consultant in private practice and the bestselling author of seven books, including *Don't Sweat the Small Stuff* and *Slowing Down to the Speed of Life*. He is also the co-author of *Handbook for the Soul*.

EMOTIONAL CONFIDENCE

Do you ever feel that your emotions run away with you? Perhaps you suspect that your behaviour is affected by old emotional hurts which need help to heal. In this practical and sympathetic book, Gael Lindenfield helps you to manage your emotions so that you can create more balance and success in both your working life and your personal life.

Emotional Confidence helps you to:

- Soothe your sensitivity
- Control runaway feelings
- Feel more assertive and positive

With a seven-step emotional healing strategy, techniques to help lift your spirits, build confidence and gain control, you will find Gael Lindenfield's advice invaluable.

Gael Lindenfield is the author of the bestselling *Self Motivation* (book and audio), *The Positive Woman*, *Super Confidence*, *Self Esteem*, *Confident Children*, *Managing Anger* and *Assert Yourself*. She works as a psychotherapist and group work consultant, running successful courses in personal development.

Robert Holden can be
contacted at

The Happiness Project

Email: hello@happiness.co.uk
or
www.happiness.co.uk